ABOUT THE AUTHOR

Osho's teaching defies categorization, covering everything from the individual quest for meaning to the most urgent social and political issues facing society today. His books are not written but are transcribed from audio and video recordings of extemporaneous talks given to international audiences over a period of 35 years. Osho has been described by the *Sunday Times* in London as one of the '1000 Makers of the 20th Century' and by American author Tom Robbins as 'the most dangerous man since Jesus Christ'.

Of his own work, Osho has said that he is helping to create the conditions for the birth of a new kind of human being. He has often characterized this new human being as 'Zorba the Buddha' – capable both of enjoying the earthy pleasures of a Zorba the Greek and the silent serenity of a Gautam Buddha. Running like a thread through all aspects of Osho's work is a vision that encompasses both the timeless wisdom of the East and the highest potential of Western science and technology.

Osho is also known for his revolutionary contribution to the science of inner transformation, with an approach to meditation that acknowledges the accelerated pace of contemporary life. His unique 'Active Meditations' are designed to release the accumulated stresses of body and mind, so that it is easier to experience the thought-free and relaxed state of meditation.

Inner WAR AND PEACE

Timeless Solutions to Conflict from the *Bhagavad Gita*

OSHO

WATKINS PUBLISHING

LONDON

This edition published in the UK in 2005 by
Watkins Publishing, Sixth Floor, Castle House,
75–76 Wells Street, London W1T 3QH

Designed and typeset by Paul Saunders
Printed and bound in Great Britain

British Library Cataloguing in Publication data available

Library of Congress Cataloguing in Publication data available

ISBN 1 84293 131 8

www.watkinspublishing.com

Contents

Preface

One of the most famous of Hindu scriptures, the Bhagavad Gita is presented in the form of a dialogue between the enlightened Krishna and the great archer and seasoned warrior, Arjuna. The dialogue takes place on the eve of the Mahabharata, the climactic 'Great War' of India that occurred some 5000 years ago.

The war grew out of a dispute about which of two branches of the royal family, the Pandavas or the Kauravas, should inherit the kingdom, the center of which was close to Delhi. Arjuna was on the Pandavas' side but on the eve of battle – as he saw many family members, friends and relatives gathering to fight on the opposing side – he was faced with the stark realization that to engage in the war would mean killing 'his own people'.

Krishna, who was related to both sides of the royal family, played the role of Arjuna's charioteer and 'life coach'. And as he speaks to Arjuna he helps him to see, step by step, that the roots of his anguish lie in his identification with his mind and all its unconscious patterns and conditionings.

In the series of talks transcribed and published in this volume, Osho calls the Bhagavad Gita 'the first psychological scripture' available to the East long before the work of Freud, Adler and Jung. And the way in which Krishna approaches Arjuna's problems – all our problems – can only be appreciated once we really understand how the human mind actually functions. This is where Osho's brilliant commentary comes in, as he explains how the patterns and conditionings of our mind create pain and misery, dilemma, conflict and war.

As he comments on the meaning of verses from the Gita and responds to questions from his audience, Osho reveals how each of us carries an Arjuna within us. It soon becomes clear that the nature of man at the beginning of the twenty-first century may not be too different from the one who fought the Mahabharata War. But in these pages, Osho is addressing a world in the throes of a crisis that is far more complex, and of a potentially far greater magnitude than when Krishna and Arjuna were living. Finding ourselves on the edge of global and not just national self-destruction, Osho expands on Krishna's psychological vision and gives us keys for personal and global peace.

The Editors

CHAPTER 1

The Psychology of War

DHRITARASHTRA:
O Sanjay,
assembled on the field of righteousness,
the ground of the Kuru,
and desirous of war,
what did my sons and the sons of Pandu do?

SANJAY:
Then the king Duryodhana
having seen the army of the Pandavas
strategically drawn up for battle,
approached his teacher, Dronacharya, and said:

'O most-honored teacher,
behold this mighty army of Pandu's sons
which your own clever pupil, the son of Drupada,
has strategically arranged.

'Here are brave warriors and great archers,
equal to Bheema and Arjuna;
men such as Yuyudhana, Virata
and Drupada the great archer.

'Also, Dhrishtaketu, Chekitana,
the valiant king of Kashi,
Purujit, Kuntibhoja,
and Shaibya the best among men.

'Mighty Yudhamanyu and powerful Uttamauja;
the son of Subhadra
as well as the sons of Draupadi –
all of them great commanders.

'Also know, O first among brahmins,
of the outstanding men on our side;
and for your information I will name
the commanders of my army.

'You yourself, then Bheeshma, and Karna,
and Kripa, ever-victorious in battle;
similarly, Ashvatthama, Vikarna,
and the son of Somadatta.

'And many other valiant heroes
ready to lay down their lives for me,
armed with many kinds of weapons,
and all highly skilled in war.

'Our army, safeguarded by Bheeshma,
is invincible in every way,
while theirs with Bheema at the helm
will be easy enough for us to vanquish.

'Therefore, standing firm on all fronts,
each in his respective place,
guard Bheeshma with your lives
every one of you.'

Hearing these words of Duryodhana addressed to Dronacharya,
the most valiant grandsire Bheeshma
the eldest among the Kauravas,

roared aloud like a lion and blew his conch shell
to gladden the heart of Duryodhana.

Then, conches and kettledrums,
tambours, drums and horns
were played and struck together
making a tumultuous sound.

Upon this,
sitting in their magnificent chariot,
which was yoked to pure white horses,
Krishna and Arjuna blew their wondrous shells.

Krishna blew his conch named Panchajanya,
and Arjuna his named Devadatta.
Bheema, an accomplisher of splendid deeds
and a man of enormous appetite,
blew his mighty conch, Paundra.

King Yudhishthira, the son of Kunti,
blew his conch named Anantvijaya,
and Nakula and Sahadeva
blew theirs named Sughosha and Manipushpaka.

And then, O Lord of Earth,
the superb archer, the King of Kashi,
the great commanding archer Shikhandi,
Dhrishtaddumna and King Virata,
and the invincible Satyaki, King Drupada
and all the sons of Draupadi,
and the strong-armed son of Subhadra,
each blew his own especial conch.

And resounding through the heavens
and through the earth,
the tumultuous uproar
rent the hearts of Dhritarashtra's sons.

And then, O King,
Arjuna, whose flag bore the crest of Hanumana,
having looked at the sons of Dhritarashtra,
armed with their weapons and ready to strike,
picked up his bow
and addressed these words to Krishna:

'O Infallible One,
place my chariot between the two armies,
so that I may clearly see these men
who stand here, eager to fight,
and know who are they
who will be fighting with me in this war.'

D HRITARASHTRA IS BLIND. But passion does not disappear with the absence of sight; desire does not disappear with the absence of sight. Had Surdas thought of Dhritarashtra, he would never have destroyed his own eyes.

Surdas destroyed his eyes believing that once his sight was gone, desire and passion would never arise in him again. But desire does not arise in the eyes, it arises out of the mind. No passion will ever be finished in this way – even if one destroys one's own eyes.

This wonderful tale of the Gita begins with a blind man's curiosity. In fact, not a single tale would be told in this world if there were no blind men. All the stories of this life begin with a blind man's curiosity. A blind man wants to see what he cannot see; a deaf person wants to hear what he cannot hear. Even if all the sense-organs were lost, the desires hidden within the mind would not vanish.

So, I would like to remind you from the very outset that Dhritarashtra is blind, and yet sitting miles away, his mind is curious, eager and troubled to know what is happening on the battlefield. Also keep a second point in mind: that the blind Dhritarashtra has one hundred sons, but that the children born of a blind person can never have any real vision even though they may have physical eyes. Those who are born of blind parents – and perhaps generally speaking people *are* born of blind parents – may have physical eyes, but it is difficult for them to gain inner sight. So secondly, it is important to understand that the one hundred sons of Dhritarashtra were acting blindly in every sense. They had outer, physical eyes but not inner ones. One who is blind can only beget blindness. And yet, this father is curious to know what is happening.

Thirdly, one should note what Dhritarashtra is saying:

O Sanjay,
assembled on the field of righteousness,
the ground of the Kuru,
and desirous of war...

The field of righteousness ceases to exist the day people gather there to fight a war. The day that fighting becomes imperative, the possibility of any religiousness surviving in this world comes to an end. Thus, at one time it may have been a field of righteousness, of religion, but now it is not. Now, people who are eager to kill one another have assembled at the very place that is known as *dharmakshetra* – the field of righteousness.

This beginning is really extraordinary. It is also extraordinary in the sense that now it will be very hard to figure out what must be happening on the fields of *unrighteousness*, on the fields of irreligiousness, if this is what is happening on the field of righteousness. What can be happening on this field of righteousness if Dhritarashtra is already asking Sanjay: 'I want to know what my sons and their opponents, who are eager for war, are doing?'

Perhaps a field of righteousness has not yet been created on this earth. If it had been, then war would no longer be a possibility. But when the possibility of war still exists, and when even a field of righteousness is turned into a battlefield, then how can we blame or criticize the unrighteous, the irreligious?

The truth is that perhaps there have been fewer wars on the fields of unrighteousness than on the fields of righteousness, of religion. If we were to think in terms of war and bloodshed, then fields of righteousness would look more like fields of unrighteousness than the actual fields of unrighteousness do.

We should understand the irony involved here – that up to now, wars have taken place in religious domains. Don't think that this is happening only now; that temples and mosques have become dens of war only today. Thousands of years ago – when it is generally believed that good people lived on this earth, and a wonderful person like Krishna was present – even then people had gathered to fight on the religious fields of the Kuru. This deep-rooted thirst for war, this deeply ingrained desire for destruction, this deeply hidden animal within, remains with man even on the fields of righteousness. Even there, this animal makes preparations for war.

It is good to remember this, and also to remember that fighting becomes even more dangerous when it comes from behind the shield of religion – because then it seems justified.

So, this religious scripture begins with the blind Dhritarashtra's curiosity. All religious scriptures begin with some blind man's curiosity. In fact, the day that there are no blind people in this world, there will be no need for any religious scriptures. So here he is, this blind man who is being curious.

OSHO,
What is the significance of Sanjay, who reports on the war to Dhritarashtra, in the Gita? Did Sanjay possess powers of seeing and hearing from afar? What is the source of his mental powers? Is this power intrinsic?

Doubts have consistently been raised about Sanjay, and this is natural. From far, far away Sanjay is reporting to Dhritarashtra about what is happening at Kurukshetra.

Yoga has always believed that the eyes we see with are not our only eyes. Man also has another eye, which can see across the barriers of time and space. But just because yoga says this, it may not necessarily be the case that what Sanjay reports will be totally right. A doubt arises in the mind: how can Sanjay see across such a long distance? Is he omniscient? No. And first of all, the power to see and hear from afar is not really such a great power. It has nothing to do with being omniscient. It is a very modest power and anyone can develop it with a little effort. And sometimes it happens that as a result of some quirk in nature this power develops in someone of its own accord.

So it is not that Sanjay is some kind of spiritual man. He is certainly special: he is able to see what is going on far away on the battleground. And it is not that he has attained the realization of some godliness or some truth because of this power. On the contrary, it is possible that Sanjay may have sabotaged himself completely by using this power.

This often happens. Extraordinary powers can lead people completely astray. That is why yoga has consistently maintained that be they common physical powers or psychic powers of the mind, one who gets entangled in these powers never reaches the truth.

However, what Sanjay could do is possible. Recently, within the last one hundred years in the West, a great deal of work has been undertaken in psychic research. So now no one has any reason to doubt Sanjay – not even on scientific grounds. Now psychologists are admitting that there are endless powers contained in man.

As a result of man traveling into space, psychologists began working in a new area. It is no longer possible to depend completely on machines: particularly when people are sent to travel in space, a terrible risk is involved. Any slight defect in the equipment and we could lose contact with them forever, and it would be impossible to trace these lost travelers. We would never be able to locate them in the infinity of space, or know whether they were alive or dead. That is why the scientists are anxiously working in their laboratories to develop a substitute system that will enable us to see across a long distance and hear and send messages without the help of technology. It will not be very long before all countries have Sanjays.

Sanjay is not a particularly spiritual man. However, he does have a special power that we all possess and which can be developed.

SANJAY:
Then the king Duryodhana
having seen the army of the Pandavas
strategically drawn up for battle,
approached his teacher, Dronacharya, and said:

'O most-honored teacher,
behold this mighty army of Pandu's sons
which your own clever pupil, the son of Drupada,
has strategically arranged.

'Here are brave warriors and great archers,
equal to Bheema and Arjuna;
men such as Yuyudhana, Virata
and Drupada the great archer.

'Also, Dhrishtaketu, Chekitana,
the valiant king of Kashi,
Purujit, Kuntibhoja,
and Shaibya, the best among men.

'Mighty Yudhamanyu and powerful Uttamauja;
the son of Subhadra
as well as the sons of Draupadi –
all of them great commanders.

'Also know, O first among brahmins,
of the outstanding men on our side;
and for your information I will name
the commanders of my army.'

When the human mind is suffering from an inferiority complex, when internally the human mind considers itself inferior, then one always begins by talking about one's own greatness. But, when the person is not ridden with inferiority, talk always begins with the mention of others' greatness.

Here Duryodhana is telling Dronacharya which great commanders and profound warriors have come together in the Pandavas' army. That Duryodhana begins like this is highly symbolic. Generally, the talk does not begin with praising the enemy; generally the talk begins with deriding the enemy; generally, the talk begins by praising oneself in comparison with the enemy. But here, Duryodhana begins his talk by identifying the heroes who have assembled in the enemy's army. This shows that whatever else Duryodhana may be, he is certainly not a man with an inferiority complex.

It is very interesting that even a good man who is suffering from an inferiority complex is worse than a bad man who is not suffering from one. Only the person who is confident in himself can begin by praising others. This is one very fundamental difference that has taken place over the past centuries. Before, too, there were bad as well as good people – and it is not that today the number of bad people has increased and the number of good people has decreased. Today, the proportion of good and bad people is also similar. So what change has taken place?

Those who continuously talk about religion spread the belief that in the old days people were good and now they have become bad. In my view this assertion is fundamentally wrong. There have always been good people and there have always been bad people. The difference that has occurred between then and now is not so peripheral; rather, it goes much deeper. In the past, even a bad person was not suffering from an inferiority complex; today even a good person is suffering from one. And here lies the profound difference.

Today, even the best man is only good on the outside. Inside, even he is not sure of himself. Keep this in mind: that when a person is unsure of himself, his goodness is not of the kind that can last for long. It is merely skin-deep: a little scratch, and even the surface will become ugly. And if a bad person is self-confident, in spite of his evil he can be transformed any day – because a quality of goodness lies crystallized at the depth: the quality of self-confidence.

I find it very significant that a bad person such as Duryodhana begins his talk in a very good way. He mentions the good qualities of his opponents first, and then he describes the heroes in his own army.

'You yourself, then Bheeshma, and Karna,
and Kripa, ever-victorious in battle;
similarly, Ashvatthama, Vikarna,
and the son of Somadatta.

'And many other valiant heroes
ready to lay down their lives for me,
armed with many kinds of weapons,
and all highly skilled in war.

'Our army, safeguarded by Bheeshma,
is invincible in every way,
while theirs with Bheema at the helm
will be easy enough for us to vanquish.

'Therefore, standing firm on all fronts,
each in his respective place,
guard Bheeshma with your lives
every one of you.'

OSHO,
On one hand we find that the total emphasis in the Shrimad Bhagvadgita is on Arjuna, while here, Duryodhana is saying that the Pandavas' army is safguarded by Bheema, and the Kauravas' army by Bheeshma. Could it be that the idea behind pitting

Bheema against Bheeshma is that Duryodhana sees Bheema as his only true rival?

This point is worth consideration. The whole war is centered around Arjuna as its main pivot, but this is in hindsight – that is, after the war, at the conclusion of the war. Those who know about the whole war and its outcome would say that Arjuna was pivotal throughout the war. But those who were standing on the threshold of the war could never have thought in this way.

For Duryodhana, the whole possibility of a war happening rested with Bheema. There were reasons for this. Even Duryodhana could never have expected a nice person like Arjuna to engage in a war such as this. Arjuna could be easily shaken – even Duryodhana had his doubts about his steadiness of mind. Duryodhana had some deep, unconscious feeling that Arjuna might run away from the war. If this war were to proceed at all, it would have to be because of Bheema alone. People like Bheema who are less intelligent but more powerful can be depended upon to fight a war.

Arjuna is intelligent; and where there is intelligence there is doubt, and where there is doubt there is dilemma. Arjuna is rational; and where there is rationality, there lies the capacity to think from a total perspective. When one has these qualities it is difficult to enter into a dangerous situation like war with closed eyes.

There is a deep similarity between Duryodhana and Bheema. Both have the same nature; deep down both have the same kind of thinking, both are the same type of person. Hence if Duryodhana saw Bheema as the central figure on the opposing side, he was right. There is nothing wrong in this. Later on, the Gita also proves this point: Arjuna is on the verge of escaping. Arjuna emerges as an escapist, and this is always highly probable as far as a person like Arjuna is concerned. This war proved costly for Arjuna: for him, entering the war became possible only after he underwent a self-transformation. Only after attaining a new level of understanding could he agree to the war.

Bheema was ready to fight at whatever level of being he found himself at the time. War is as natural to Bheema as it is to Duryodhana. Hence, it is not coincidental that Duryodhana should see Bheema as the central figure. But this is at the beginning of the war; Duryodhana does not know how the war is going to conclude; what the end will be. But we know.

Remember, often life does not end in the same way that it begins. The end is always unknown; it is always invisible. Mostly what we think will happen doesn't happen. Life is an unknown journey. Hence, whatever is believed in the first moments of life, in the first moments of any event, does not necessarily turn out to be the outcome at the end. We can engage ourselves in shaping our destiny but we can never become the one who decides it. The outcome is always something different.

Duryodhana's clear understanding was that Bheema would be the central figure. And had Bheema been the central figure, then perhaps what Duryodhana was saying about being victorious would have come true. That Duryodhana's viewpoint did not prove to be true and that an unexpected element came into the picture is worth reflecting on.

Duryodhana forgot Krishna, he forgot that Krishna would be able to bring Arjuna back into the war if he decided to escape. We, too, never remember that the invisible, the intangible may also have a hand in our lives. Our calculations are made according to what can be seen. We never remember that at some point the invisible may also penetrate, the invisible may also enter into the midst of everything.

Here in the midst of everything, the invisible has entered in the form of Krishna, and consequently the whole story has taken a different turn. What could have happened didn't happen; and that which had the least possibility of happening did happen. The arrival of the unknown cannot be predicted. Whoever reads this tale for the first time cannot be but shocked when he finds Krishna driving the escaping Arjuna back into the war – certainly the reader is shocked.

When Ralph Waldo Emerson read this tale for the first time, he shut the book, he was horrified – because what Arjuna was saying would be accepted by all so-called religious people. The argument Arjuna was making was exactly that of a so-called religious person. When Henry Thoreau came across Krishna counseling Arjuna to enter into war, he too was horrified. Henry Thoreau has written that he never believed, he never had the slightest idea, that the story would take such a turn – Krishna counseling Arjuna to enter into war. Gandhi, too, faced the same difficulty; he was troubled for the same reason.

But life never proceeds according to set principles. Life is an extraordinary phenomenon. It never runs on railway tracks, it flows like the current of the river Ganges – its course is never pre-determined. And when the invisible unknown appears in the midst of it all, it disturbs everything. Whatever was planned, whatever man has woven, whatever man's mind has thought – everything goes topsy-turvy.

Duryodhana had never imagined that this invisible presence would enter into the war. So what he is saying is just an initial statement of the kind we all make in the first stages of any situation in our lives. Meanwhile, the invisible, the unknown, keeps intervening and the entire story changes.

If we look at our lives in hindsight, we will see that whatever we intended to happen went wrong. Where we expected success, we met failure; what we had set our hearts on was never attained. We expected happiness to follow as the result of obtaining something, but when we got it, it led to sorrow. And that which we never dreamed of having, the mere glimpse of it, suddenly opened up fountains of joy and happiness. Everything goes topsy-turvy.

But people who are so intelligent that they take the outcome into consideration in the beginning are very few in this world. In the beginning we all pay attention only to the beginning. If only we could take the end into consideration first, the story of life could be very different.

However, if Duryodhana were to take the end into account first, the *war* could not take place. But Duryodhana can never take the end into consideration. He will take the end for granted – that it will happen only like this. That is why he says over and over again that although the other side's army is great, the final victory will be his; that his warriors are anxious to make him victorious, even at the cost of their lives.

Even if we put our whole power behind it, the untruth can never be victorious. Even if we give our very lives, the untruth can never be victorious. But there is no way that a Duryodhana can have a realization, an understanding, of this fact. The truth, which initially might appear to be losing, always wins in the end. Untruth appears to be winning initially, but meets defeat in the end. Truth appears to be losing in the beginning but becomes victorious in the end. But how can one possibly see the end from the beginning? The person who is able to becomes religious. The person who fails to see this keeps slipping, like Duryodhana, into a blind war.

OSHO,
There is the will of the invisible unknown and there is the will of the individual. Since they come into conflict, how is an individual to know what is the will of the unknown?

The question is, how is an individual to know what is the will of the unknown? The individual is never able to know. But if the individual can let go of himself, if he can erase his ego, he will know the will of the unknown immediately – because he has become one with it.

A drop cannot know what an ocean is until it dissolves itself in the ocean. An individual can never know the will of the whole as long as that individual maintains his separate identity. But if he can dissolve himself and cease to be an individual who is separate from the whole, then only the whole will remain. And because the individual's will no longer remains, the question of knowing the will of the whole does not arise. Then the individual will live the way that the unknown, the whole, makes him live. In this situation, no individual will, no individual desire for any particular outcome, no personal longing for anything, no attitude of imposing one's own will upon the will of the whole remains anywhere, because the individual himself is no more.

As long as the individual is there, the will of the whole can never be known. And when the individual is no more, there remains no need to know the will of the whole – because then whatever takes place is happening through the will of the whole, the unknown; the individual has become just an instrument, a vehicle.

Further on, and throughout the Gita, Krishna counsels Arjuna precisely this: that he should leave himself in the hands of the unknown, that he should surrender himself to the unknown – because then those whom Arjuna worries will be killed in the war are already killed at the hands of the unknown, of the whole; because then Arjuna will not be at all responsible for the deaths of those whose deaths he feels he is responsible for. Of course, if he keeps himself separate as an individual, he will certainly be responsible. But if he can let go of himself and fight as an instrument, as a witness, then no responsibility will rest on him.

If the individual can disappear into the whole, if he can surrender himself totally, if he can give up his ego, then it is simply the will of the whole, the will of existence that is being fulfilled all the time. It is being fulfilled this very moment; there is no way we can alter its fulfillment. But we can fight, we can ruin ourselves, we can destroy ourselves in the hope of altering the will of existence, the will of the whole.

I have often told a small story about two little straws that are drifting in a flooded river. One straw that happens to be lying diagonally across the current is trying to hold back the flood, is screaming that it will not let the river go forward. Although the river is moving ahead and the straw is unable to control it, yet it goes on shouting that the river will be stopped: it is boasting aloud that whether it lives or dies, it will stop the river.

But the straw is still drifting. The river neither listens to its voice nor knows that the straw is struggling against it. It is a tiny straw; the river is completely unaware of it, and it makes no difference to the river. But for the straw it is a matter of great consequence. Its life is in great difficulty. It is drifting, but fighting, it will ultimately reach the same destination as it would have reached if it had not been fighting. However, as it *is* fighting, this moment in between, this period in between, will become one of pain, sorrow, conflict and anxiety for it.

The straw next to it has let go of itself. It is not lying across the river; it is lying straight, in the direction that the river is flowing – and it thinks that it is helping the river to flow. The river is completely oblivious of this straw too. The straw thinks that since it is taking the river along with it to the ocean, the river will eventually reach there too. And the river is totally unaware of its help.

All this makes no difference to the river but for both the straws it is a matter of great consequence. The one who is taking the river along with it is feeling great joy; it is dancing in great delight. The one who is fighting against the river is in great pain. Its dance is not a dance at all: it is a nightmare. It is nothing but a twisting of its limbs, it is in trouble, it is being defeated; while the one who is flowing with the river is winning.

An individual is unable to do anything except that which is the will of the whole. But he has the freedom to fight, and by fighting he has the freedom to cause himself anxiety.

Sartre has made a valuable statement: 'Man is condemned to be free.' Man is compelled, he is condemned, he is cursed to be free. However, man can use his freedom in two ways. He can pit his freedom against the will of existence and create a conflict. In this case his life will be a life of sorrow, pain and anguish, and ultimately he will meet defeat.

Another individual can make his freedom an object of surrender to existence – and his life will be a life of bliss, it will be a life of dance and of song. And what will the end result be? The end result will be nothing but a victory for him. The straw that thinks it is helping the river is bound to be victorious. There is no way it can be defeated. The straw that tries to block the river is sure to meet defeat. There is no way it can ever win.

So it is impossible to know the will of existence, but it is certainly possible to become one with existence. And if this is the case, then one's own will disappears and only the will of existence remains.

OSHO,

In scientific discoveries there is something of the individual's own that is contributed. It is difficult to understand how the will of existence, of the whole, enters into scientific discovery.

Normally, it seems that it is the individual's will that is working in scientific discovery – but that is only a superficial appearance. If one looks at it more deeply it will not appear so. You will be surprised to know that the experiences of the world's great scientists with regard to science are quite different from the ideas created in colleges and universities.

For example, Madame Curie has written that once, for several days, she was bothered by a problem. She tried to solve it but couldn't. Getting tired and upset, she finally gave up: one night at two o'clock in the morning she decided to forget about the problem and went to bed leaving the incomplete papers on her desk.

When Curie woke up in the morning, she found to her surprise that the half-finished problem was completed. The doors were closed and no one had come into the room. Even if someone had entered the room, it was impossible that a problem which Madame Curie herself could not solve had been solved by someone else. After all, the woman was a Nobel Prize winner. There were only servants in the house, and it would have been a miracle if any one of them had solved it.

But there was no doubt that the problem had been solved. It had been left half-done, and now the remaining half was completed. She checked all the doors, and still found it hard to believe. She could not accept the idea that maybe God had descended from above. Anyway, no God *had* come from above: when she looked more closely, she found that the rest of the handwriting was hers.

Then she started recalling that during the night she had had a dream. She remembered dreaming that she got up and solved the problem, that she woke up in the night and solved the problem.

After that, it became a regular practice for her – whenever she was unable to solve a problem – to place it under her pillow and go to sleep. During the night she would wake up and solve it.

Throughout the day, Madame Curie remained an individual. At night, in sleep, the ego disappears; the drop meets the ocean. The problem that her conscious mind was unable to solve was solved by the unconscious mind, which deep down is united with the universal self.

Once, Archimedes couldn't solve a problem. He was in serious trouble because the emperor had commanded him to solve it. Archimedes' entire reputation depended on his solving the one problem; but he became exhausted and no solution came. The emperor was sending messages every day asking for an answer.

Someone had presented the emperor with a very precious ornament. But the emperor suspected that he was being cheated, and that something else was mixed with the gold. The problem was to find out, without destroying the ornament, whether or not some other metal had been mixed in with it. In those days no means had been developed to find this out. It was a sizeable ornament and it was possible that its weight had been increased by mixing something else with the gold.

Archimedes became tired and troubled. But one fine morning while he was lying in his bathtub, the problem was suddenly solved. He forgot everything and dashed out naked into the street. Had Archimedes been present he would have never forgotten that he was naked. He went out into the street shouting, 'Eureka! Eureka! – I've got it! I've got it!' and he ran toward the palace.

People took hold of him and asked what he was doing: 'Would you appear before the emperor naked like this?' He replied, 'I did not realize what I was doing!'

The man who ran out into the street naked was not Archimedes. Archimedes could never have appeared naked on the street. It must have been that in that moment he had ceased to be an individual. The problem was not solved in an individual's consciousness; it was solved in a state of impersonal, universal consciousness.

He was in the bathroom lying in the bathtub, relaxing. A moment of meditation occurred and penetrated deep inside him… and the problem was solved. Did the bathtub solve the problem that he himself could not solve? Could the bathtub have really solved it? By lying in water, is it ever possible to solve a problem that one cannot otherwise solve? Does intelligence increase by lying in water? How can becoming naked solve something that cannot be solved with clothes on?

No, something else had happened. For a short while Archimedes ceased to be an individual. For that brief period he became one with the whole.

If we read through the experiences of all the great scientists of the world, such as Einstein, Max Planck, Eddington, Edison, we find that they have one experience in common: whatever it was that came to be known, it wasn't 'I' who came to know it. It has happened time and again that when 'I' came to know something, in that moment 'I' wasn't there – and the act of knowing happened. This is precisely what the sages of the Upanishads say, and the same is said by the sages of the Vedas, by Mohammed and by Jesus.

When we say that the Vedas have not been created by man, it doesn't mean that God appeared and wrote the book. There is no reason to say such ridiculous things. 'Not created by man' simply means that this occurrence – of putting the Vedic mantras and verses into words – took place in a moment when the person himself wasn't there; in a moment when his 'I' was not there. When such a phenomenon took place, when the statements of the Upanishads descended on someone, when the Koran descended upon Mohammed, when the statements in the Bible descended upon Jesus, these people were not there.

The experiences of religion and science are not different. They cannot be, because when a truth is realized in science, the route to its realization is the same as it is in the realization of a religious truth. There is only one way for truth to be revealed: when the individual is not there, the truth descends from the whole. An empty space occurs within us and the truth descends into that empty space.

Whosoever has received any ray of truth in this world, through any route whatsoever – be they a musician, a painter, poet, scientist, religious seeker or a mystic – has received it only when they themselves were not present.

Religion understood this long ago. The experience of religion is ten thousand years old, and throughout these ten thousand years, the religious seeker, the religious mystic, the religious meditator, has relaxed into the experience that it is not 'I' who realizes the truth.

It is a difficult matter. When for the first time something descends into you from the whole, it becomes very difficult to make the distinction as to whether it is yours or from the whole. When this happens for the first time the mind is tempted to assert its claim; and the ego also likes the idea that it is its own. Gradually, however, when these assertions become more transparent and you come to know that there appears to be no link or relationship between you and the truth that has been revealed, the distinction between you and the whole, the universal, becomes apparent.

Science is still very young – it is only two or three hundred years old – yet during this time the scientist has become humble. Fifty years ago a scientist would say, 'We have discovered.' Today, he will not say this. Now, he says, 'Everything seems to be beyond our reach.' Today's scientist is speaking the same mystical language that the mystics of the past did.

There is no need to hurry – just wait a hundred years more and the scientist will be speaking exactly the same language as we find in the Upanishads. They will have to speak the very language that Buddha spoke; they will have to speak the same language that St Augustine and St Francis spoke. They will have to speak it because as their experiences of truth deepen, their belief in the individual as a personality diminishes. The more the truth reveals itself, the more the ego disappears – and one day the individual realizes that whatsoever has been known is because of the grace of the whole: 'It has descended upon me; I am nowhere in it. And I am responsible for whatever I didn't come to know, because I was so strongly present that I could not have known it. I was so solidly present that truth could not have descended there.'

Truth descends into an empty mind, and the presence of 'I' is necessary only if untruth is to be realized.

No, the will of the whole, of existence, will never become an obstacle to scientific discoveries. In fact, whatever discoveries have been made so far have happened through a connection with the whole, through surrender. Truth has never entered, and will never enter, other than through the door of surrender.

OSHO,

This statement of yours that the unconscious mind is united with the whole, with existence, creates difficulties. Jung has explained this earlier by relating mythology with the collective unconscious. But when Freud says that the unconscious is also connected with Satan, it only adds to the problem.

Freud believes that our unconscious mind is not only connected with the divine but also with the devil. Actually *God* and *Satan* are our words. When we don't like a certain thing, we say that it is connected with Satan; and when we like a certain thing, we say that it is connected with God. What I am saying is simply that the unconscious mind is connected with the unknown, and to me the unknown is godliness, and as far as I am concerned, Satan is included in this godliness, is not separate from it.

In fact, our minds want to believe that what we dislike must have been done by the devil, and what is not wrong or inconsistent must be the work of the divine. We have assumed that we are at the center of life, and so everything that appeals to us is done by the divine, and everything we don't like is done by the devil: the devil is the enemy. It is man's ego that has put both Satan and God at its service.

Nothing exists except godliness. What we call Satan, or satanic, is nothing but our non-acceptance. What we call 'evil' is simply our non-acceptance. If we could look deeply into what we call bad we would immediately find good hidden there. If we could look deeply into sorrow we would find happiness there. If we could watch a curse closely, we would find a blessing hidden inside. Actually, good and bad are just two sides of the same coin.

I am not referring to the unknown as the divine in the sense of it being the opposite of the devil. The entity I am calling the unknown is the source of all our lives, is the very basis of existence. It is from this source of existence that both Ravana, the symbol of evil, and Rama, the symbol of goodness, emerge. It is from this source of existence that darkness and light both emerge.

We feel fear in the darkness, so our minds want to believe that the devil must be the creator of darkness. Since we like the light, our minds want to believe that the divine must be creating that light. But as such, there is nothing bad in darkness or good in light.

One who loves existence will find godliness as much in the darkness as in the light. The reality is that because of the fear we carry about darkness we are never able to know the beauty of darkness. We are never able to appreciate the flavor, the mystery of darkness. Our fear is man-made. We have emerged from the caves, we have passed through the wild... Darkness was dangerous there; wild beasts could attack, night was frightening. That is why when fire appeared we accepted it as a god – because then the night became safe. We got rid of fear by lighting a fire. So in our experience, darkness has become associated with fear. In our hearts light has become associated with fearlessness.

But darkness has its own mystery and light has its own mystery too. Whatsoever happens in this life that has any significance happens with the cooperation of both darkness and light. We bury the seed in the darkness, but the flower appears in the light. We sow the seed in darkness under the ground, the roots spread in that darkness, but the flowers blossom in the sky, in the light. Leave a seed in the light, and the flower will never appear; bury a flower in the darkness, and the seeds will never be created. A child is created in the deep darkness of the mother's womb where not a single ray of light reaches. Later, when it has developed, it appears in the light.

Thus, both darkness and light are the basis for the same life energy. And division, polarity, and contradiction in life are just man-made.

Freud saying that the unconscious mind is also joined with the devil.... Freud was bound up with Jewish thinking. He was born into a Jewish family; since childhood he had learned about the conflict between God and Satan. Jewish people have made a division: one side belongs to Satan and the other belongs to God. Actually, it is a division made by the human mind. So Freud thought that whenever bad things were surfacing from the unconscious, Satan must be responsible for them.

No, there is nothing like Satan. If we do see Satan anywhere, we are making a fundamental mistake. A religious person is incapable of seeing the devil anywhere. Only godliness exists. And the unconscious – from where the scientist finds the truth, or the religious person finds the truth – is a door to godliness. As we move more deeply into this, it will certainly become understandable.

Hearing these words of Duryodhana addressed to Dronacharya,
the most valiant grandsire Bheeshma
the eldest among the Kauravas,
roared aloud like a lion and blew his conch shell
to gladden the heart of Duryodhana.

Then, conches and kettledrums,
tambours, drums and horns
were played and struck together
making a tumultuous sound.

Upon this,
sitting in their magnificent chariot,
which was yoked to pure white horses,
Krishna and Arjuna blew their wondrous shells.

Krishna blew his conch named Panchajanya,
and Arjuna his named Devadatta.
Bheema, an accomplisher of splendid deeds
and a man of enormous appetite,
blew his mighty conch, Paundra.

King Yudhishthira, the son of Kunti,
blew his conch named Anantvijaya,
and Nakula and Sahadeva
blew theirs named Sughosha and Manipushpaka.

OSHO,

Since Krishna blows his conch in response to the terrifying
sound of Bheeshma's conch, couldn't the sounding of Krishna's
conch be taken as a reaction rather than an independent action?
Does the mention of this conch blowing by Krishna and Arjuna
in the first canto of the Gita mean anything other than the
making of a declaration?

The question has been raised whether the sound of Krishna's
conch is a reaction to the sound of Bheeshma's conch. No, it is simply a response. The sound of Krishna's conch is merely a rejoinder
– not for war or fighting, but just as an acceptance of the challenge.
Whatever that challenge may bring, whatever that challenge may
unfold, wherever that challenge may lead, it is accepted.

It would be useful to understand the nature of this acceptance a
little more.

Life is a challenge every moment, and the one who does not
accept this is dead – even though he is still living. Many people die

while they are still alive! Bernard Shaw used to say that actually people die quite early, although they are buried much later. Almost forty years pass between their death and their burial.

The moment a person stops accepting the challenge of life he is dead – from that very moment. Living means accepting the challenges every moment. But this challenge can also be accepted in two ways: it can be with anger, and then it becomes a reaction; or the acceptance can be with happiness, delight and joy and then it becomes a response.

It should be noted that when Bheeshma blew his conch the description says that he did so with delight, causing rejoicing among the other warriors. Great joy and exultation spread all around when he blew the conch.

This is acceptance. Whatsoever life is bringing... even if it is war, that too is accepted. If life is leading one into a war, that war is also accepted. Certainly this action deserves a response. Consequently, Krishna and the Pandavas blow their respective conches.

It is also worth considering that the first conch sound comes from the Kauravas' side. The onus for starting the war rests with the Kauravas. Krishna is only responding; from the Pandavas' side it is merely a response. If there must be a war, they are ready to respond to it – although they have no inclination for war as such. The Pandavas could also have blown the conch first. But no, this much responsibility, the responsibility of dragging everyone into a war, only the Kauravas would take.

The beginning of this war is very symbolic. There is another thing to notice here: that it is Krishna who takes the lead in giving the response. Since Bheeshma has initiated a challenge from the Kauravas' side, it does not seem fitting that Krishna should be the one to respond. The proper thing would have been for the warriors who were assembled there to participate in the fighting to respond. Krishna was only there as a charioteer. Neither is he a soldier, nor has he actually come to participate in the fight – there is no question of his actually fighting. It is the commander of the Pandavas' army who should have responded by sounding his conch.

But no – and this is very significant – the response has been initiated through Krishna's conch-sound. It symbolizes that the Pandavas consider this war as nothing more than a responsibility laid upon them by existence itself. They are ready for the call that has come from the whole. They are only willing to fight as an instrument of existence. That is why this rejoinder, accepting war, has been initiated through Krishna.

And it is right. It is right even to meet defeat while fighting on the side of existence, and it is not right even to be victorious when fighting against existence. Now for the Pandavas, even defeat will only be a rejoicing, even defeat *can* only be a rejoicing – because now the battle is no longer theirs; if it is anyone's at all, it belongs to existence. So it is not a reaction; it is a response. There is no anger involved in it.

Had Bheema blown the conch, it could have been in reaction. Had Bheema given the reply, it would certainly have been in anger. Since the reply has come from Krishna, it is in the form of a joyous acceptance in the sense of: 'All right, if life has brought us to a point where war has finally become imperative, then we leave ourselves in the hands of existence.'

And then, O Lord of Earth,
the superb archer, the King of Kashi,
the great commanding archer Shikhandi,
Dhrishtaddumna and King Virata,
and the invincible Satyaki, King Drupada
and all the sons of Draupadi,
and the strong-armed son of Subhadra,
each blew his own especial conch.

And resounding through the heavens
and through the earth,
the tumultuous uproar
rent the hearts of Dhritarashtra's sons.

And then, O King,
Arjuna, whose flag bore the crest of Hanumana,
having looked at the sons of Dhritarashtra,
armed with their weapons and ready to strike,
picked up his bow
and addressed these words to Krishna:

'O Infallible One,
place my chariot between the two armies,
so that I may clearly see these men
who stand here, eager to fight,
and know who are they
who will be fighting with me in this war.'

Arjuna is requesting that Krishna let him see the men with whom
he is to fight. There are two or three points here that are worth
understanding.

Let us first examine Arjuna's request to take him to a place from
where he can see those with whom he is going to fight. This shows
that, for Arjuna, this war is a responsibility thrust upon him from
the outside – it is not a call coming from his own interior world. It
is an obligation that is being forced upon him; it is not a desire
coming from within. For Arjuna, this war is something he is being
compelled to do; he has no other choice except to fight. That is why
he is inquiring, asking, to see with whom he will be fighting. He
wants to see who they are – these people who have come so eager
to fight, so eager for a war.

A person who himself is eager for war does not care to see
whether the opponent is eager to fight or not. A person who is
eager for war is blind. He never looks at the enemy, he only
projects the enemy. He doesn't want to look at the enemy; in
fact, whomsoever he meets is an enemy for him. He doesn't need
to see the enemy; he creates, he projects the enemy.

When a battle is raging within, enemies appear on the outside.
Only when there is no war going on within does one feel the need

to investigate who is anxious and ready to have a fight. So Arjuna asks Krishna to place his chariot at the strategic point from where he can see those who have assembled there, eager to fight.

The first rule of war is to know well the enemy one is going to fight. In all wars, in all wars in life – inner or outer – identifying the enemy, understanding the enemy is the first rule. Only those who know, who understand the enemy well, win wars.

That is why the warmonger is not able to win wars. He is so surrounded by the smoke of his own desire for war that it becomes difficult for him to know the enemy. His eagerness to fight a war is so great that it becomes difficult for him to know and understand the enemy he is fighting against. And if you don't know whom you are fighting against, then your defeat is sealed from the very beginning.

Therefore the calm and composure needed in time of war in order to win that war is more than is needed at any other time. The capacity of witnessing, required in time of war in order to win that war, is greater than in any other situation. Arjuna is saying: 'Now let me see, now let me observe from the state of a witness those who have come to fight.'

This needs to be understood.

Observation is at its minimum when you are angry. When you are in anger, the capacity to observe is almost entirely lost. And the fact is that the capacity to observe is never more needed than when you are angry. The irony is that if there is observation, there is no anger, and vice-versa. Both cannot be simultaneously present. If a person who is angry becomes interested in observing, anger will disappear.

Arjuna is not angry here; that is why he is able to talk about observation. What he is saying is not out of anger. It is as if the war were just an extraneous matter for Arjuna. It is not affecting him in any place: he simply wants to observe as a witness who has come to fight, who is anxious to fight.

The statement regarding observation is very valuable. Whenever a person goes to any war – whether it is with outer enemies or inner enemies – right observation is the first key to be followed. Even if you are to fight with the inner enemies, right observation is the first key

First one should have a good look at whom the fight is going to be with. If the fight is going to be against anger, then look at the anger; if it is going to be against sex, then look at sex; and if it is to be against greed, then look at greed. Even if one has to have a fight outside, first take a good look at whom the fight is going to be with. Who is this person? A thorough observation of this kind is possible only when one has the capacity for being a witness. Otherwise it is not possible.

So, the Gita is now about to begin. The stage is set. But looking at this sutra it seems that even a person who doesn't already know the rest of the story of the Gita but has an understanding of what observation means can very well say – simply on the basis of this sutra – that it will be very difficult for Arjuna to fight, that this man will not be able to fight, that he will certainly have difficulty in fighting.

One who is ready to observe will find fighting difficult. Because he is observing, he will not be able to fight. In order to fight one's eyes have to remain closed, in order to fight one has to be mad – there cannot be room for any observation.

Thus, even without further knowledge of the Gita, anyone who understands the phenomenon of observation can say, on looking at this sutra, that this man Arjuna is not dependable; this man is not dependable for war. He can easily withdraw himself from a war – because when he looks, he will find it all so meaningless. Anyone who is observing will find everything so futile that he will feel like removing himself from it.

What Arjuna is saying is highly indicative of his state of mind. In this statement, he is showing his state of mind very clearly. He is not saying that he is anxious to fight: 'O my charioteer, bring me to a place from where I can destroy my enemies in the best possible way.' Arjuna is not saying this – even though this is what he would be expected to have said. Instead, what he is saying is, 'Take me to a place from where I can see who has come to fight and from where I can observe how eager they are to have this fight.' This word *observation* shows that here is a man of reflection – and a man of reflection is bound to fall into indecisiveness.

Only those who are either thoughtless like Bheeshma or Duryodhana or who are in the state of 'no-thought' like Krishna can fight a war. Reflection, thinking, is a state in between the two.

These are the three states. Thoughtlessness is a state prior to the state of thinking. War is a very easy thing in this state. There is really nothing to be done in order to enter into a war; a man in this state of mind is at war all the time. Even when such a man loves, his love proves to be nothing but a war. Even when such a man loves, his love proves to be nothing but hatred. Even when such a man goes into friendship, it proves to be nothing but a step toward enmity. After all, in order to have an enemy one first needs to make a friend. It is difficult to create an enemy without making a friend. So even when a thoughtless mind goes into friendship, only enmity can come out of it. War is a natural occurrence in this state.

The second state is that of thinking, reflection. Thinking is always unsteady; it is always wavering. Arjuna is in this second stage. Here he is saying, 'Let me observe. Let me look and understand. Then I may enter into the war.' Has anyone in this world ever been able to go to war after looking and understanding? Looking and understanding can pave the way for escaping from war, but not for going into it.

Krishna is in the third state. This is the state of no-thought. Thought is also absent here, but it is not a state of thoughtlessness. Thoughtlessness and no-thought seem to be alike but there is a fundamental difference between the two. The man of no-thought is one who, having realized the futility of thinking, has gone beyond it.

Thinking shows the futility of everything: even of life, even of love, even of the family, even of wealth, even of the world, even of war. But if one goes on thinking, then in the end, this thinking shows the futility of thinking itself. And it is at this point that the person enters the state of no-thought. Then, in this state of no-thought everything becomes possible for this person – in exactly the same way as it is for a thoughtless person. But the very quality of this person and his actions is different. He is like a small child.

When someone attains to saintliness in old age, he again becomes like a child. However, the similarity between saintliness and the child exists only on the surface. A sage's eyes become as innocent as those of a child, but in a child everything is still dormant, has yet to manifest. Hence, a child is a volcano: it has not exploded yet, but that is the only difference. His innocence is superficial: underneath, everything is getting ready to explode. The seeds are germinating inside him; they are sprouting. Sex, anger, and enmity – everything will surface in time. Right now, everything is being prepared. A child is a time bomb: it will take some time and then it will explode.

But a sage has gone beyond all this. All those seeds that were supposed to sprout within him have done so, and having proved futile have been dropped. Now nothing remains inside: his eyes have again become innocent; everything has again become pure.

Someone asked Jesus who would inherit his kingdom of heaven. Jesus answered, 'Those who are like children.' Jesus did not say those who *are* children – because children cannot inherit. He said those who are *like* children, not those who are children. So one thing is clear: those who are not children but who are like children will be entitled to inherit.

If children could enter heaven then there would be no problem: everyone would enter. No, children cannot enter; only those who are like children, who have transcended, can enter.

So, there is a great similarity between an ignorant man and a man of supreme understanding. The man of supreme understanding becomes as simple as an ignorant one looks. However, inside the simplicity of the ignorant, a complexity is still hidden which can manifest at any time. The man of supreme understanding is one who has lost all complexity.

One who is thoughtless can still think. One day he *will* think:

the power of thinking is still lying dormant in him. But one who has reached the state of no-thought has transcended thoughts: he has entered into meditation, he has entered samadhi, the supreme meditation.

This is the problem that will present itself throughout the Gita. This is the inner conflict that will manifest throughout the Gita. Arjuna can enter into the war in only two ways: either he can become thoughtless and step downward and stand where Duryodhana and Bheeshma are, or he can rise to the point where Krishna is standing and becomes a man of no-thought. Then he can enter into the war.

But if Arjuna remains as he is – in between, engrossed in thinking – then he will head toward the forest, he cannot go to war. He will escape; he will run away.

CHAPTER 2

The Roots of Violence

'I would like to see those who are assembled here, ready to fight,
and wanting the evil-minded son of Dhritarashtra to flourish.'

SANJAY:
Thus addressed by Arjuna, Krishna placed
his supreme chariot between the two armies
deliberately in front of Bheeshma, Drona and the other rulers,
and said:
'Behold, Arjuna, these Kurus assembled here.'

Thereupon Arjuna beheld the uncles, grandfathers and teachers,
maternal uncles, brothers, sons, and grandsons,
as well as comrades, assembled there.

Also fathers-in-law and friends in both the armies.
Seeing all his kinsmen thus arrayed, Arjuna,
overcome with mercy, uttered these words in great anguish:
'O Krishna, seeing my own kinsmen standing before me, eager
to fight,
'My limbs give way, my mouth becomes dry, my body trembles,
and in the dreadful thrill of horror the hairs on my body stand aloft.

'My bow, Gandiva, slips from my hand; my skin is aflame
I cannot remain steady. My mind appears confused.

'O Krishna, I see all the portents are opposing this,
and I do not foresee any virtue in slaying my own people in battle.

'I do not long for victory, O Krishna,
nor for the kingdom, nor for its pleasures.
Of what use, O Krishna, will this kingdom be to us,
or pleasures, or even life itself?'

ARJUNA IS NOT OBSESSED with war, but he is not against war either. And he has no aversion to violence. In fact, his whole life's education and training, his lifelong conditioning, is all for violence and war.

But it is worth understanding that the more violent a mind is, the more full of attachment it is. Violence and attachment live together, side by side. A non-violent mind transcends attachment. In fact, one who wants to be non-violent has to let go of the very idea of attachment. The very sense of 'mine' is violence, because as soon as I say 'mine', I have begun to separate myself from that which is not mine. As soon as I address someone as a friend, I have begun to make someone else my enemy. As soon as I draw a line around those who are mine, I have also drawn a line around those who are strangers to me. All violence is an outcome of the boundary created between those who are 'mine' and those who are outsiders, 'not mine'.

That is why Arjuna suddenly became weak, limp. All his limbs gave way: not because he suddenly became averse to war or because he found anything wrong with the violence that was about to ensue, or because a sudden pull toward non-violence took place in his mind. Arjuna became weak because his mind was suddenly gripped by the other side, by the opposite side of violence; by its much deeper component, by its fundamental basis. His mind was gripped by the feeling of 'mine-ness', of attachment.

Mine-ness, attachment, is nothing but violence. It will be difficult to understand the whole of the Gita without first understanding this. To those who cannot understand this point, it seems as if Arjuna was actually leaning toward non-violence and that Krishna pushed him toward violence. If someone were leaning toward non-violence, Krishna would never want to push him toward violence. In fact, even if Krishna wanted to, he would not be able to.

The situation here is that Arjuna is not leaning even one iota toward non-violence. Arjuna's mind has moved to and is stuck at the very foundational point of violence. Mine-ness is nothing but the very foundation of violence.

Arjuna saw his own people – loved ones, relatives. Had they not been his beloved ones and relatives, Arjuna would have slaughtered them like cattle – but he found it difficult to do so because these were his own people. Had they been strangers he would have felt no difficulty in cutting them to pieces.

Non-violence can only be born in the consciousness of a person who has gone beyond the feeling of 'mine' and 'yours'. The reason behind Arjuna's troubled mind is not that he is attracted toward non-violence, but that he has touched the very basis of violence.

It is natural that the basis, the foundation stone of violence surfaced in such a moment of crisis. Had the enemies been strangers, Arjuna would not have even noticed that he was a violent person or that he was doing anything wrong in killing them. He would have never felt that war was against religiousness. His limbs would not have given way; instead, on seeing these strangers they would have become even tauter. His arrow would have been set on the bow, his hands would have grasped his sword – he would have been delighted, exhilarated.

But at this point, Arjuna became completely sad, and in that state of sadness he encountered the real basis of the violence that was within him. What he saw at that moment of crisis was 'mine-ness'.

It is a surprising thing that we are often only able to see into the depths of our minds during moments of crisis. We do not see these depths in ordinary moments. In ordinary moments we live ordinarily. It is only during extraordinary moments that what is hidden in the deepest part of us begins to manifest.

Arjuna saw 'my people'. In that horrendous situation of war, in that immediacy of war – when the war is just about to start – he sees 'my people.' If Arjuna had said, 'War is useless, violence is useless', the book of the Gita would not have been born. But what Arjuna said is, 'Our own people are assembled here and my limbs are giving way at the mere thought of killing them.' In fact, it is only natural that one who has built the whole edifice of his life upon the foundation of 'mine-ness' will find his limbs giving way at the thought of killing them.

A death occurs in the neighborhood, but it does not touch people's hearts. People simply say, 'The poor man died.' We are unable to brush it away like this when it occurs in our own homes. Then it affects us, because when a death occurs in our homes, when one of 'our own' dies, we also die, a part of our own selves dies. We had an investment in this person who has died, we used to get something from this person's life. This person was occupying a certain corner of our hearts.

So when a wife dies it is not just the wife who dies. Something in the husband dies too. The truth is that the husband came into being when the wife came into being. Before that there was not a husband or a wife. When a son dies, something in the mother also dies – because the woman only became a mother at the birth of her son. With the birth of a child, the mother is also born, and at the death of a child, the mother also dies. We are connected with the one we call ours. When he or she dies, we also die.

It is not surprising that when he saw his own people assembling to fight the war, Arjuna felt as if he were committing suicide. It is not the idea of others' deaths that shook Arjuna. It is the idea of his own death, the possibility of a suicidal experience, that made him shaky. He felt, 'Where will I be if all my own people die?'

This is worth giving some thought to.

Our 'I' is nothing but a name of the sum total of what we call 'our own people'. What we call 'I' is the name for all the accumulations of 'mine'. If all those who are 'mine' are to leave, then I will be no more, then I cannot remain. This 'I' of mine is attached partly to my father, partly to my mother, partly to my son, partly to my friend... to all of these people.

What is even more surprising is that this 'I' is not only attached to those whom we call our own, but it is also attached to those whom we consider outsiders or 'not-mine'. Although this attachment is outside our circle, nonetheless it is there. Hence, when my enemy dies, I also die a little, since I will not be able to be exactly the same as I was while my enemy was alive. Even my enemy has been contributing something to my life. He was my enemy. He may have been an enemy but he was *my* enemy. My 'I' was related to him too: without him I will be incomplete.

Had Arjuna seen that it was others who were going to be slaughtered, that would have been a different matter altogether. But what he saw, deep down, was: 'Actually I have been eager to kill no one else but myself. It would be a suicide. What would be the point of continuing to live when all 'my very own' are dead? Even if I were to gain everything, it would be worthless if none of 'mine' were alive'.

This is worth considering more deeply. Whatsoever we accumulate is less for ourselves than it is for those whom we call 'our very own'. The house that we build is less for ourselves than it is for those whom we call 'our very own' – for those 'very own' who will live in it, for those 'very own' who will admire and praise it – and also for those 'very own' and 'others' who will become full of envy and will burn with jealousy. Even if the most beautiful mansion on this earth is mine but none of 'my very own people' are around to see it – either as friends or as enemies – I will suddenly find that this mansion is worth less than a hut. This is because the mansion is only a façade: in reality it is simply a means to impress 'our very own' and those who are not our very own. If no one is around, whom will I impress?

The clothes you wear are more intended to dazzle others' eyes than to cover your own body. Everything becomes meaningless when you are all alone. You ascend thrones less for any pleasure that you may get from ascending – no one has ever attained any bliss from merely sitting on a throne – rather than for the sake of all the charisma that you are able to generate amongst 'your very own' and 'others' by being on it. You may remain sitting on the throne, but if all the people around it disappear, you will suddenly find that sitting on it has become ludicrous. You will get down from it and perhaps never sit on it again.

In that moment Arjuna felt, 'These are my very own people who have gathered on both sides. These are my very own people who are going to die – so what is the point of a victory?'

Victory is never desired for the sake of victory. The real interest in victory is because of the ego-fulfillment that it brings to one amongst 'one's very own' as well as amongst strangers or those who are not one's very own. 'I may gain the whole empire, but what is the point?' It will have no meaning at all.

The anguish that has overtaken Arjuna's mind should be properly understood. This anguish is born out of 'mine-ness'. This anguish is a product of a violent mind. And it is because of this state of anguish that Krishna had to give Arjuna so many jolts. Had a person like Mahavira been in Arjuna's place, the whole matter would have ended right there and then: it could not have been prolonged any further. Had it been a person like Mahavira, then maybe the whole matter would not have even come up. Perhaps Krishna would not have said a single word to a person like Mahavira – it would make no sense. The whole matter would have been finished without a word.

The truth is that the Gita is less about what Krishna said and more about what Arjuna caused him to say. Its real author is Arjuna and not Krishna. The state of Arjuna's mind has become the basis of the Gita. And it is clearly visible to Krishna that a violent man has reached the philosophical peak of his violence, and at the root of all this talk of running away from the violence is that same violent mind.

Arjuna's dilemma is not that of a non-violent man trying to run away from violence; Arjuna's dilemma is that of a violent man trying to run away from violence. This truth needs to be rightly understood.

'Mine-ness' is nothing but violence. It is a deeper violence; it is not seen. The moment I call someone 'mine', possession has begun. Possessiveness is a form of violence. The husband calls his wife 'mine'; possession has begun. The wife calls her husband 'mine'; possession has begun. But whenever we become a person's owner, right there and then we damn that person's soul. We have just killed that person; we have destroyed that person the moment we claim ownership over him or her.

In fact, by owning a person we are treating them not as an individual but as an object. Then a wife becomes 'mine' in the same way that a house is mine. Naturally, wherever there is the relationship of 'mine', love is not the outcome. What manifests is only conflict.

This is why in this world as long as a husband and wife or a father and son keep claiming their ownership over each other, only conflict can happen between them – never friendship. The assertion of such ownership is the cause of the friendship's destruction. Such an assertion of ownership puts everything awry; everything becomes violent.

Whenever there is an assertion of ownership, only hatred is created; and where there is hatred, violence is bound to follow. That is why all our relationships have become relationships of violence. Our families have come to be nothing but relationships of violence.

So here, seeing where he would be if all his own people were destroyed; seeing the futility of being victorious – of having the kingdom and all that comes with it, but with all his own people annihilated – has not made Arjuna a non-violent man.

Had this happened, Krishna would have blessed him and asked him to leave, and the whole matter would have come to an end. But because he is talking in terms of 'I' and 'mine-ness', Krishna knows that Arjuna is a totally violent man, and that his talk of non-violence is just phony.

If someone is talking in terms of 'I' and in favor of non-violence, then know that his non-violence is phony – because the flower of non-violence never blossoms in the soil of 'I' and 'mine'. A life of non-violence never evolves from the basis of 'mine'.

OSHO,

Arjuna went to the battlefield, saw his relatives, elders, teachers and friends and was filled with sorrow. He felt anguish... his mind was violent. At the same time Duryodhana, Yudhishthira, Dronacharya and many others whose relatives and friends were there and whose minds were also full of violence and 'mine-ness' were on the battlefield too. Why, then, did only Arjuna fall into a state of anguish?

This is true. Duryodhana was certainly there, so were other warriors – so why didn't they feel this anguish? They too were full of this feeling of 'mine', they too were full of violence, but they didn't fall into a state of anguish.

There is a reason for this. Violence can be blind and thoughtless; the feeling of mine-ness can be blind and thoughtless. But violence can also have eyes and can be thoughtful, and so too can the feeling of mine-ness.

The problem for Arjuna is that he is *not* thoughtless. He is a thoughtful man. Thinking throws one into a dilemma, and it is thinking that threw Arjuna into a dilemma. Duryodhana can also see, but the violence in him is so blinding that he is unable to realize that by resorting to violence he will destroy all those without whom even the outcome of his violence will lose all meaning. In his blindness he cannot see this.

Arjuna is not so blind. And that is why he is special, unique, on that battlefield. He is special in the sense that although his preparation and upbringing in life has been the same as Duryodhana's, the preparedness of his mind is different. He has a mind capable of thinking and doubting. He can doubt, he can inquire, he can raise questions. He has got the fundamental keys of inquiry.

And our greatest questions are not those that we raise about the universe. Our greatest questions are not those in which we inquire who created the universe. Our greatest questions are not those in which we ask whether there is a God or not. Our greatest questions are those that are born out of our own inner conflict, our own mental dilemma. But it takes thinking, reflection and contemplation in order to see the conflicts and dilemmas of one's own mind.

Arjuna is able to think, he is able to see that the violence he is going to commit will kill those very people for whose sake there could be any justification for engaging in violence in the first place. Arjuna is not blind, and this very fact is his affliction as well as his blessing.

It will be good to understand this.

Arjuna is not blind: that is his trouble. Duryodhana is not in trouble – war is a passion for him. For Arjuna, war has become a crisis and an affliction, which in a different sense is also a blessing for him. If he can go beyond this crisis, he will enter the state of no-thought. If he can go beyond this crisis, he will arrive at the state of surrendering to the whole. If he can go beyond this crisis, he will enter the state of renouncing mine-ness. But if he fails to go beyond this crisis, then this war will certainly prove to be a terrible crisis for him and it will turn him into a schizophrenic. In that case, either he will run away or he will fight halfheartedly and be defeated.

A battle that is fought reluctantly is bound to bring defeat – because fighting reluctantly means that half of the mind is on the run while the remaining half is involved in the fight. For the one who is moving in two opposite directions within himself, defeat is certain. Then it will be Duryodhana who wins because he is fighting with an undivided mind. Although he is falling into a ditch, he is doing so with an undivided mind; although he is going into darkness, he is doing so with an undivided mind.

In fact, only two kinds of people can go into darkness with an undivided mind. One is blind – because whether there is darkness or light makes no difference to him, and the other is the one who has the light of consciousness – because then his very existence will dispel the darkness.

Either Arjuna should become like Duryodhana and fall below, descending from thought into thoughtlessness, and then he will go into the war, or he should become like Krishna and move upward from thought to the state of no-thought – becoming so illuminated, so full of inner light that he can experience statements such as 'no-one dies, no-one gets killed'. Only then will he see that all these things happening around him are more than a dream.

So either he can enter the war by seeing a great truth of such immensity as this, or he can enter the war by subscribing to such a great untruth that he will attain to happiness by killing the very people for whose sake the war is really being fought.

Arjuna can be free from anxiety either by descending into Duryodhana's untruth or by ascending to Krishna's truth. So Arjuna is in tension.

Nietzsche has said somewhere that man is a bridge, a link joining two different shores. He is in tension. Either he becomes an animal and finds pleasure, or he can become divine and attain to bliss. But as long as he remains a human being he can find neither pleasure nor bliss – he can merely be pulled between the two; he will remain filled with anxiety and tension.

That is why we do both things in life. We drink and turn into an animal. It gives some pleasure. Sex gives some pleasure – we go back into an animal state. We find some pleasure when we fall below the level of thought. The main reason why people in the world are so attracted toward alcohol is that it helps them become an animal again. We reach to the same level as animals when we get drunk. At that level we become like carefree animals, because an animal has no worries.

No animal goes insane except those who work in circuses, because a circus animal comes very close to being in the same state as man. And man is very close to being in the state of a circus animal.

No animal is insane; no animal is faced with psychosis, worry, or a disease like insomnia. No animal commits suicide – because in order to commit suicide much anxiety has to accumulate.

It is an interesting fact that no animal feels boredom. A buffalo keeps grazing the same grass every day and never gets bored. There is no question of her getting bored because a state of thoughtfulness is needed in order to get bored. That's why, among human beings, the more thoughtful one is, the more bored one is. The more thoughtful one is, the more worried one is. More thoughtful people can easily become mad or insane. But this is only one side.

The other side is that one who can transcend the state of potential insanity can become liberated, and one who can transcend the state of anxiety can attain a conscious, blissful state – a carefree state. And one who can go beyond tension can attain to the experience of relaxation that happens only by relaxing into godliness, into the whole.

Arjuna is the symbol of man, Duryodhana is the symbol of the animal, and Krishna is the symbol of godliness. Thus, there are three symbols on this battlefield.

Arjuna is not steady; he is in a shaky state that lies between the states of Duryodhana and Krishna. He can attain to carefree-ness; he can be at ease if he becomes a Duryodhana or a Krishna. This will not be possible as long as he remains an Arjuna. Remaining an Arjuna there is tension, there is difficulty. His difficulty is precisely this: he cannot become Duryodhana, and he is not able to work out how to become Krishna. And at the same time he cannot remain being as he is because he is merely a passing wave: it is not possible to endure for long.

No bridge is meant to be made into a home.

When Akbar built Fatehpur Sikri, he inscribed on a bridge: 'A bridge is for crossing, not to live on.' This is right. Anyone making a bridge his home will certainly get into difficulties.

One can return to either one of these states: one can become an animal or one can become divine. But one thing is certain – to remain a human being is not man's destiny. To be a human being is to be in crisis. Man is not the end. Rightly understood, man is neither animal nor godly. He is unable to be an animal because he has passed through the animal stage and he is unable to be godly because he has yet to reach up that far. Man is simply an existence that swings between godliness and the animal.

We touch these two poles several times each day. In anger, a person touches the animal, in peace, the same person touches godliness.

During twenty-four hours we travel many times between hell and heaven, many times. One moment we are in heaven, the next moment we slip into hell. When we are in hell, we repent and strive again for heaven. We have hardly settled down in heaven again than we start falling back to hell. Tension, by its very nature, creates an attraction to the opposite.

Take, for example, the pendulum of a clock: when it goes to the left we feel as if it is only going to the left. But, those who understand the science of a clock know that while the pendulum is moving to the left, it is also gathering momentum to go to the right. It is gathering energy to go as far to the right as it went to the left. In fact, it is only going to the left so that it can go to the right, and it is only going to the right so that it can go to the left.

Man is constantly moving like a pendulum between the animal and the divine. Arjuna is a symbol of man – particularly of today's man. Modern man's consciousness is exactly like Arjuna's. That is why both things are simultaneously evident in the present world. On the one hand man is eager to raise his consciousness to samadhi, to superconsciousness, and on the other hand he is eager to take it to the animal level with the help of LSD, mescaline, marijuana, alcohol and sex. Often, the same person will appear to be doing both things. The person who comes to India on a spiritual quest will keep taking LSD in America. He is doing both simultaneously.

In his unconscious state man can turn into an animal. However, it is not possible to remain unconscious for long – because even the pleasures of unconsciousness are experienced only in a conscious state. Even the pleasures of unconsciousness are not experienced in the unconscious state. The pleasure of a drink is not felt when a person is drunk; he comes to feel it only when he becomes sober. When you are asleep you do not know the pleasure of sleep; it is only after waking up in the morning that you recognize how beautiful and relaxing the sleep was. In order to feel the pleasure of unconsciousness it is necessary to return to the conscious state.

Arjuna represents human consciousness and this is why he is so special. And the Gita is so special because it portrays the basis of man's deep inner state of mind: Krishna's constant struggle with this state, which is represented in Arjuna; this dialogue, this debate that Krishna is having with Arjuna; Krishna's monumental efforts to pull Arjuna back again and again toward the divine – and again and again Arjuna's limbs giving way as he wants to fall back into the animal state... . This inner struggle is Arjuna's lot, but not Duryodhana's. Duryodhana has not a care in the world. If Arjuna were like Duryodhana, he too would not have a care in the world. But he is not like him.

There are those amongst us who, like Duryodhana, have no cares. They are building houses, they are clambering onto the thrones of Delhi and other capitals, they are busy making money. But those of us who are like Arjuna are restless and troubled. Restless, because where they find themselves does not seem to be a place worth making into a home. They have evolved a long way from where they originally began, so it is not possible to fall back, but they have no idea whatsoever about the place that they have not yet reached. How do they get there, where is the shrine located? They have no idea at all about this.

A man of religiousness will inevitably find himself in crisis. An irreligious man is not in crisis. Compared with the man sitting in a prison, the man sitting in a temple seems to be more worried. The man sitting in a prison seems to be less anxious; he has not a care in the world. He is at one end, on the shore. He is not on the bridge. In a sense he may appear to be fortunate, worth envying. How carefree he is! But hiding inside this so-called good fortune of his is a very deep misfortune. He will remain on this shore. As yet, not even a spark of humanity has been born inside him. Trouble, anguish, begins with being human – because in this state of being human the doors to the possibility of attaining to godliness open up.

Arjuna does not want to become an animal – and this situation could make him just that – but he has no idea how to attain to godliness. Yet deep down, unknowingly, the desire is there inside him to attain to godliness. That is why he is inquiring and raising questions; that is why this search is arising.

Religiousness can be born in anyone in whose life there are questions, in whose life there is a search, a discontent. Religiousness has no possibility of entering the life of anyone whose life has no anxiety, no questions, no doubts, no inquiry and no discontent.

The seed that is breaking open so that it can sprout will certainly feel anxiety. The seed is a tough thing, the sprout is very delicate; the seed is very carefree, the sprout faces great anxiety. Breaking through the rocks, cutting through the soil, such a delicate thing as a sprout comes out to an unknown and unfamiliar world, a world that it is completely unacquainted with. A child could snap it, an animal could eat it, anybody could trample over it. What will or will not happen to the sprout... nothing is certain around this. On the other hand, if the seed remains enclosed within itself, then it will be completely secure and safe, carefree – no trampling over it by a child, no unknown dangers. It is closed within itself.

Duryodhana is like a closed seed, having no cares. Arjuna is like a sprout, worried, restless. He is anxious to know what will happen next: will flowers blossom forth or not? He has dropped just remaining a seed, but will the flowers appear now? He is eager to grow, he is eager to blossom, and it is this eagerness that keeps him constantly asking Krishna questions.

Thus, there is anxiety, there are questions in Arjuna's mind – but not in the mind of Duryodhana.

OSHO,

Since man is confronted again and again with inner dilemmas, what should be the basis for overcoming them? How can we turn this state of inner dilemma into growth? And what should be the main and fundamental factor before us when we are finding a resolution to an inner dilemma?

Arjuna is facing the same question, and he too wants to solve it in the way that every man usually does. To be in a dilemma is the nature of man – not of the soul, not of the body, but of man.

If one tries to solve this dilemma hastily, what happens is that we fall back into the animal state. Haste will take us backward. It is a familiar path: one can easily return. To pass through the state of inner conflict is a real discipline for self-growth. To go patiently through a state of inner conflict is real asceticism, and only by facing this dilemma can one transcend it. So, if someone makes a hasty resolution, a hasty decision simply to avoid the inner dilemma, this kind of decision will not help. He will fall down, he will fall backward.

Animals are very definite; they have no doubt. They live in certainty, they are very confident. They seem to be great believers! But their belief is not real theism – because unless one has known atheism first, one's theism has no meaning. One who has never experienced the pain of saying 'no' cannot reach to the bliss of saying 'yes'. The trust of someone who has never doubted is worthless. But someone who has doubted, who has lived through his doubt and transcended it – this alone has some strength, some authenticity.

One way is to make a hasty decision, a hasty resolution – and man uses many routes to arrive at such a decision. If he catches hold of some scripture, the decision, the answer, is immediately there. The scripture will tell him in very definitive language to do such and such a thing and to have faith in it. But one who arrives at a decision by resorting to the scriptures denies himself the status of being human. He had an opportunity to evolve, but he rejected it. Or one can catch hold of some teacher, some guru. But whoever does so is losing the opportunity to grow. There was a crisis, life left him to go through it alone, unaided – but he saved himself from the inconvenience. He carried on without passing through the crisis.

Had the gold gone through the fire it would have emerged shining. But that person never passed through the fire. Instead, he sheltered behind a guru. Naturally, the gold did not purify itself.

I am not asking you to reach a decision. How can you reach a decision? The answer of someone who is in a quandary is surely going to be full of inner conflict too. How can you decide when you are in a quandary? One who is full of inner conflict cannot find a resolution – and he should not either.

Live the dilemma, go through the heat and suffering of it, die and be consumed by it, experience it. Don't run away from its fire, because what is manifesting as fire will burn away all the dirt, all the rubbish, and the pure gold will remain.

Pass through the dilemma; understand it is human destiny. You will have to go through it; live it. Don't hurry. Don't make a hasty decision. Yes, if you pass through it, the decision will come. Pass through it and the trust will emerge by itself – you will not have to get it from somewhere.

A trust brought in from the outside is of no value. The very fact that the trust had to be brought in shows that the mind was not yet ready for it, it has been prematurely brought in. A trust that has to be enforced only means that behind it there exists a mind full of conflict. This conflict will remain alive beneath the outer layer of this trust. And although this kind of trust may work superficially, it will be of no help at a critical time.

When a difficult moment confronts you, when death faces you… although you firmly believed that the soul is immortal, although this firm belief remained with you when you read the Gita, although you were certain about the immortality of soul while going to the temple every morning; now, when the doctor is standing next to you with a grim face, and when there is all this commotion amongst your concerned family members as your pulse begins to fall... in this moment you will suddenly come to realize that you don't know if the soul is really immortal or not.

The soul cannot become immortal because your Gitas say so – although your Gitas say so because the soul *is* immortal. But that is a different matter. The soul cannot become immortal because they are saying it. You believing someone else's words will make no difference.

Yes, pass through the inner conflict; bear its pain. This is an opportunity, and don't try to avoid it.

Arjuna is also trying to run away from this situation of dilemma, but Krishna is not helping him to avoid it; rather, he is trying to prolong it. Otherwise Krishna would have said: 'Don't worry. I know all about it. Don't indulge in meaningless talk. Just have faith in me and jump.' He could have talked like this; then there would have been no need for him to deliver such a long Gita.

The Gita, long as it is, is a great tribute to Arjuna's inner conflict. The interesting thing is that Arjuna keeps on asking the same thing again and again, and Krishna never says to him, 'You have asked this already. Why are you asking it again?' Arjuna asks the same thing over and over. None of his questions are different from one another; only the wording is different. His inner conflict keeps appearing again and again. But Krishna doesn't say to him, 'Be quiet! How dare you not have faith in what I say? How dare you doubt me?' No. Arjuna goes on repeatedly asking the same things. His inner conflict keeps appearing in newer and newer forms.

Krishna is not interested in creating any belief in Arjuna. Krishna is certainly interested in taking him to the point of trust. And there is a great difference between belief and trust. Belief is that which we impose upon ourselves without resolving the doubt, while trust is the outcome of the doubt falling away. Trust is the destination that is reached by journeying through doubt. Beliefs are blind supports that we clutch at out of our fear of doubt.

Hence I would say: live the dilemma, live it with intensity. If you live it mildly, it will take a long time. If you put the gold into slow fire, it can take lifetimes for it to shine to its purity. Live intensely.

Dilemma is the essential way in which man is tested, and from facing this dilemma his worthiness to attain to godliness is born. So live. Don't escape; don't look for consolations. Just realize that this is the destiny: dilemma is your destiny. Fight it; enter into the dilemma with intensity.

What will be the outcome of this? The outcome will be twofold. As soon as a person agrees to go completely into his inner conflict, a third point emerges within that person – a third power besides the other two is born in him. As soon as a person agrees to live through his inner conflict, three things instead of just two start functioning in him. This third force – which takes the decision to live through the dilemma – is outside of it, is uninvolved in it.

I have heard:

Saint Theresa was a Christian nun. Once she had three pennies, and one morning she said to the townspeople that she had enough money and wanted to build a big church. The people were puzzled, because until the day before they had seen her begging. People were asking how, all of a sudden, she had found so much money that she could propose building a church.

She showed them her begging bowl that contained three pennies.

The townspeople said, 'Theresa, have you gone mad? We always knew that there was something wrong with your mind.' Actually, those who don't turn toward the divine always find something wrong with the minds of those who do.

Theresa replied, 'As well as myself, I have the three pennies and existence: Theresa, plus three pennies, plus existence.'

The people said, 'Where is this existence?'

Theresa said, 'It is the third force which you do not see, because you have not yet been able to find this third force within yourselves.'

The one who discovers this third force within himself also becomes immediately capable of seeing it in the whole universe. You are only looking at the dilemma, without realizing that the one who sees it, the one who knows it, cannot be a part of the dilemma but will always be outside it.

When the two are fighting inside you and you become aware of this, you are inevitably separate from the two – otherwise how could you be watching them? Had you been associated with either one of the two, you would have become identified with that one and separate from the other.

But you say that there is a conflict: that your left hand and your right hand are fighting with one another. This fighting between the two hands can be observed as a conflict, because behind the two hands *you* are present as a third force, a third power. Otherwise, if you were just the left hand, why would you ever see any inner conflict with the right hand? The right hand would be the other to you – where would an *inner* conflict be?

Inner conflict is there because the third one is also present – watching, saying that a big conflict is taking place in the mind. Sometimes the mind says this and sometimes it says that – but who is the one who is mentioning this conflict?

Enter the conflict and go on recognizing, becoming acquainted with this third one. As you enter into the conflict, gradually you will begin to see this third one, the witness. And the day this witness is seen, conflicts will begin to fade away. The reason why there is conflict is because this third one is not seen. As soon as it is seen, synthesis begins.

So do not escape from dilemma, from inner conflict. The process of inner conflict is essential. Only by passing through is that which is beyond this conflict, the transcendent, attained.

The whole Gita is nothing but an effort to bring Arjuna to this third point. Throughout the Gita, Krishna's whole effort is to bring Arjuna to a point from where he can see this third one. His whole effort is for Arjuna to come to recognize this third one.

This third one is within everyone as well as without, but unless it is first seen inside, it cannot be seen on the outside. Once it is seen inside, then nothing but this third one begins to be seen on the outside as well.

OSHO,

You have described Arjuna as a symbol of human attributes. So in view of Sartre's statement about man being condemned to be free and therefore anxiety-ridden, wasn't it human for Arjuna to tremble at the idea of killing his own nearest and dearest? Wasn't the idea of avoiding war, even if it was born out of attachment, simply human nature?

Furthermore, just as the dilemma of Shakespeare's Hamlet was 'to be or not to be', Arjuna's anguish was 'to kill or not to kill'. In his *Gita Rahasya*, Tilak finds a parallel between Arjuna's state of anguish and Hamlet's. Is this right?

What Sartre says is absolutely applicable to Arjuna. Arjuna's crisis was also an existential one.

The Western existential thinkers – Sartre, Camus, Unamuno, Jaspers, Heidegger – have exactly the same state of mind as Arjuna. So beware! Krishna can also be born in the West, because there is a strong possibility of Krishna also being born wherever Arjuna's state of mind exists.

The entire West is in an existential crisis. Man's state of anxiety is hanging over the West as the only reality. What to do and what not to do – this or that? What to choose and what not to choose? Which value is worth choosing and which value is not? Everything has become uncertain.

Remember, the existential thinking that was born in the West came into being between the two wars. Sartre, Camus, and Unamuno are all outcomes of the last two world wars. These last two wars have created the same state of mind in the West as the Mahabharata did in Arjuna. These last two wars have shaken up every Western value. Now the question there is: 'To fight or not to fight?' What can fighting contribute? And the situation here is the same: 'What is the sense in fighting if all our own people are going to die?' And in the face of such a critically frightening situation as war, all the values and rules created in times of peace become questionable – which is not at all surprising. So you have asked a right question.

Sartre is in exactly the same state of mind as Arjuna was, but the danger here is different. The danger is not from Sartre's state of mind. Sartre is in Arjuna's state of mind, but he believes himself to be in Krishna's state of mind. And therein lies the danger. Actually, he is in the same state of mind as Arjuna, so if he were to inquire, that would be all right; if he were to ask questions, that would be all right. But instead he is giving answers: and this is where the danger lies.

The danger lies in the fact that Sartre is not inquiring; he is not asking what is right. Rather he is providing an answer that nothing is right. Sartre is giving an answer that nothing is right, that life has no value, that all existence is meaningless.

The answer that Sartre is giving is that there is nothing divine in the universe, there is no soul, there is nothing that survives after death; that the whole of existence is nothing but anarchy; that it is all accidental and there is no meaning in it anywhere. These are the answers he is providing and herein lies the danger.

Arjuna could have provided answers too; but he is just inquiring. If Arjuna answers, there are bound to be dangers. But Arjuna is only inquiring. And according to me, if one sees – as Sartre does – that there is no value in anything, that there is only valuelessness, that there is no meaning in life, no purpose; if that is really what one sees, then there remains no meaning, no point in Sartre saying anything either! Then he should just become silent. In such a situation only his silence seems to be meaningful. All talking is useless.

But no, Sartre is not silent. Rather, he is anxious to speak, to explain, to convince others of his viewpoint – so there is some fear behind it. The fear is that Sartre is not sure inside himself about the truth of his explanation. Perhaps, by explaining to others, he is eager to see it reciprocated on their faces. If they agree with the statement, if they consider it to be right, then it must be right. Then he can also believe that it is right.

As long as Sartre is inquiring, it is all right. But the existentialist thinkers in the West are labeling an inquiry as an answer. And when an inquiry poses as an answer, when the disciple poses as a master, when questions pose as explanations, a crisis of values develops – as it has in the West.

Everything has become muddled in the West; everything has become topsy-turvy. And there appears to be no way out of this muddle. No way is visible – not because the way doesn't exist, the way always exists, but if we have already made it our firm belief that there is no way out, and if this becomes our sole answer, then the way certainly becomes impossible to see.

Arjuna doesn't subscribe to this. He is desperately inquiring: there *must* be a way. 'I am seeking, I am inquiring. Please tell me.' He is beseeching Krishna: 'Please tell me, please explain to me. I am ignorant, I don't know anything.' Arjuna is humble. Arjuna's ignorance is humble. Sartre's ignorance is not humble. Sartre's ignorance is very assertive, and that is the danger. Nothing causes as much danger as assertive ignorance.

But it often happens that ignorance is very vocal. Arjuna is inquiring. He is saying, 'I am ignorant, I am in doubt, I am engulfed by this crisis. Please show me the way.' But he is still searching in the hope that there must be a way.

In my view, Arjuna is more courageous than Sartre – because the search for a way, even when one is in such deep distress, is certainly a matter of great courage. Sartre is not that courageous. His statements appear to be very courageous, but he himself is not so courageous.

Actually, it often happens that when a man passes through a dark alley he whistles. The whistling may appear to be quite a courageous act to those sleeping nearby, but this is not actually so. It only shows that the man is frightened. This whistling is not a proof of his courage; it is merely an effort to hide his fear.

There is an effort to deny the volcano, the chaos that the two world wars have produced in the West; to deny the enormous whirlwind that has been generated from the depths and which has resulted in the ground giving way and the earth being rent apart. Since there is no meaning in life, where is the need to fear the meaningless, the absurd? Since nothing has any value, where is the need to bother in searching for any value? Since there is no godliness what good is prayerfulness? Since there is nothing to hope for, there is no point in worrying about hopelessness.

An attempt to be free from anxiety, even in this state of hopelessness, only indicates a weak heart and a lack of courage. In fact, it is only when hope falls into a state of intense despair that it becomes clear if hope truly exists or not. When efforts to search for the light in a dense, deep darkness begin, only then does it become clear whether or not the desire for light is connected with a profound courage, an intense aspiration and a tremendous determination.

The Sartre, the existentialist way of thinking in the West is to accept this despair in a helpless way. The despair is there, but the West cannot get out of it so cheaply. That is why existentialism is nothing more than a fashion. And this fashion has begun to erode, has begun to die. Now, existentialism is not much of a living concept. In the West, the young are now disclaiming it, it has become old-fashioned: 'Let us drop this nonsense.'

But, the harmful effects of the hopelessness and despair that has been passed on by Sartre's generation are evident in the upcoming generation. This generation says: 'All right, then we shall dance naked on the street. After all, you are the ones who said everything is meaningless. Then what is the point in wearing clothes? We shall create all sorts of sexual relationships – since you are the ones who said there is no meaning in life anyway, so what is the use of having a family? We will not show respect to anyone, since – as you say – when nothing is sacred, what is the point of being respectful? And finally, we shall not worry about tomorrow.'

Students are dropping out of the universities in America and Europe. When their parents ask them to continue with their studies, they say: 'Who knows whether there will be a tomorrow? You have said that everything is uncertain, so what difference does it make if we become educated?' These young people say, 'Students were also studying in the colleges in Hiroshima, and then the atom bomb fell, and everything was over. If we are studying, and you are still preparing atom bombs, no one knows when you may drop them on us. So, allow us to live! Whatever few moments we have got for our lives, please allow us to live them.'

Thus, in the West, the expanse of life, in terms of time, has been completely shattered. Man is lodged on the moment. The feeling is: 'Do whatever has to be done right now. No one knows what will happen next moment. And how can you trust in the next moment anyway, because the next moment is nothing but death.'

In the West, time has become synonymous with death. Both have the same meaning. Whatever is available now, that is it. The rest has no value.

Recently, a man committed several murders, and when the court asked him why, he said, 'What's the problem? When everyone has to die sooner or later, I have simply facilitated the death of these people. They were going to die anyway, and murdering them meant I could have some pleasure. What is so wrong with my having that pleasure?'

When there is no place for value at all, then what the murderer says seems all right.

Sartre's generation has suffused the West with a hollowness because it does not have any answers, it only has questions – and it has declared those questions to be the answers.

Had Arjuna been the winner, a similar hollowness would have been generated in this country. But he didn't win; Krishna won. It was a great struggle between Arjuna and Krishna. Had some idea entered Arjuna's head, had he fallen victim to some craze for becoming a guru and therefore labeled his inquiries and questions as answers and assumed that his ignorance was wisdom, then the same situation as the one that has occurred in the West because of existentialist thinking would have been engendered in this country too.

The situation is the same, but as yet, the West still doesn't have a Krishna. But under such conditions a Krishna can be born in the West too.

Hence, it is not very surprising when movements such as Krishna Consciousness catch hold of Western people's minds. It is not surprising when young people start beating drums and chanting the name of Krishna on the streets of Western countries. It is not surprising at all – and it is not accidental either.

Nothing happens accidentally in this universe. Even when a flower blossoms, there is a long chain of reasons behind it. If someone is wandering on the streets in London beating a drum and singing 'Hare Krishna', it is not accidental. There is a deep pain in the minds and hearts of the West. Arjuna has appeared, but where is Krishna? The question has arisen, but where is the answer? The answer is being searched for. This search for the answer has been born.

So this was a very appropriate question.

I call Arjuna a symbol of man. And the sense of attachment, of 'mine-ness' that caught hold of Arjuna is also human nature.

Let me tell you a statement of Nietzsche's. He says: 'Unfortunate will be the day when man gives up his desire to go beyond himself. Unfortunate will be the day when the arrow that takes man beyond man will not be drawn on his bow. Unfortunate will be the day when man will be satisfied with just being a man.' Man is not the destination, he is only a resting place – he has to be transcended, crossed over. Arjuna himself is not the destination; he is only a resting place.

It is natural for man to be fond of his own people; it is natural for man to be afraid of killing his own people; it is natural for man to fall into the dilemma of either/or, this or that, to do or not to do. It is natural for him to be caught up in anxiety. But that which is natural for man is not necessarily the ultimate point of life. And that which is natural for man is natural for him alone – and with it also comes worry, pain and tension, restlessness, suffering and insanity.

If we consider man as he is as a criterion for what is natural, then this naturalness is as natural as cancer and tuberculosis. Pain and suffering are a part of the nature of tuberculosis. If we look at man from the animal side, the animal end, then he is an evolution. And if we look at him from the side of godliness, then he is a disease. Man is an evolution if seen from the animal side and a disease if seen from the side of the divine.

This English word *disease* is a good one. It is made up of two words, *dis* and *ease*, and means restlessness, not at ease. So, seen from the side of godliness, man is a disease, a restlessness. And if animals ever think about us, they will never even consider that we are more highly evolved than they are. They may be thinking that people are those animals who went crazy, who went out of their minds. Animals may well be thinking this as they see man going to psychiatrists for mental check-ups, creating mental asylums and hospitals, worrying day and night. Occasionally, when they gather together, they must be wondering – just as fathers often think about their sons – how much they have tried to convince these poor fellows not to become man. But they would not listen and now they are suffering.

Animals are our forefathers; we have come through the same route. Certainly, they must be thinking that despite their entreaties this particular generation got spoiled, went astray. But they have no idea what possibilities have opened up because of this straying. A tremendous pilgrimage has opened up because of man's going astray.

Obviously, someone who is sitting at home does not have to go through as many problems and troubles as someone who is on a pilgrimage. There is dust on the path, there are ditches and holes on the path; there are all the mistakes and the errors that occur on the path; there is always the possibility of going astray on the path. The path is unknown, without any map. It is uncharted, one has to discover it and walk; one has to create the path by walking. But it is those who walk, those who go astray – who become lost, who fall down, suffer and go through the pain – that reach.

Arjuna's state is a natural state for man, but he himself is filled with pain, he himself is not willing to remain a man. He either wants to become like Duryodhana, or he wants someone to help him to the state of realization where everything that is happening is perfectly fine, he wants someone to raise him from his present state of being an Arjuna. This is his anxiety and sorrow. Exactly this is his pain.

'My limbs give way, my mouth goes dry, my body trembles, and in the dreadful thrill of horror the hairs on my body stand aloft.

'My bow, Gandiva, slips from my hand; my skin is aflame I cannot remain steady. My mind appears confused.

'O Krishna, I see the portents are opposing this, and I do not foresee any good from slaying my own people in battle.

'I do not long for victory, O Krishna, nor for the kingdom, or for its pleasures. Of what use, O Krishna, will this kingdom be to us, or pleasures, or even life itself?'

Arjuna's limbs have lost their strength, his mind has deserted him; the bow has slipped from his hands. He appears so weak that he says he is doubtful if he will have enough strength to remain seated in the chariot.

A few things need to be understood here.

Firstly, the body is only a reflection of our mind. Whatever takes place deep within the mind is reflected through each and every fiber of our body. The mighty Arjuna suddenly feels so weak that he finds it difficult even to remain seated in his chariot. This was not so a moment before. In this single moment he has not fallen sick; in this one moment nothing crippling has happened to his body, he has not become old. So what has happened?

In this single moment only one thing has happened: his mind has lost its strength. His mind has become feeble, his mind has become divided into self-opposing parts. Whenever the mind is divided into self-opposing parts it immediately makes the body sick and helpless. Whenever the mind becomes synthesized into a single harmony, immediately the body becomes healthy and wholesome. Arjuna's bow slipping from his hand, the trembling of his limbs, his hair standing on end, is all indicative. It is indicative of the fact that the body is nothing more than a reflection of the mind.

In the past, this was not believed to be so. Scientists said that the mind is nothing more than a reflection of our body, and those who based their thinking on this mistaken notion said the same thing. Brihaspati, Epicurus, Marx and Engels all said that this consciousness of ours is merely a by-product; this mind within us is simply a by-product of our body. It is only following the body.

William James and Carl Lange each contributed to an amazing theory that arose late in the nineteenth century, which remained in vogue for years. The theory came to be known as the James-Lange Theory. What they said was very interesting. Both tried to prove that the commonly held belief that a man first becomes frightened and then runs is wrong. They said that this was a mistaken idea – because if the body is the principal thing and the mind is merely a by-product, then the reverse should be true. They said that a man feels fear because he runs.

Normally it was believed that because a man gets angry, his fists and teeth clench, blood runs through his eyes, his breathing becomes heavy, and he gets ready to attack. James and Lange said that this was a misunderstanding, that the phenomenon will first take place in the body because the body is the primary thing. It will merely be reflected in the mind. The mind is just a simple mirror and nothing more. Hence, they said, the phenomenon is the reverse: because man clenches his fists and presses his teeth together, because blood runs faster in his body, because his breathing becomes heavy, anger takes place.

James and Lange each presented a number of arguments to prove their point. Now, this is a very curious example of logic. It is worth seeing how logic can mislead one and take one on mistaken routes. They said, 'Let us see if a man can show fear without running away from the fearful object or scene and without allowing any physical symptoms of fear. Let's see if any man can be angry without his eyes turning red, without clenching his fists or pressing his teeth together.'

This is difficult; how in the world can you manage this? So they said that if anger is not possible without all those symptoms, it means that anger is a sum total, an outcome of them all – nothing more than that.

I don't know why no one said to James and Lange that actually the reverse of what they were saying takes place. An actor can show anger – he can make his eyes red, he can grind his teeth, he can clench his fists, and yet there is really no anger inside him. An actor can show his love – and perhaps no one else can show as much love as an actor can – but inside him there is not a trace of love.

Arjuna is functioning in exactly the opposite way from the James-Lange Theory. James and Lange would never agree with what he is saying. They would say he is talking nonsense, that what he ought to say is: 'Because my bow is slipping down, because my hairs are standing on end, because my body is becoming weak and my limbs are giving way, therefore, O Krishna, great anguish is arising in my mind.' But Arjuna is not saying this. The anguish has arisen in him first – because there is no other reason for his body to become weak and his hair to stand on end. There is no outer cause for all this to happen. In that single moment nothing has changed externally, everything has remained the same. But inwardly everything has changed.

At the Lhasa University in Tibet, some elements of yoga were an essential part of the curriculum. One yoga experiment was regularly practiced there. It was known as 'Heat Yoga' and all students were required to pass it. It was a technique to create heat in the body through the mind. It sounds strange – just through the mind!

It would be snowing outside and the men would stand naked, sweating in the cold.

They would not even stop at that. Students were examined at night in an open field where they were asked to stand naked in the snow on the shores of a lake. Wet clothes – shirts, jackets, etcetera, dipped in the freezing water – were kept close by. The poor students would stand there and the one who could dry the largest number of clothes on his body by creating bodily heat would receive the highest points.

When some Western doctors saw this and looked at it closely, they were simply astounded. They said, 'Whatever happened to the James-Lange Theory?' It was snowing outside, the doctors were shivering even under the heavy clothes they were wearing – so what were these boys doing standing naked? Their bodies were there, ready to respond in the manner that they should in such a given situation, but their minds were denying it. Their minds went on suggesting that they were standing in fierce sunshine, that it was really hot, that their bodies were burning like fire – and so their bodies had to sweat profusely.

What happened to Arjuna was nothing but the whirlpool that had arisen in his mind reaching and manifesting in his body. Very rarely in our lives do the whirlpools in our bodies reach to our minds. Almost always it is the whirlpools in our minds that reach our bodies. And yet, for our whole lives, we only keep worrying about the body.

If Krishna had had even a touch of our so-called 'scientific brain' he would have said to Arjuna, 'It seems you are struck down with flu.' If he had read Marx, he would have said to Arjuna, 'It seems that your body is lacking some hormones. Come and get yourself admitted to some general hospital.' But he said nothing of the sort. Instead, he began to advise the physically failing Arjuna in another way. He began to explain something else to Arjuna's mind; he began trying to change Arjuna's mind.

There are only two processes of transformation in this world. One is the process that transforms man's body, and the other is the process that transforms man's consciousness. Science focuses on the process that transforms man's body; religion focuses on the process that transforms man's consciousness.

This is where the difference between the two lies – and hence I say that religion is a deeper and a greater science than science itself. It is the supreme science, because it begins with the center. A scientific mind would certainly begin with the center, because the impacts made upon the circumference may not necessarily reach to the center, but the impacts made upon the center certainly reach to the circumference. Harm caused to a leaf may not necessarily reach down to the roots of a tree – often it will not, and there is no need for it to – but harm caused to the roots will certainly reach up to the leaves. It has to; there is no way it cannot reach.

At what level does Krishna deal with Arjuna, seeing him in this state of mind? Had Krishna dealt with Arjuna on the physical level, the Gita would have become a book on physiology. It would have been merely a scripture on the physical. But Krishna deals with him on the level of consciousness; hence, the Gita has become a work on psychology.

The point where the Gita develops into a psychological scripture is when Krishna pays absolutely no attention to the phenomenon of Arjuna's physical state. He neither examines his pulse nor gives him a thermometer. He simply cares as little as possible about what is happening to Arjuna's body; Krishna's is concerned with what is happening to Arjuna's consciousness.

This needs to be given some more thought.

As I have said, even today the human race is gripped by a consciousness almost exactly the same as Arjuna's. Even today the symptomatic effects on the human body are the same as they were on Arjuna's. But the treatment we are giving people today begins with the body, and that is why even after a complete treatment, the person remains as sick as ever – because no treatment is being given from the side of his consciousness.

This is what Arjuna is saying, 'My mind is forsaking me. I have become completely drained of energy, powerless.'

What is power? One power is the one which resides in the muscles – which has not changed at all in Arjuna's case. And still, in this moment, Arjuna could fall down even from the push of a small child. His muscles would be no use; a small child could defeat him. So this muscular power doesn't seem to be of much consequence.

There is yet another power which comes through the will. The truth is that the real power or strength is that which is born out of the will.

The strength that comes through the will has been completely lost – because from where will this will come? Once the mind is in a dilemma, in conflict, the will falls to pieces. The will only crystallizes when the mind is single-pointed. When the mind falls into dilemma, into conflict, the will is lost.

We too are weak, we too have no will. The will has been lost in our 'What to do and what not to do? What is proper and what is improper?' All the ground beneath our feet has been lost. The Arjuna in us is in suspension, is in limbo.

This is the state of each and every person. This is why, although there are marvelous truths in the Koran, in the Bible, in the Tao Te Ching and in many, many other scriptures of the world, the Gita remains special. And the sole reason is that it is less a religious scripture and more of a scripture on psychology. There are no empty statements in it such as: 'There is God' or 'There is soul'. There are no philosophical statements and there is no philosophical syllogism in it. The Gita is mankind's first text on psychology; hence its value is incomparable.

If I could have my way, I would like to call Krishna the father of psychology. He is the first person who tries to integrate the conflict-ridden mind, the anguished mind, and the scattered will. We can say that he is the first man who uses psychoanalysis – not only psychoanalysis but also psychosynthesis.

Unlike Freud, Krishna is not merely a psychoanalyst; he is a psychosynthesist. He not only analyzes and investigates the mind to find out its fragmentations, he also investigates how it can attain to individuation – how Arjuna can become integrated.

Arjuna's state of mind is the state of mind of us all, but perhaps we are never in such an acute moment of crisis as he is. Even our crises are so lukewarm that we go on enduring them. If our crises could be as intense as his, as dramatic as his, perhaps we too would become eager for integration.

I have heard:

Once a psychologist dropped a frog in a pail of boiling water. Instantly the frog jumped out of it. He was placed in the same situation as Arjuna! Since the water was boiling, the poor frog could not adjust himself to it – so he jumped out.

Later, the same psychologist put that frog in a different pail of water and began to heat it up slowly. He brought it to a boiling point in twenty-four hours. As he kept on warming the water very gradually the frog went on accepting it – just as we all do. The water became a little warmer and the frog too became a little warmer. The frog thought there was no real need for him to jump out; that it could be endured. So he went on adjusting himself – just as we all do.

In twenty-four hours he became fully adjusted. By the time the water did boil the frog remained adjusted because he did not notice any difference – the water temperature has risen bit by bit and there was nothing drastic between any two successively rising bits that could make him feel the need to jump.

The frog went on accepting it, bit by bit. He died. The water kept on boiling, he got boiled in it, but he didn't jump. The frog could have jumped – there is nothing more natural for a frog than to jump – but he couldn't even manage that.

Here too Arjuna is finding himself in a totally boiling situation. It is an extreme situation; hence Arjuna abruptly drops his bow and arrows. We cannot even drop our weighing scales or yardsticks in our shops and businesses – or even our writing pens – and here is Arjuna who has suddenly become so weak he is just sitting in his chariot.

What has happened? To get adjusted to the crisis so fast and with such intensity became very difficult.

I would like to say to you: Don't go on slowly adjusting your-selves. No, not everyone has the situation of a Mahabharata arising in his or her life. And that is very compassionate on the part of existence – because if everyone had to face a Mahabharata war it would be a big problem.

Life is a Mahabharata, but stretched out over a longer term. It doesn't have the same urgency, the same degree of intensity or the same kind of density to it: everything takes place slowly and grad-ually. We go on adjusting ourselves up to the last moment when death knocks on our doors. We reconcile ourselves and thus no revolution ever takes place in our lives.

In Arjuna's life the revolution is certain. Whether this way or that, he will have to pass through a revolution. The water at boil-ing point – it is a situation in which he will have to do something. He could run away, as many people do... that would be the easiest thing, that is the shortcut, that seems to be the closest route – escaping.

This is why people embrace a sannyas that escapes from life, a life-escaping renunciation. They simply escape to the forests. They say, 'No. No more city life! We are going to the forests.' But they still carry a copy of the Gita along with them, which is amazing: they read their Gita in the forest.

Arjuna could have done the same thing. He *wanted* to escape to the forests, but he came across the wrong man. He met Krishna, who said to him, 'Stop! Don't run away!'

Can escapists attain to godliness? No, escapists cannot. Those who run away from the realities of life cannot reach godliness. Those who are unable to face life can never encounter the whole face to face – because those who develop numb limbs from just facing life, whose swords start slipping from their hands, whose hair stands on end, whose hearts begin to tremble – just from see-ing life... No, they cannot stand before the whole.

Life is a preparation. Its every step is a preparation for encoun-tering the supreme truth. And here is Arjuna, fleeing from facing a very minor reality of life – but his preparations for fleeing are total.

Now, it is very interesting that he is not able to remain seated in the chariot. He says there is not enough strength left in him even to remain seated in the chariot. But if he were allowed to escape to the forest, he would find he had plenty of strength to do that; he would immediately run faster than he has ever done before. A person who is unable to gather enough strength to encounter life finds the same strength to run away from it. Then there seems to be no lack of strength or power; the strength is there. If Krishna were to ask Arjuna to escape from everything, he would become instantly happy, delighted. But that happiness wouldn't last long. If Arjuna were to go to the forest, in a very short time he would become sad. Even if he were sitting under a tree in a sannyasin's robe, he would soon be collecting wood and other material from the forest and carving out a bow and arrows for himself. The man would still be the same.

We cannot run anywhere to get away from ourselves. We can run away from everyone and everything but not from ourselves. Wherever I go I will be with me.

So, after a short while, once Arjuna had realized that there was no one looking at him, he would have started hunting birds and animals. After all, the person who has escaped is still the same Arjuna as ever. And the birds and animals are not 'his very own', are not his nearest and dearest; hence, he would have had no difficulty in killing them. He would have done so with great pleasure.

Arjuna cannot be a sannyasin, because there is no way that someone who is unable to muster enough courage even to be a worldly man can become a sannyasin. The fact is that sannyas does not mean escaping from the world. Sannyas means transcending the world.

Sannyas is the transcendence of the fire and heat of this world. Only he who transcends it utterly becomes worthy. Sannyas is not an opposition to the world or an escape from it. Sannyas is the outcome of a total understanding of the world and the struggles one goes through in it.

So Arjuna has arrived at a stage that is favorable to sannyas.

Should he become an escapist, then that route is available right now to him. But if he chooses to face the struggle, then there are difficulties ahead. The whole purpose of the Gita from now on is to remove Arjuna's physical weakness, is to bring back his resolve and will. It is a total effort to restore his power, resolve and individuality; and to give him his soul.

All the discussions that I am going to have here will be from this same viewpoint; that they can be of use to your psyche too. And if as yet there is no Arjuna within you, then you need not come; then this will be of no use to you. Then it will be meaningless for you. If there is no inner conflict, no struggle, no restlessness within you, then you need not listen. Then it will be irrelevant for you.

These talks can only be meaningful to you if there is conflict and dilemma inside you, if there is restlessness and tension, if there is a difficulty in being decisive, if the person within is divided into fragments, and you are not integrated.

CHAPTER 3

The Yoga of Anguish

'My bow, Gandiva, slips from my hand, my skin is aflame
I cannot remain steady. My mind appears confused.

'O Krishna, I see the signs are against all this,
and I do not foresee any good from slaying my own people in
this battle.

'I do not long for victory, O Krishna,
nor for the kingdom, nor for its pleasures.
Of what use, O Krishna, will the kingdom be to us,
or pleasures or even life itself?

'Those for whose sake we desire the kingdom,
enjoyments and pleasures, stand here arrayed for battle
renouncing all hope for life and riches.

'Teachers, uncles and sons; also grandfathers, maternal uncles,
fathers-in-law, grandsons, brothers-in-law and all other kinsmen.

'I do not want to kill them, O Krishna, even if I am killed instead.
Not even for the kingdom of the three worlds, let alone for this
earth.

'What happiness can befall us, O Krishna,
from killing the sons of Dhritarashtra?
Though they are tyrants, to kill them would be a sin.

'My bow, Gandiva, slips from my hand, my skin is aflame
I cannot remain steady. My mind appears confused.

'O Krishna, I see the signs are against all this,
and I do not foresee any good from slaying my own people in this
battle.

'I do not long for victory, O Krishna,
nor for the kingdom, nor for its pleasures,
Of what use, O Krishna, will the kingdom be to us,
or pleasures or even life itself?'

ARJUNA IS MAKING a very conditional statement, one that is all
bound up with conditions. He is not free from the illusion of
'happiness'. Quite simply he is asking what use happiness can be if
it comes from killing his own people, what use a kingdom can be
if it is gained after killing one's own kinsmen.

He is ready to have the kingdom and its joys and pleasures – *if*
they can be had without slaying his own people. Happiness is possible through attaining the kingdom, about that he is in no doubt.
Authentic good is possible through attaining the kingdom, about
that he is in no doubt. The only thing he has doubts about is killing
his own people.

It will be helpful to understand this state of mind. We also think
in a similar way in terms of conditions. Vaihinger has written a
book called *The Philosophy of As If*. It seems that our entire lives are
based on 'if': 'If such and such a thing happens in a certain way,
then happiness will be mine; if it doesn't happen in this way then
happiness won't be mine. If such and such a thing happens in a
certain way, then true benediction will be mine; if such and such a
thing doesn't happen in this way, then it cannot be mine.' But about
one thing we are certain, about one thing we are clear: happiness is
possible, only the conditions for it need to be fulfilled.

But the funny thing is that anyone who makes terms and conditions with life can never attain to happiness. And why? Because the
person whose illusions of happiness are still intact, who has not yet

been disillusioned as far as happiness is concerned, can never find happiness.

Only the person who realizes the truth that happiness is not possible in this world will find happiness.

This looks very paradoxical. The person who thinks that it is simply a question of managing certain conditions in order for happiness to be found in this world only ends up finding newer and newer sorrows. Actually, if you are seeking sorrow, you need to seek it under the guise of happiness. The proper way to find sorrow is to look for happiness. While we are looking for it, it appears to be happiness, but once found, that same happiness brings sorrow, and once we are in this sorrow, there is no escape.

If Arjuna were to ask: 'Where is the chance of happiness in this world, where is the chance of authentic good in this world, does having a kingdom serve some authentic, real purpose?' – if he were to raise such questions, then they would be questions that are not bound up with conditions, and then the answer would be entirely different. But what he is saying is, 'How is it possible to attain happiness by killing one's own people?'

In his understanding, happiness is possible – and as long as his own people are not killed, he is ready to have it. He believes that authentic good is possible; he also believes that there is meaning and purpose in having a kingdom – but only if his own people don't get killed.

The kind of realization that happened to Mahavira or Buddha – that having kingdoms is futile, that searching for happiness in this world is futile – has not happened to Arjuna. All of Arjuna's statements indicate his conflicting state of mind. He doesn't actually *know* that all the things that he calls futile are futile. Even when he asks what meaning, what good, there is in a certain thing, all the time he knows in his heart that meaning *is* there, that good *is* there – just his preconditions have to be fulfilled first. Arjuna has no doubt whatsoever that happiness will be achieved provided his 'if' is fulfilled.

I have heard that Bertrand Russell was dying… it is just a joke. Hearing the news, a priest rushed to his side, cherishing the hope that there would be a good chance that this lifelong, learned atheist would fear death and remember God. But the priest didn't have the courage to go near Russell even in his dying moments. He remained standing behind the crowd of friends who had gathered there, waiting for some opportunity to tell Russell to ask for forgiveness.

Suddenly Russell turned in his bed and said, 'Oh, God!' Seeing that Russell had even uttered the name of God, the priest thought that this was an opportune moment. He went closer to Russell and said that it was the right time, and that at least now he should ask for God's forgiveness.

Russell opened his eyes and said, 'Oh God – if there *is* any God – Bertrand Russell – if there *is* any entity called a soul in him – asks for your forgiveness – if any forgiveness is possible. If Russell has committed any sins, he asks for your forgiveness – *if* any forgiveness is possible.'

In this way our whole lives are surrounded by 'ifs'. Bertrand Russell was straightforward and honest, but we are not so.

Arjuna is also not clear. He is very confused; he is very entangled. The knot of his mind is tangled and bound up. He is saying that it is possible to achieve happiness provided one's own people are not killed. He is saying that winning the kingdom can bestow authentic good provided one's own people are not killed.

This very 'if' is Arjuna's knot. And the illusions, desires and aspirations – as far as happiness, kingdom, wealth and fame are concerned – of a person who talks like this are not yet shattered. In the back of his mind he is very ready to receive all of these things; the only condition is that all his 'ifs' are also taken care of.

This is why Krishna has to work continuously on Arjuna. All the effort he has to make is focused upon Arjuna's self-contradictory thinking. All the way through, it is apparent that Arjuna desires the very thing that he talks of giving up. He is asking for the very thing that he is running away from, he is embracing the very thing he wants to save himself from. Arjuna's state needs to be properly understood.

Such an Arjuna lives within us all. Whatsoever we are pushing away with one hand, we keep grabbing with the other; or whatever we are pulling with one hand we go on pushing away with the other. No sooner have we walked one step to the left than we take another step to the right. If we take one step toward godliness, we immediately take another step toward the worldly.

Arjuna is like a bullock cart that has bullocks yoked to both ends. He is being pulled from both ends. He is saying, 'Of course happiness exists in the world – that is why my mind is being pulled towards it. He is also saying, '…and my mind is running away from it because to attain that happiness I will have to kill my own people.' This self-contradiction of Arjuna's is worth keeping in mind, because the whole story of the state of Arjuna's mind is nothing but an expansion of this very self-contradiction.

OSHO,
We have just witnessed the state of mind of a deeply anguished Arjuna. An anguished person moves away from the sense of self; which means he moves into *viyoga*, separation, from his self-nature. And the first chapter of the Gita is named *Arjuna Vishaad Yoga*, which means the yoga of Arjuna's anguish – Arjuna's journey through the spiritual discipline of anguish in order to be united with his self-nature. How can this be so? What connection is there between anguish and yoga? And in what sense has the word yoga been used in the Gita?

The yoga of anguish! There are many meanings of *yoga*. There are even meanings that are exactly the opposite of our commonly-held understanding of yoga.

So it is right to ask this question: How can anguish be yoga? Bliss can be yoga, but how can anguish be yoga? But anguish can be yoga precisely because it is only an inverted form of bliss; it is bliss standing on its head. You are still a man whether you are standing on your feet or on your head. Even what we call the opposite of our self-nature is just our self-nature standing on its head. Whatever we call insanity – even though it is a perversion of our self-nature – is still a part of our self-nature.

Gold that is mixed with dirt is called impure gold. We may ask why we call it 'gold' when it is impure – but it has to be called gold; even with these impurities it remains gold. It has to be called gold because the impure element in it can be burned away and the gold that was mixed with the dirt can again become pure.

It is called 'the yoga of anguish' because the anguish in it can be burned away and the yoga, the meditation in it, can be saved – and the journey to *anand*, to bliss, can be made.

No one has ever come upon such a state of anguish that he cannot return to his true self-nature. Even in the deepest state of anguish the path leading back to one's true self-nature remains intact. It is for the remembrance of this path that yoga is being mentioned – and this anguish is happening for that very reason.

Why is anguish there in the first place? A rock never feels anguish. It never feels anguish because it can never feel bliss either. This is the reason why anguish is felt. In a deep sense it is because of a memory of bliss. It is a remembrance of the fact – somewhere deep within our consciousness the understanding is there – that our consciousness is not able to be what it actually can be, is not able to attain what it actually can attain; that what is possible is not actually happening. This is the reason why anguish occurs.

Hence, the greater a genius a person is, the deeper into anguish he will go. Only idiots don't fall into anguish – because they have no means of comparing. An idiot has no idea what he can become. For someone who knows what he can become, for someone who knows that bliss is possible, the darkness of anguish will become more pronounced; he will feel the anguish more intensely. One who knows about the morning will find the darkness of the night to be very dark. But for one who has no idea about the morning, even the night may appear to be the dawn – and he may find the night quite acceptable.

Even the state of Arjuna's anguish is being called 'yoga' here, because an awareness of anguish only becomes possible when it is contrasted with our self-nature. Otherwise it cannot be seen. No one else on the battlefield is going through such a yoga of anguish: Duryodhana is not going through anything of the sort! A friend has asked me, 'You have talked about Duryodhana, but what do you think about Yudhishthira? I agree that Duryodhana is not feeling anguish, and in any case he is not a good man. But Yudhishthira *is* a good man; he is Dharmaraj, the lord of religiousness. Why isn't anguish happening to him?' This needs to be given some thought.

One would expect Yudhishthira to be in anguish, but he is not. The reason is that Yudhishthira is a so-called religious person, and even a bad person is better than a so-called religious person – because sooner or later the thorn of badness will start pricking that bad person. But that pricking, that pain never happens to a so-called religious person because he has already taken it for granted that he is a religious person, so how can he feel anguish?

Yudhishthira is complacent about being religious. It is a false complacency, but that is how he is. Actually Yudhishthira is the image of a traditional, religious man.

There are two categories of religious people. The first contains those whose religion is borrowed, borrowed from the past. The other contains those whose religion comes out of their inner revolution.

Arjuna is a man of religion who is standing on the threshold of an inner revolution. As yet, he is not religious, but he is standing on the threshold of the revolution. He is passing through the pain out of which religiousness can be born in him. Yudhishthira is satisfied, contented, with the religion he has inherited from the past. That is why he can be a religious man and a gambler at the same time and have no misgivings arising in his mind about this. He can be religious *and* he can go to war to gain a kingdom with no misgivings. He is religious and yet everything irreligious goes on aplenty around his so-called religiousness – and he is not in the least bit troubled.

Usually, the people who go to the temple or the mosque or the *gurudwara* or the church are the ones who find they are in rapport with Yudhishthira. Such a man is contented. He reads the Gita every day, he has memorized the entire Gita. He is a staunchly religious man, and there the matter ends. He knows everything that is worth knowing, and that is that. But such a man is like an empty cartridge: there is nothing left behind that can be fired, there is no gunpowder left. And such an empty cartridge looks nice because it doesn't carry much danger inside it.

If we take this meaning, Yudhishthira *is* Dharmaraj, the lord of religiousness. He is a custodian of the religion that he has inherited from the past; he is a symbol, a reflection of the religion that he has received from the past, from tradition, from orthodoxy. Hence he isn't troubled.

The so-called religious man is always compromising. In every situation he manages to compromise between religion and irreligion. The so-called religious man is a hypocrite. He has two faces. One is his religious face that he keeps to show to others. But he has a second, his real face that he uses to function, to get things done. To him, there is never a conflict between these two faces.

This is the key, the secret of hypocrisy. No inner conflict is ever born in him; he never feels he is divided in two. He is very fluid; he moves easily from one side to the other, he has no difficulty whatsoever. He is like an actor. An actor changes his roles and has no difficulty with it. He may have been Rama, the hero, yesterday, and today he can move into the role of Ravana, the villain, with no problem at all. He will put on Ravana's clothes and start speaking in Ravana's language.

What I am saying is that a so-called religious man is even worse than an irreligious man. I say this because the irreligious man will not be able to bear his pain for long; sooner or later he will feel the thorn. But the man who has made compromises can endure the pain forever. This is why Yudhishthira has no pain, is utterly complacent.

Now this is very interesting. Both the irreligious man and the so-called religious man are utterly complacent about this war, while Arjuna, who is neither complacent about being irreligious nor complacent about being so-called religious, is worried.

Arjuna is a very authentic man. His authenticity lies in the fact that he is worried, that he has questions, that he is unable to reconcile himself with the situation he finds himself in. This very restlessness, this very pain, becomes the source of his growth.

It is called the yoga of anguish because Arjuna is able to attain to anguish. Blessed are those who attain to anguish, because those who do so will have to seek a way out. Unfortunate are those who never attain to anguish – because then of course the question of their attaining to bliss does not even arise.

Blessed are those who attain to the experience of separation, because herein lies the desire for union. Hence the pain of separation, *virah*, is also yoga. It is a desire for union, it is a path that is seeking union. Of course yoga is union, but separation is also yoga because separation is only a longing and a thirst for union.

And anguish is also yoga. Of course yoga is bliss, but *vishaad*, anguish, is also yoga because it is the process through which bliss is born. Hence this *adhyaya*, this chapter, has been called 'Vishaad Yoga'.

OSHO,
You mentioned Bertrand Russell a little while ago. Citing Bertrand Russell's self-satisfied, atheistic position, Ved Mehta asked Paul Tillich why the experience of emptiness, of hollowness, did not happen to Russell during his life, even though he was an atheist.

Tillich replied, 'Such people can deceive themselves. There are so many people who simply cannot see the color green.'

Could Russell be one of them? Arjuna himself could not see the magnificent sight of the universal oceanic form through his physical eyes.

Secondly, commenting on Albert Camus' 'philosophy of despair' Paul Tillich says in one place that despair in itself is

religious. But from what I hear you say regarding the Gita, it seems
to me that Arjuna's anguish was irreligious. Please comment.

If Arjuna's anguish is satisfied in being anguish, if it ends up still
remaining anguish, if it becomes closed, then it is irreligious. If
anguish becomes a journey, if it becomes the Gangotri – the source
of the Ganges – and the river Ganges flows out of it and reaches to
the ocean of bliss, then it is religious.

Anguish in itself is neither irreligious nor religious. If anguish
closes the person up, then it will become suicidal, but if it keeps the
person flowing, then it will become self-transforming.

Paul Tillich says that despair in itself is religious. This is a
half-truth; he is not saying the whole truth. It is a half-truth, an
incomplete truth. Anguish *can* become religious; the possibility of
its becoming religious is there, the potential is there, *if* it becomes
a flow.

When anguish goes around in circles, when it revolves within
itself, only then is it suicidal and irreligious. It is very interesting
that a person with a suicidal temperament reaches a point where
either he has to transform his very soul or he has to commit
suicide. One thing becomes certain: the old way of being will no
longer do. Because of this fact one could also say that suicide is
religious – but that again would only be a half-truth, similar to the
statement of Paul Tillich that you have quoted here.

Yes, there are two alternatives facing the person who has reached
the point of committing suicide. Either he kills himself, which will
be absolutely irreligious, or he transforms himself – which is the
profounder alchemy of killing oneself, and which will be religious.

Buddha and Mahavira both arrived at a point where either they
committed suicide or they were transformed. Arjuna too is standing at a point where either he dies, finishes himself, or transforms
himself and raises his consciousness to new levels.

Paul Tillich's statement is incomplete and there is a reason for
this. It is incomplete because Christianity is based on a partial truth
– and Paul Tillich happens to be a great contemporary interpreter

of Christianity. He certainly has a penetrating insight, but a penetrating insight is not necessarily a comprehensive one too.

The image of Jesus that Christianity has adopted is one of despair. It doesn't have any other image of Jesus. It doesn't have any laughing image of Jesus; Christianity has no dancing, joyous picture of Jesus. It doesn't have any concept or image of Jesus proclaiming *satchitanand* – truth, consciousness and bliss. The only image it has of Jesus is of him hanging on the cross, his head resting on his shoulder, his eyes sad... a Jesus in the final moments of his death. That is why the cross became the symbol of Christianity. Such despair and such a cross are not religious in themselves. They may become so – or they may not.

If Paul Tillich says that people like Bertrand Russell are deceiving themselves – because Russell is an atheist, because he has no faith in the divine – then he is saying something absolutely wrong. One could ask Paul Tillich why Russell doesn't have the feelings of emptiness and meaninglessness that Sartre and Camus and other such people who have no faith in the divine have. Surely if Russell is an atheist, he should experience emptiness.

Not necessarily. In my view, there are also two kinds of atheism: the kind that is closed in upon itself and the kind that is outgoing. An atheist who becomes closed in upon himself, as anguish can become closed in upon itself, will become empty – because the one who bases his life on 'no' is bound to become empty. A man who says his life is based on 'no' – what else can he become other than empty? Nothing ever sprouts from the seed of 'no', no flowers ever blossom from the seed of 'no', life never grows from the seed of 'no'. Life will certainly become empty if 'yes' is also not there somewhere. Atheism does not necessarily have to rest on a 'no'. Atheism can also rest on a 'yes'.

Bertrand Russell's atheism is based on 'yes'. He denies the divine but he does not deny love. And only ignorant theists would call a person who does not deny love an atheist – because the person who is not denying love is in fact, at a very deep level, accepting the divine. His acceptance is not a formal acceptance. Of course he will not ring the worship bell in a temple in front of some statue of the divine. But there is no reason whatsoever to assume that those who do this are theists either – because what has ringing a bell to do with theism?

The divine is not very far away from the one whose life has the ring of love in it. Love is not a thread of denial, of exclusion; love is a thread of acceptance, of inclusion. Love is a very deep 'yes' towards the whole of existence.

I call Bertrand Russell an atheist only in the formal sense. In the formal sense Russell is an atheist – just as there are many who are theists in the formal sense – but Russell's atheism is actually flowing toward theism. It is flowing, there is a fluidity in it, it is unfolding. He takes pleasure in flowers – but our theist goes to the temple and offers flowers and yet is unable to take any pleasure in them. While plucking a flower it never occurs to him that he is plucking the divine. He plucks a living flower just for the sake of presenting it to some stone idol. Deep down this man is an atheist. He has no 'yes', no reverent feeling toward existence – nor does he have any feeling for what is divine in existence. He has no feeling whatsoever. If someone destroys his stone idol, he is ready to kill, he will destroy the living form. Theism has no connection with this man's heart. His theism is nothing but a self-deception.

Bertrand Russell's atheism is not a self-deception, because I can see that Russell is a sincere man. And a sincere man cannot become a theist so easily. It is only dishonest people who can become theists so easily – because can you find a more dishonest man than someone who can say 'yes' to the existence of something divine without even searching? Where can you find a more self-deceiving person than the man who accepts the existence of even such a great and vital phenomenon as godliness just by reading some book?

Experiencing the ultimate is not child's play. It has nothing to do with the texts you may have read in some books. What has it got to do with the theories that are taught by your parents?

The realization of the ultimate is the outcome of a highly intense and painstaking search in life. It is attained after passing *ever a person of knowledge is only of a point along their journey.* [handwritten marginal note]

through immense anguish. After passing through immense endeavor and discipline in meditation, after passing through many 'no's, after much pain and meaninglessness... and with great difficulty. Perhaps after a long search and journeying through lifetimes, after much wandering, after lifetimes of successes and failures, after having gone through all this pain of giving birth, only then – only after all of this does the experience that transforms a person probably come, does this state of religiousness probably happen. *[handwritten marginal note: lifetimes of learning]*

In my view, Bertrand Russell is on such a journey; hence, he is not empty. Sartre, on the other hand, is empty. His atheism is closed, it circles in upon itself, it rotates in circles within him. If this is the case, then the person is bound to become empty from within. And how can flowers blossom in a life that is based on the negative, on nothingness? It is like trying to sow seeds in the desert. Flowers can never blossom there.

There is no bigger desert than 'no'. At least the earthly deserts have oases, but in the desert of the 'no' there isn't an oasis, there is no greenery. Greenery only grows where there is a 'yes', an affirmation. Only a theist can be fully verdant and fulfilled. Only a theist can attain to flowers, never an atheist.

Atheism can be of two kinds, and theism can also be of two kinds. Atheism becomes dangerous when it is closed in upon itself, and theism becomes dangerous when it is borrowed. The danger of theism lies in its borrowing, and the danger of atheism lies in its becoming closed in upon itself. All the theists on this earth are borrowers. If a person is not honest enough even to be an atheist, it will be utterly impossible for him to take the giant step of becoming a theist.

As I see it, atheism is the first step towards becoming a theist. Atheism is the training. The practice of saying 'no' is a preparation for saying 'yes'. And how much strength can the 'yes' of one who has never said 'no' have? How much life, how much soul can there be in the 'yes' of one who never could gather the courage to say 'no'?

In my view, Bertrand Russell is passing through this phase of atheism, of a person who is searching. He cannot say 'yes' without searching first. This is only appropriate, right, religious. I call Russell an atheist, but a religious atheist. And I call the so-called theists, theists – but irreligious theists. These statements seem to be paradoxical, but they are not.

Arjuna's anguish is very religious; it has a momentum. Having a man as precious as Krishna so close by, he could easily have said, if he had wanted to, 'Oh master, whatever you say must be right. I am going to fight the war.' But he doesn't say this; rather, he struggles with Krishna.

The courage to struggle with Krishna is no ordinary courage. One's very heart feels like saying 'yes' in the presence of a person like Krishna. Saying 'no' to such a person is painful; one finds it painful even to raise a question to someone like Krishna. But here is Arjuna continuing to question. He puts the person of Krishna to one side and doesn't give up his questioning. He doesn't fear what others may say about him.

Arjuna is without faith. He is a skeptic, he doubts, he is not a trusting man. The usual thing when confronting a man like Krishna is to accept him as the master and just follow him. But that sort of theism is a borrowed theism. No, Arjuna is seeking authentic theism, and that is why the Gita is so prolonged, becomes such a long journey. Arjuna just keeps on asking and asking... .

Krishna, too, is amazing. He could have used the weight of his glory. Had he had any desire to be a guru, he could certainly have done that. But one who is truly religious never has any desire to become a guru. When godliness itself is present everywhere, there remains no need for the individual to be a guru. And one who trusts in existence doesn't look at questions with skepticism or with condemnation, because he knows that existence is there to take care, and that if this person is raising questions, he is already journeying; that he will reach, and he should just be allowed to reach in his natural way.

Once the Ganges has set out on its course, it is bound to reach the ocean. As yet it may not be aware that there is an ocean, but since it is flowing there is no cause for worry; it *will* reach it. The ocean doesn't say, 'Stop and believe that there is an ocean.' Should the Ganges stop and assume that there is an ocean, it will never be able to *know* that there is an ocean. By coming to a halt it will turn into a dirty puddle and will consider that puddle to be the ocean.

Arjuna is not this kind of a theist. Rightly understood, there is some similarity between Arjuna's and Bertrand Russell's personalities – just as I said yesterday that there is some similarity between Sartre's and Arjuna's. That similarity is only to the extent that just as Sartre is worried, so is Arjuna. The similarity ends there, because Sartre turns his anxiety into a philosophy, while Arjuna just turns it into a question. So in this way, he is closer to Bertrand Russell.

Bertrand Russell is an agnostic; to the end of his life he goes on questioning. That he did not come across a Krishna is a different matter, but that too is all right. He will come across one on some future date; no harm is done. But the fact that he is inquiring means that his journey is happening.

I believe that the theists on this earth like Paul Tillich are insincere compared with Bertrand Russell. Paul Tillich may be a man who is deceiving himself, but not Russell. And people like both Paul Tillich and Bertrand Russell have always been on this earth. My own understanding is that Bertrand Russell has progressed more toward theism than Paul Tillich. Paul Tillich is just a theologian.

It is very interesting that the biggest enemy of religiousness in this world is not irreligion but theology. The greatest enmity towards religiousness is found in theocracy. Those who live under a theocracy never become religious. There are reasons for this. The reason is that religion is something beyond the intellect and theology is always something below the intellect. Theology never goes beyond the intellect, and intellect never reaches up to religion.

Paul Tillich is living only through the intellect. It is not that Bertrand Russell is denying the intellect. He is living fully through his intellect but he is not submitting himself to it: he even questions the intellect, he is also skeptical about the intellect; he feels that the intellect too has its limitations. In Arjuna there is a deep synthesis, as if both Russell and Sartre are there, existing together in him.

Arjuna's anguish is a religious anguish, because it will lead him to trust.

'Those for whose sake we desire the kingdom,
enjoyments and pleasures, stand here arrayed for battle
renouncing all hope for life and riches.'

Arjuna's delusions can be seen at every step. He is saying, 'These fathers, sons, friends, dear ones for whose sake we desire the kingdo... .' He is lying. Nobody desires anything for the sake of others; everyone desires things only for himself. If a father and son desire something for each other, it is only because he is *my* father, or he is *my* son – and that too only to the extent to which this 'my-ness' exists.

Of course the fact remains that without these people, happiness would no longer remain juicy, because the actual happiness that one obtains is very small. It is others noticing it that brings the greater joy, and without this the quantity of happiness that one encountered would be as good as nothing. Even if someone attains the largest kingdom, he will not find as much happiness in having it as in the feeling of being able to prove to his nearest and dearest that he has attained it.

And there are limits to the reach of a person's thinking. For example, a girl sweeping the streets will not feel jealous if a queen decked out with diamonds and necklaces passes by, because the queen will fall beyond her range, the queen doesn't come within the range of her thinking. But if another sweeper girl from the neighborhood walks past wearing an artificial piece of glass jewelry, that will make her terribly jealous, because this girl is within her range. Man's jealousies, ambitions, all work constantly within a limited range.

If you want to achieve name and fame, then it has to be in front of your own people and acquaintances – only then will you enjoy it. If it comes to you amongst strangers, you won't enjoy it very much at all – because it is not much fun to parade your ego in front of strangers. The fun is in surpassing your own people. The fun is in showing your own people that they can't achieve what you can.

Jesus has said somewhere that prophets are never honored in their own town. They can't be honored – although they would like to be.

When Jesus was visiting his own town, the people there would say, 'Look at this carpenter's son! Isn't he the son of Joseph the carpenter? How can he have attained enlightenment? Just the other day he was cutting wood, and now he has attained wisdom!' People would laugh at him.

Behind such laughing is this same difficulty: that of the range of concern – the difficulty there is in accepting that a carpenter's son can now be at such a great height. The person comes from within their range of concern, so such a thing is very difficult to accept. It is very unlikely that a prophet will be honored in his own town, because he happens to come from within the range of that town's jealousy.

Vivekananda never received as much honor in Kolkata as he did in America. On his return to Kolkata, there were welcome ceremonies and receptions and commemorative functions for a few days, but that was that. Then the people in Kolkata would say, 'Hey, isn't he the boy from that clerical family? How much self-knowledge do you think he can attain?'

Ramateertha received great honor in America but not in Kashi. Once a pundit stood up in a meeting in Kashi and said, 'You don't even know the ABC of Sanskrit and yet you dare to talk about having known the *brahman*, the ultimate reality? First go and learn Sanskrit.' And poor Ramateertha set out to learn Sanskrit.

So we all have a range, a boundary, a zone. Perhaps even Ramateertha couldn't enjoy receiving an honor in New York as much as he would have enjoyed receiving it in Kashi. Ramateertha never got upset, troubled or worried as long as he stayed in America, but he felt unhappy in Kashi. He would talk about ultimate realization, but in Kashi he couldn't gather enough courage to say, 'What has Sanskrit got to do with knowing the brahman? To hell with your Sanskrit!' He couldn't gather even this much courage. Instead he hired a tutor and began learning Sanskrit. Can you understand the hurt behind all this?

What Arjuna is repeatedly saying is an utter lie. He is not aware of this, because falsehood is also so infused in man's blood that it is very difficult to detect it. Actually, the real falsehoods are precisely those that have become infused with our blood. The lies that we become aware of do not go so deep, it is the lies that we cannot detect, that we are not conscious of, that have become our flesh and bones. Arjuna is speaking the same kind of lie that we all do.

The husband tells his wife, 'I am doing everything for you.' The wife tells her husband, 'I am doing everything just for you.' Nobody is doing anything for anybody. We all live in an egocentric way. We only do as much as will satisfy our egos, even for those who seem to fall within the boundaries of our egos, our sense of self. What we do for them is in direct proportion to how much they are a part of our egos and satisfy this sense of self.

When a wife begins to talk about divorce, she ceases to be your wife and then all your doing for her stops. The very friend we were ready to die for, we can now be ready to kill. We forget everything. Why is everything forgotten? Because as long as someone was strengthening my 'I', he was 'mine'. Once he no longer does that, he is no longer 'mine'.

No, Arjuna is saying something false, but he is not aware of it. If he had been aware of it, then things would have been altogether different.

He *will* become aware of it slowly, slowly. He is wrong to have said, 'Those for whose sake we desire the kingdom...' What he should have said was: '...without whom there would be no fun in having the kingdom....' The fact is that we desire things solely for our sakes, and the real fun is in seeing that our own people notice what we have achieved. What pleasure is there in having a kingdom, in going on an ego trip, in front of strangers and people we don't know? When you reach the skies in front of those who know you, only then can you say with great egotism, 'Look what I have achieved!'

Remember, we do not only compete with our enemies. We compete with our friends even more deeply. Our real competition is with those whom we know. With strangers there is none whatsoever. That is why two strangers can never become such enemies as two real brothers can. Only in front of people we know do we wish to prove 'I am something'.

Arjuna is making a false statement, but this is not clear to him. He is not saying it knowingly. Lies that we tell knowingly are very superficial. It is the lies that come out of us unconsciously that are really deep – we have mixed them with our own blood, we have made them one with our very selves over lifetimes. Arjuna is telling such a lie when he says, 'Those for whose sake we desire the kingdom... what use will such a kingdom be to me without them?'

No, the proper thing, the correct thing, for him to have said would have been that of course one desires the kingdom for oneself, but of what use is it if those very people whose eyes one was trying to dazzle are no longer around?

But as of yet he is unable to say this. If only he could, Krishna is again and again ready to stop talking in the Gita. But whatsoever Arjuna says reveals that he is making statements that are contrary to his reality.

Had Arjuna even once made some straightforward, some true statement – one single, authentic assertion – in that very moment Krishna would have become quiet. He would have said, 'The matter is finished. Come, let us turn our chariot back.' But the matter is not over because Arjuna continues with his double-talk. What he actually wants is different from what he says; what he talks about is different from what he is. His dilemma lies somewhere deeper in him – but all the time he is indicating that it is something that it is not, and that it can be found somewhere where it is not.

We must proceed with this clear understanding, only then will we be able to understand Krishna's answers. As long as we do not understand the dilemmas and the complexities that are behind Arjuna's questions it will be difficult to understand the depths and clarities contained in Krishna's answers.

OSHO

In the context of killing his own people, when Arjuna says that he doesn't see any ultimate spiritual good in it, he is obviously keeping his distance from the idea of worldly, material good. Is the context here merely material happiness? And if so, then how will he ever become truly religious?

From where Arjuna is, it can only be referring to material happiness. It is not that the theist doesn't have a relationship with material happiness, of course he does, but the more he seeks it, the more he will find that attaining it is impossible. And only when the search for material happiness leads one to experiencing its impossibility does the spiritual search begin.

So the search for material happiness does have a significant contribution to make in the search for spiritual happiness. The most significant contribution this search makes is that it inevitably takes one into frustration and anguish.

Now, it is a very interesting thing about life that not only those steps which are connected with the temple of the divine take us there, but also those steps which are not connected with it. This appears to be very paradoxical: not only does the ladder which is connected to heaven help us to reach there, but even more so, and even before that, the ladder which is connected to hell has been helping us. And in fact, unless the journey that leads to hell turns out to be completely futile, no journey towards heaven can ever begin. Until it becomes perfectly clear that the road one is following is going to hell, it doesn't become clear which is the way to heaven.

Material joys function as negative warning signs on the path to spiritual happiness. Again and again we seek happiness through material pleasures, and again and again we fail. Again and again we desire something, and fail to get it every time. Again and again we aspire, and each time we fall back.

There is a Greek story about Sisyphus. Camus has written a book about it: *The Myth of Sisyphus*. Sisyphus is being punished by the gods by having to take a rock up to the top of a mountain. And the other half of the punishment is that as soon as he reaches the top – tired, sweating and gasping from dragging the rock – the rock slips from his fingers and falls back down again into the valley. Again he goes down, and takes the rock up to the top of the mountain, and again the same thing happens – and goes on happening again and again. This punishment continues, endlessly repeating into eternity.

Sisyphus goes back to the valley and starts dragging the rock up again. Each time he sets out with the hope that this time he will succeed, that this time he will manage to bring the rock up to the top, that he will show the gods how wrong they were and tell them, 'Look, Sisyphus has finally brought the rock up to the top!'

He drags the rock up again, toils hard for weeks and months and somehow, half-dead, reaches the top of the mountain. But no sooner he is there than the rock slips away and rolls back down into the valley. And Sisyphus goes down again.

You may say that he seems to be a crazy person: why doesn't he drop the idea and stay where he is? If you have *truly* come to realize this, then religiousness will soon unfold in your life.

We are all Sisyphuses. Our stories may differ, our mountains may differ, our rocks may differ, but we are all Sisyphuses. We go on doing the same things again and again. Again and again the rock slips from the mountaintop and falls into the valley, but the human mind is very strange, it repeatedly consoles itself: 'It seems something went wrong this time, next time everything will work out well.' And so it starts all over again. If such a mistake were happening only for one or two lives, it would still be tolerable, but those who know say that this has been happening for endless lifetimes.

The desire for material pleasures has an essential role in the spiritual search, because its failure, its utter failure, is the first step towards the search for spiritual bliss. That is why I don't call someone who is seeking material happiness irreligious. He too is seeking religiousness but in the wrong direction; he too is searching for bliss but in a place where it cannot be found. But at least he has to discover this much first: that he cannot find it there. Only then will he look in a different direction.

Someone asked Lao Tzu: 'You say that nothing can be gained from the scriptures, but we have heard that you have read the scriptures.'

Lao Tzu replied, 'No, I have gained a lot from the scriptures. The greatest thing that I have learned from them is that nothing can be learned from them. Now this is not a small achievement. Nothing can be learned from the scriptures, but this too could not have been understood without first reading them. I read a lot, I searched a lot – and then I came to the realization that nothing can be gained from them.'

This is not a small reward for such effort, but because of its negative character we don't notice it. Only when it becomes clear that nothing can be attained from words, from the scriptures, only then will we start searching in existence, in life. If we cannot find happiness in the material, only then will we begin searching for it in peace. If we cannot find it outside, only then will we start looking for it within. If happiness cannot be attained through material things, only then may we perhaps begin to search for it in the spiritual. But this second search actually only begins when the first search has failed.

So, what Arjuna is talking about here certainly only refers to material happiness: 'Of what value is a material gain that only comes after all one's loved ones have been lost?'

But herein, the very first step of his spiritual search is being taken, and therefore I would insist on calling him a religious man

– and by this not meaning someone who has attained religious-ness, but someone who is thirsty to do so.

OSHO,

You said that the Bhagavad Gita is a scripture of psychology and comes very close to modern psychology. Are you limiting the word *psyche* by assigning it the meaning of *mind* – because the original meaning of the word *psyche* is 'soul'? Would you stop at calling the Gita a scripture of psychology or would you also call it a scripture of spirituality? Please explain.

I would call the Gita *manovigyan*: a science or scripture of psychology. And by *mana* I don't mean soul; by *mana* I only mean the mind.

Many may feel difficulty and trouble with this. They may say that I am bringing the Gita down; that I should call it a spiritual scripture. But I would like to say to you that there can be no spiritual scripture. At the most, scriptures can pertain to the mind. And yes, the scripture of the mind may lead one to the point where spirituality begins, but this is all that can happen.

There is nothing like a spiritual scripture – there cannot be. There is spiritual life, but there are not spiritual scriptures. The most words can do is make one capable of touching the ultimate heights and depths of the mind. So I would not make the Gita worthless by calling it a spiritual scripture – there is no such thing. Every scripture that claims to be a spiritual scripture... and it is not the scriptures that make this claim, it is their adherents who claim that they are spiritual scriptures, and by doing so they unnecessarily put them out of the range of usefulness to man.

Spirituality is an experience that is beyond words and beyond description. It is beyond explanation and, as the scriptures themselves keep saying, cannot be attained through the mind. It is attained beyond the mind, and that which is attained by going beyond the mind cannot be written in words.

This is why the ultimate reach of any scripture is the mind. If it can take one as far as that point, it is a great scripture. And the jump that takes place beyond that will be the beginning of spirituality.

I call the Gita a scripture of psychology because it contains the threads that lead one to the point from where this jump takes place. But no scripture is a spiritual scripture.

Yes, there can be spiritual statements. For example, the Upanishads are spiritual statements. But they do not contain any system in them; hence they are not of much use to man. The Gita, however, is tremendously useful.

interesting

A statement such as 'There is only brahman' is all very well, but we do not know this – it is a bald statement. The one who knows says, 'It is.' The one who doesn't know says, 'Maybe.'

So the Upanishads can only be useful when you have experienced spirituality. Then, when you read the Upanishads you can say, 'That's right. I have also had the experience that only brahman is.' Thus the Upanishads can confirm your experience – but only after you have already experienced it for yourself.

The interesting thing is, however, that once you yourself have known, there is no longer any need for the Upanishad to confirm it. Now that you know for yourself, whatever you say becomes an Upanishad.

The Upanishad can at the most become an endorsement for a *siddha* – for one who has arrived home – but there again, a siddha has no need for any endorsement. So the Gita can be useful for a seeker, but it is of no use to a siddha. But the real question is about the seeker, and the real inquiry of a seeker is not about spirituality.

Arjuna's real problem is not spiritual. It is psychological, it is a problem of the mind. So if someone were to suggest that even though Arjuna has a psychological problem, Krishna should give him a spiritual solution, no communication between the two would be possible.

A solution should be at the same level as the level at which the problem lies. Only then can it have any meaning. Arjuna's problem is psychological, not spiritual. His confusion is psychological.

It is very interesting that there is absolutely nothing like a spiritual problem. Wherever there is spirituality, religiousness, there is no problem; and wherever there is a problem, there is no spirituality.

It is something like this: if my house is in darkness and I tell you that there is darkness there, you may say, 'Let me fetch a lamp and see where this darkness is.' Then you will fetch the lamp and I will fail to show you the darkness. You may say, 'I have the lamp; show me, where is the darkness?' This will put me in trouble, and if I say, 'Please leave your lamp outside,' you can retort, 'How will I see the darkness if I leave the lamp outside?' True, because in order to see, one needs light. Then the only thing I can say to you is, 'Forget about it! The darkness cannot then be seen, because where there is light there is no darkness, and where there is darkness there is no light. There is no connection, no communication between the two.'

So there is no such thing as a spiritual problem; all problems are psychological. Spirituality, religiousness, is not a problem. It is the solution.

Where there is spirituality, religiousness, there exists no problem at all. And with no problem, where is the need for a solution? Spirituality itself is the solution; and that is why we have called the door to spirituality the door to religiousness, *samadhi*.

Samadhi means: from here begins the solution; from here on there will be no problem. Hereafter there will be no questions – there will be no room for any questions. Samadhi is the name of such a door. It means one has arrived at the door, and beyond it lies the world of solutions – where there are only solutions and solutions, where there are no problems anymore. But there will be many problems before reaching this door called samadhi. And all these problems are psychological.

Understood rightly, it means that mind is the problem. The day there is no mind there is no problem either. Spirituality means having the experience of no-mind.

That is why when I call the Gita a scripture of psychology, I am saying the utmost that can be said about a scripture. More is not possible. Those who try to label it as a spiritual scripture do harm to it, make it worthless and throw it into the garbage – because no one has a spiritual problem. Everyone's problem is of the mind.

So, when I say that Krishna is the earliest, the first proponent of psychology I am saying the utmost that can be said about him. Yes, he is a psycho-synthesizer. There is no psychosynthesis of the spirit, of the soul. The whole game is of the mind, the whole problem is of the mind – beyond the mind there is neither any trouble nor any problems. That is why there exists no scripture beyond the mind.

All masters and disciples are within the boundaries of the mind; beyond the mind there is no master, no disciple. Beyond the mind there is no Arjuna, and no Krishna. That which exists beyond the mind has no name. The whole thing, the whole process, is a matter within the mind. And that is why the Gita is so special.

There are numerous spiritual statements. They are precious, but nevertheless they are bare statements. One man says, 'This is the truth' – but that doesn't solve anything. Our problems, our troubles, are on some entirely different level, and they need to be addressed at that same level. Krishna is talking at exactly the level where Arjuna is.

Were Krishna to talk from his level, then the Gita would be a spiritual scripture, but then it would not have been possible to make Arjuna understand. Arjuna would have simply said, 'Forgive me. What you are saying may be so, but it has no connection with me.' In that case a dialogue between Krishna and Arjuna would not have been possible. There would have been an enormous communication gap between the two of them: one in the skies, the other in the nether lands. Krishna's statements would have gone over Arjuna's head.

But Krishna is holding Arjuna's hand and starting to resolve his problems from the very place where Arjuna is. That is why the Gita is a very dynamic psychological system. As Arjuna grows, step-by step, so the Gita rises. If Arjuna slides back down, the Gita slides back with him. If Arjuna falls on the ground, Krishna bends down; when Arjuna stands up, Krishna stands up with him. All the time Arjuna is the focus, not Krishna.

In the Upanishads, the sage is at the center; he is giving his statements. He is saying, 'I say what I have known.' Of course that has no direct relevance to you. That is why I am calling the Gita 'statements given by a teacher'.

If Krishna were to speak like an enlightened being, there would be no connection with Arjuna. To remain at Arjuna's side he has to bend down very low, and then speak to him. Slowly, as Arjuna rises Krishna also rises with him. And Krishna leaves the final sutras of the Gita at a point where the mind ends and spirituality begins. The discussion comes to an end after that – it becomes meaningless after that.

So, my statement is a well-considered, conscious statement. I don't say things unknowingly; I don't say anything just like that, unknowingly. I have very consciously said that the Gita is a scripture of psychology.

And the future belongs to psychological scriptures. There is no future for metaphysical scriptures. Metaphysics is dead; there is no place for it anymore. The man of today says: 'These are my problems; solve them.' There will only be room for those who can solve them. Now the world belongs to Freud, Jung, Adler, Fromm and Sullivan, not to Kapil and Kanad. And the Gita only has a future if Krishna has the courage to stand beside Freud, Jung and Adler in the future – otherwise it has no future.

I am making my statement after great consideration, very knowingly. I cannot call the Bible a scripture of psychology – I cannot. There are some statements in it that are psychological, but deep down even they are spiritual.

What I mean by 'spiritual' here is that Jesus is making statements about what he has known. And actually, that has caused the trouble. Jesus is talking about things pertaining to heaven, but the listeners understand them as earthly matters – which is why he was crucified. There are reasons why Jesus was crucified, and the responsibility for most of them lies with Jesus himself.

Jesus was talking about the kingdom of God and was saying: 'I will make you the inheritors of the kingdom of God', and people understood it to mean that he was going to make them owners of earthly kingdoms. The Jews reported to the authorities that this man is dangerous, rebellious, that he was trying to usurp the state. Pilate asked Jesus, 'Are you trying to take over the kingdom?' Jesus said he was taking over the kingdom – but he was referring to an altogether different kind of kingdom: the kingdom of God. Now no one anywhere knew anything about that kingdom, so they said, 'This man is dangerous; he should be crucified.'

No one is listening at the same level as Jesus is speaking from. Especially with Jesus, there isn't a single person listening from the same place as he is speaking from. So there is no bridge between Jesus and his listeners.

Krishna is an extraordinary teacher. He takes Arjuna right through from the primary level to finally leaving university. It is a long journey. It is a very long and very subtle journey. My wish is that we too can make this same kind of journey here.

OSHO,

You have said that man goes on passing through the cycle of coming and going, birth after birth. Isn't this recurrence necessary in order to attain a newer, fresher life? If not, then when does one transcend this repetition? Can't a master or scripture be of some help in this transcendence? Please explain.

There is an endless recurrence to life. This has its usefulness – it brings maturity. It has its dangers too – it can also bring inertia. Passing through the same thing twice, there are two possibilities: either you will experience it more deeply while passing through it for the second time, or the second time you may not experience it even as much as you did while passing through it for the first time. Both possibilities are there.

You hardly ever look at the tree that may be standing in front of your house; you must have seen it so many times that now there is no need to look at it. It is most unusual for husbands and wives to ever look at each other. Thirty odd years may have passed in living together and they have already looked at each other, long ago, in the early days of their marriage. Since then, no occasion has arisen to really look at each other again. In fact, they haven't found any reason to look at one another. But on the other hand, one would not miss looking at an unknown woman passing on the street!

The fact is, the unfamiliar is very easily observed. We become blind toward the familiar – a blind spot develops toward it. There remains no need to see a familiar person.

For example, close your eyes and try to remember your mother's face – and you will see how difficult it is to do so. You can easily recall the face of a film actress, but as you close your eyes and try to see your mother's face, it will start disappearing. Her features will soon get mixed up; it becomes so hard to catch her image. You have seen her face so often, so closely, but you have never looked at her with an attentive mind. Closeness turns into unfamiliarity.

So repeatedly passing through the same experiences – life after life – there are two possibilities. And as far as what you would like to do is concerned, the choice is up to you. The freedom is yours. Either you can become unconscious and mechanical as most of us have become...

You can go on moving mechanically, doing more or less the same things day after day. For instance, you were angry yesterday, and also the day before yesterday, and the day before that – last year too, and the year before last as well. It would be more than enough just to keep an account of this present life. If you have lived for fifty years so far, then how many times have you become angry, and how many times have you repented after that anger? Each time your repentance has been followed by anger, and anger has been followed by repentance – and so on and so forth. Gradually the whole thing has been turned into a routine.

Looking at a person, you can easily guess that right now this man is angry and soon he will express his repentance about it. If you have observed this same person getting angry three or four times already, you will not only be able to recount what he may have already said so far in his anger but also what else he is going to say. And you will also be able to predict what he will say while he is repenting after his anger: he will swear never to get angry again, although he has sworn that before too, and it doesn't mean a thing. This whole business has turned into an unconscious routine.

However, if a person has been consciously angry, then every experience he has of anger will help him to become free from it. And if that person has gone unconsciously into anger, then every experience of anger will lead him further into the deep unconsciousness of anger.

So, being born again and again opens up both possibilities. The way we use it depends on us. Life provides only the opportunities; what we make of them is up to us. By becoming repeatedly angry, one can become adept at an even deeper anger if one wants. And another man, after having been angry again and again and after having seen its stupidity, its futility, and the fire and insanity of it, can become free of it forever – if he chooses to.

A person who goes on becoming more and more unconscious and stupefied with anger becomes irreligious. He belongs to the mundane world. And a person who goes on becoming more and more conscious about anger becomes religious; a revolution takes place in such a person's life. So it is up to each person what he or she would like to make of his or her life.

Life is not preordained. It is an opportunity. What you will make of it depends on you. This very freedom is the proof that you are a soul, this very freedom is the dignity of your being a soul.

Having a soul means that you have the power to choose whatever you want to do. And the interesting thing is that you may have passed through some act or situation thousands of times, and yet you can drop out of it, break away from it, this very moment if you decide to.

But what happens is that the mind has a tendency to flow on the course that offers the least resistance. If you drop a glass of water on the kitchen floor, in a short while it will evaporate, leaving behind just a dry streak. Now there is no water left; nothing but a dry mark has remained, indicating that at some earlier time water was flowing there. If you drop water on that same floor again, the chances are that ninety-nine percent of the time the water will follow that same track, because it offers the least resistance. Compared to other parts of the floor there are fewer dust particles on that dry track; flowing along it is easier – and the water will flow there.

Things that we have done many times have turned into dry track-marks, and are known in psychology as our conditioning. Once again the same act takes place along the same track; once again the energy is created and flows. Looking for the way of least resistance we end up taking the same route.

But the dry track-mark never asks us to flow through it. It never says if you don't flow through it there will be a lawsuit against you in the court. It never says that there is some law stating that you have to flow this way, or that existence is ordering you to flow through here. That dry mark is simply an open opportunity, but the choice is always yours. Should the water decide not to flow through that dry track, it can flow and make a new track. A new dry track-mark will be left behind; a new conditioning will have been formed.

Religiousness is decisiveness and resolve both. It is an effort to make things happen differently from how they have always been happening. It is a determined choice that repeating what has been happening up until yesterday can be avoided – through understanding it. We can call it meditation, we can call it yoga, or we can call it by any other name we may like.

Read one more sutra and the rest we will discuss in the evening.

'Teachers, uncles and sons; also grandfathers, maternal uncles, fathers-in-law, grandsons, brothers-in-law and all other kinsmen.

'I do not want to kill them, O Krishna, even if I am killed instead. Not even for the kingdom of the three worlds, let alone for this earth.

'What happiness can befall us, O Krishna,
from killing the sons of Dhritarashtra?
Though they are tyrants, to kill them would be a sin.'

It is worth giving a thought to what Arjuna is repeatedly saying. Two or three things need to be understood here. Arjuna is saying that he is not willing to take the kingdom of the three worlds if that means killing his own people – so how much less willing is he to do it just for this earth? It seems as if Arjuna is talking about making a great sacrifice, but this is not the case.

Once I went to see an old sannyasin. He sang a song of his for me. The general content of the song was: 'O emperors, you may be happy sitting on your golden thrones, but I am happy even living in my dust and dirt. I spurn your golden thrones – they are good for nothing. I am happy living in my dust and dirt.' This was the major theme of the song, and the audience was captivated by it. People in India become very easily enchanted, and this is what happened with this audience: they started nodding their heads in appreciation of the song.

I was very surprised to see them doing so, while the sannyasin seemed to be delighted. He asked me, 'How was it?'

I said, 'You had better not ask me. You have put me into a difficulty.'

He insisted, 'Please say something.'

I replied, 'I am wondering how it is that no emperor has ever said, 'O sannyasins, you enjoy living in your dust and dirt – but we don't give a damn! We are quite happy on our thrones.'

No emperor has ever written a song like this, but sannyasins have certainly been writing songs like that old sannyasin's for hundreds of years. We need to discover why.

In reality, this sannyasin *does* envision in his mind that a golden throne will give him happiness. He is just consoling himself. He is saying, 'Stay on your thrones! We are happy in our dust and dirt.' But who is asking him to go and sit on the throne? If he is happy in his dirt, then great! Let the one who is sitting on the throne feel envious of him. But the man on the throne never writes a song that goes: 'If you are happy in the dirt then remain there…' He has no need of any consolation. While sitting on his throne he is not jealous of the sannyasin's dirt. But the sannyasin in the dirt is certainly jealous of the throne. And the jealousy is deep-rooted.

Now here is Arjuna, consoling himself. Of course he is interested in attaining the kingdom, and yet he is saying, 'Even if I gain the kingdom of the three worlds after killing all these people…' – although nothing of the sort is actually being gained; no one is actually offering him anything – '…it is worthless.'

Having said this about such a large kingdom, he moves to the next conclusion: 'Then what is the sense in having this kingdom on earth?' Having first created a grand idea in his mind like relinquishing the kingdom of the three worlds, he can then easily remark: 'Relinquishing this kingdom on earth is no big deal for me.'

But neither does he really want to give up the kingdom on earth, and if Krishna were to make a proposal to him, 'Look, we will give you the kingdom of the three worlds', Arjuna would suddenly find himself in a great dilemma. So Arjuna is simply talking, simply consoling himself.

It is very interesting to see how many sorts of tricks we use in order to console ourselves. Someone is looking at his neighbor's big house and saying, 'What's the big deal in having a big house?' But this very remark shows that the man *does* see that having a big house is a big deal. Without any doubt it *is* a big deal for him – otherwise he would never have noticed the big house in this way. He is simply trying to console himself by saying that having a big house is no big deal: 'And that is why I never tried for it. Had there really been something in it, I would have immediately attained one. But since there is nothing in it, I have never tried for one.'

Arjuna is saying very much the same thing: 'What is the big deal in attaining the kingdom of the three worlds? And obviously attaining this kingdom on earth is even less important – and killing so many of my own people for such a small kingdom!'

Slaughtering so many of his own people is what is bothering Arjuna the most, not the slaughtering as such. It is the slaughtering of his nearest and dearest that is troubling him.

Naturally his entire family is standing on that battlefield waiting to fight. Such a situation is rare in war. This war is unique. And the poignant intensity of the Mahabharata War lies in the fact that one family is divided into the two sides of the war.

Even with this division, everyone is not an enemy. One should say that the difference – and this is worth thinking about – between those who are facing each other is less in terms of enemy and friend. The difference is actually between who is less of a friend and who is more of a friend. The division is not of the kind where the enemies are on one side and the friends are on the other. Had the distinction been that clear – 'Our own people are on this side and on the other side are strangers' – a division would have become very easy, and then Arjuna would have had no difficulty in killing. But the division here is very unusual. And the unusualness of this is highly significant.

The unusual nature of this divide is that those who are more of a friend are gathered on one side and those who are less of a friend are gathered on the other. Of course, they too are friends, they too are loved ones – the teacher himself is on the opposite side. This is what I am saying is significant.

And such a situation is significant because things in life are not divided into watertight compartments. Things in life are not simply divided into black and white; life is an expanse of gray. In one corner it is black and in the other it is white, but in the remaining vast expanse of life the black and the white are mixed.

Here the division is not so clear-cut – that so-and-so is an enemy and so-and-so a friend. The division is that this person is less of a friend and this one is more of a friend; so-and-so is less of an enemy and so-and-so is more of an enemy. There are no absolute terms in life. Here, nothing is completely separate. And this is the complexity. Here, everything is divided into 'more' and 'less'.

For instance we say, 'this is hot' and 'this is cold'. However, *cold* really means less hot, and *hot* really means less cold. Sometime try an experiment. Warm one of your hands a little on the stove and put the other hand in ice and make it a little cold. Then submerge both hands in a pail of water and you will find yourself in difficulty. You will be precisely in the same situation in which Arjuna is. One of your hands will tell you that the water is cold, and the other hand will tell you that the water is hot. And the water is the same, it cannot be both hot and cold simultaneously.

In life, everything is relative; nothing is absolute. Here all divisions are of less and more. This is precisely what has become Arjuna's difficulty.

Anyone who takes a good look at life will face precisely this same problem. All divisions in life are between 'a little less' and 'a little more'. Someone is a little more our own, someone a little less. Someone is a little closer, someone is a little further away. Someone is ninety percent or eighty percent or seventy percent our own, and someone else is ninety percent or eighty percent or seventy percent not our own. Nevertheless, even the one who is a 'not our own' holds some percentage of being 'our own'. And even the one who is 'our own', to some extent, he too is not our own.

That is the reason why life has its complexities. If it could be divided exactly into friends and foes, into good and bad, things would be very easy. But that is never the case.

There is a little of Ravana, the villain, in Rama, the hero, and a little of Rama in Ravana too. That is why someone is able to love even Ravana – which would otherwise be impossible. Someone is able to see Rama somewhere even in Ravana; someone loves even Ravana. Someone is able to be inimical even to Rama – somewhere that person must see traces of Ravana in Rama.

So Arjuna's difficulty is that the people standing there are all his own. It is one family – just a line has been drawn down the middle. Arjuna's own people are on the other side, too, just as they are on his side. So, whatsoever the outcome, the people who die there will be his own.

This is the ongoing pain of all life; this is the situation of all life. So what has become a question mark for Arjuna is not something that has surfaced just on this battlefield; it is a question that surfaces in all fields of life.

Now Arjuna has become perplexed. On the other side stands Drona – he learned from him, and now he is supposed to shoot him with arrows. Arjuna learned the art of archery from him. He is Drona's chief disciple, and Drona has done everything in his life for Arjuna, as he has done for no one else. For Arjuna's sake Drona even got Eklavya's thumb cut off, and now this same disciple is ready to take his life. This is the very student whom he has raised with his own sweat and blood, in whom he has poured all his art and skill – and today he will have to draw his bow and aim at this same disciple!

This is a very strange war. This is one family, but in it there are so many connections and cross-connections, so many combinations and intimacies, now rent apart.

But if we look at life, if we look deeply at life, we will find that all wars are wars between people who belong to one another, because this earth is nothing but one family. If India fights Pakistan, it is a fight within a family. The children who yesterday were raised and educated here in India are now today in Pakistan. The land that we identified with as 'ours' is now in Pakistan. The Taj Mahal, which they called theirs until yesterday and for which they could have laid down their lives, is now here in India. So in life everything is connected.

Tomorrow if we fight with China.... India has given everything to China, and China has preserved India's greatest heritage: Gautama the Buddha. No one else would have been able to. And tomorrow, if we start to fight against her....

So, seen in the right perspective, the whole of this life, this whole earth, is one big family. And all wars fought on this planet are within a family, and all wars create the same situation that has arisen in Arjuna's mind. Arjuna's dilemma is completely natural; his anxiety is utterly valid, and the fact that he has become shaken like a dry leaf is completely natural too.

Now what is the way out of this dilemma? Either he should close his eyes and plunge blindly into the war, or he should close his eyes and run blindly away. These seem to be the only two ways out. Either he should close his eyes and say, 'Who cares who is fighting? Whosoever is not on my side is not my own. If he has to die, then so be it!' and close his eyes and throw himself into the war – this is simple – or close his eyes and run away. This too is simple.

But the way out that Krishna is suggesting is not so simple. It does not belong to the path of least resistance. The other two belong to the path of least resistance: both of them are dry imprints, track-marks. Whichever one of the two he chooses to follow, things will be simple. Probably in his numerous past lives he has passed through both of these. They are very obvious options.

But Krishna suggests another route, a third route, one that Arjuna has never taken before. And it is this third option that is valuable. In life, whenever you are faced with two options, remember the third one before coming to any decision, because this third one is always significant. Those two options are always the same and you have always chosen them – again and again. Sometimes one, and when you have tired of that one then the opposite one, and when you have tired of the opposite one then this first one again. You have been forever opting for these two.

The third choice, which is the really significant one, never occurs to us. Krishna will be proposing this third one, and we shall be talking about it in a later chapter.

CHAPTER 4

Beyond Justifications

'Hence, O Krishna, it is not worthy of us
to kill the sons of Dhritarashtra – our own kinsmen.
For how can we gain happiness
By killing our own people?

'Even though these people,
whose sensibilities are already ravaged by greed,
cannot see the wrongness of destroying their own people
and the sin of betraying their friends.

'But Krishna! Why should not we,
who are aware of this sin
and can see the wrongness that comes from doing this,
avoid it?

'As the clan weakens,
Its virtuous traditions decline,
and many transgressions arise within it.

'As these transgressions increase,
the women of the clan become corrupt.
And once our women are corrupt, O Krishna,
descendant of the Vrishni clan,
spurious births take place.

'These spurious offspring, these destroyers of the clan,
are simply doors to hell.
And their forefathers also fall
because the ritual offerings to them
have been forgotten.

'The good and ancient traditions of the clan and its lineage
disappear because of these defects
caused by such clan-destroying offspring.

'O Krishna, those who have lost their noble clan traditions
dwell forever in hell.
Thus I have heard.'

OSHO,
You said that the Gita is a scripture of psychology and not a
spiritual scripture. But you also explained that there is always a
part of Rama, the hero, in Ravana, the villain, and Ravana, the
villain, in Rama, the hero. So isn't it also possible that there is
some part that is spiritual in this scripture of psychology?

SPIRITUALITY, IN MY VIEW, is an experience that cannot be
articulated. Indications can be given, but indications are not
articulation. The moon can be pointed to with a finger, but the
finger is not the moon.

When I say that the Gita is a work of psychology, I don't mean
that it is something like Freud's psychology. Freud's psychology
stops at the mind. It gives no pointers whatsoever towards what is
beyond the mind. Mind is the end – beyond that nothing else
exists. The Gita is the kind of psychology that points towards the
beyond, but the pointing itself is not what actually exists beyond.

The Gita is indeed psychological, but through that psychology,
indications are made towards the self, towards spirituality, towards
the ultimate existence – yet this does not make the Gita a spiritual

text. It is only a milestone, a sign with an arrow pointing towards the ultimate destination. But it remains just that: a milestone. It is not the destination.

There are no spiritual scriptures. Yes, there are scriptures that are pointers towards spirituality, but all pointers are basically psychological. They should not be seen as spiritual. Spirituality is something that is attained by finding a pointer, and there is no way to articulate such spiritual attainment – not even partially. Even its reflection is not possible.

There are reasons for this. It will be good to look at a few of them briefly.

Firstly, when a spiritual experience takes place, in that moment, no thought exists in the mind. How can an experience where thought is not present be expressed with the help of thought? Only the experience in which thought is present, only the experience in which thought is a testifier, can be expressed through thought. But thought is unable to express the experience in which thought is not present.

Spiritual experience is an experience of no thought. Thought does not exist in that moment; hence it is unable to bring forth any message about that experience. That is why the Upanishads keep relentlessly saying, '*neti, neti*'. They are saying, 'neither this, nor that.' If you ask them what it is, they say, 'neither this, nor that.' Whatsoever man can say, it is nothing of that.

Then what is this experience that falls beyond all expression?

Buddha even forbade eleven questions from being asked to him. 'There are dangers involved,' he said. 'If I don't answer, I will appear to be hard on you. If I answer, then it will be an injustice towards the truth – because these questions cannot be answered. So please don't ask them, don't put me in difficulty.'

So when he visited a village it would be announced that no one should ask these eleven questions. These eleven questions are related to spirituality.

When people pressed Lao Tzu to write down his experiences, he would say, 'Please, don't put me in difficulty, because whatsoever

I may write will not be my experience. And there is no way to put into words the experience that is mine, that I would like to write about.'

But people didn't listen to him. So finally, under pressure from his friends and loved ones, he wrote his book. But right in the beginning of the book he wrote, 'That which can be said is not the truth. The truth is that which cannot be said. Keep this in mind when you are reading my book.'

In this world, whosoever has the experience of spirituality has also felt that it should not be expressed. It simply *cannot* be expressed. The mystics keep saying that to give expression to this experience is like a dumb person trying to describe the taste of molasses. Not that the dumb person does not know the taste of molasses; he knows, but he is unable to describe it.

You may think you are able to, but that too is a mistake. You also have been unable to describe the taste. Not only the one who is unable to speak but also those who can speak have been unable to describe it. And if I am to insist on your describing it, then the most you can do is put the molasses in my hand and ask me to taste it. There is no other way. But at least molasses can be put in your hands so you can taste it, whereas even that is not possible with spirituality.

There are no spiritual scriptures in the world. Of course there are scriptures that give pointers towards spirituality – the Gita is one of them – but these pointers are within the mind. They point to beyond the mind, but they themselves are within the mind. Their science is the science of psychology; their basis is psychology. Even the highest flight of scripture is psychological: the highest possibility of words is still within the realms of the mind, the ultimate boundary of any expression is still mental. As long as there is mind, expression is possible. Where the mind ceases, all remains unexpressed.

So when I called the Gita a psychology, I didn't mean it to be something like Watson's psychology, something like behaviorism, or something like Pavlov's 'conditioned reflex'. All these psychologies are closed in on themselves and they are not willing to accept any reality beyond the mind. Some of them are not even ready to accept the reality of mind itself. They say: 'Mind is just a part of the human body. Mind means brain. There is no mind anywhere else. Mind is simply a product of our blood, bones, and marrow. Mind is nothing separate from the body.'

The Gita is not this kind of psychology. The Gita is the kind of psychology which indicates all that which is beyond the mind. But nevertheless, it still remains psychology. I will not call it a spiritual scripture – and not because there is some other spiritual scripture somewhere: there is no spiritual scripture anywhere. The very proclamation of spirituality is: 'My existence is not possible in any scripture. I cannot be contained in words. I cannot be bound by any boundary lines of the intellect.' Spirituality is an experience that transcends all boundaries, that makes all words futile and all expressions hollow.

Osho,
There is a statement by Manu somewhere that says: 'It is all right to kill the tyrant.' So permission is given by the scriptures – and Arjuna knows very well that Duryodhana and his accomplices are all tyrants. Yet in his heart Arjuna hesitates to kill them. What is the reason for this?

The first thing is that what Manu is saying is simply social ethics; he is talking about a social code. Manu's statements are not spiritual. Manu's statements are not even psychological. His statements are a part of social norms and behavior. Hence, if you want to place Manu somewhere you will have to place him with Marx and Durkheim – and others like that. Manu's status is not of any deep significance.

Manu is fundamentally a maintainer of social order, and no social system is ever absolute. All social systems are time-related. Anyone doing even a little thinking will always rise above the social order, because a social system is created with the last man in mind

– just as it is said that the ablest teacher is the one who remembers the least able student in the class while he is teaching. This is certainly true, but then such a teacher immediately becomes useless to the student who ranks first in the class.

As far as the social order is concerned, it is the last person who is taken into consideration and for whom the basic laws are made. Arjuna is not an ordinary person; his is not a mediocre mind. Arjuna is rational, he is intelligent, he is exceptionally talented. For such a person life becomes a matter of deep reflection.

Manu says there is nothing wrong in killing a tyrant. But for a thoughtful person things are not so simple. After all, who is really a tyrant? And even if someone is a tyrant, is it right to kill him or isn't it? Moreover, what if the tyrant is from one's own family? Manu does not have even a thought about this. With the term 'tyrant' he has simply assumed that he is an enemy. Here, the tyrant is 'one's own' – and not just one, they number hundreds of thousands. And there are a million kinds of intimate relationships within these – millions.

So Arjuna's situation is very different. He is not in the usual situation where there is a tyrant and someone who has become that tyrant's victim. This is what he is reflecting upon, this is exactly what he is saying: 'If I win the kingdom by killing all these people, is it a worthwhile bargain?' He is questioning: 'Is this a worthy trade-off to win the kingdom at the cost of all these lives? Does it make any sense to pay such a heavy price to gain the kingdom?' This is exactly what he is inquiring about.

Arjuna's state of mind comes from a much higher level of reflection than the laws of Manu do. In fact, laws are always lifeless and rigid. They only have a functional value. They become meaningless in critical situations.

Arjuna's crisis is very special. It is special in three ways. Firstly, it is very difficult to determine who the tyrant is. Had the Kauravas won the war, you would have had a completely different knowledge of who the tyrant was – because then the story would have been written in a different way, and the writers of the story would have been different. Storywriters gather around the victorious, they don't get close to the defeated.

Hitler lost the Second World War, and so we all know who was 'the bad guy'. But if Hitler had won, and Churchill, Roosevelt and Stalin had lost, then for sure we would know that these other fellows were 'the bad guys' and not Hitler. What we are able to think and judge in hindsight, after an event or situation has occurred, is not so clear-cut in the middle of the event or situation. Generally, the writer of history writes the history of the victorious, and generally history crystallizes around the victorious.

So today we know that the Kauravas were the tyrants. But right in the moment of war things are not so plain and clear that we are able to judge who is the tyrant, who has done wrong. It is never that clear.

China keeps saying that India attacked her. India keeps saying that China attacked her. It will never be clear who attacked: to date it has not been ascertained who was the invader. Yes, the one who wins writes the history and the one who is defeated is branded as the invader. The loser is not able to write the history. But is being defeated in itself the proof of being the invader?

It is always easy to make a judgment after the event, because by then the picture is much clearer. But it is not so easy to do this in the middle of a situation.

Mistakes are always made on both sides. There can be a difference of degrees, but the mistake is never one-sided. It is not that only the Kauravas are responsible for all this evil and the Pandavas have no responsibility for it. It isn't so. The differences are only of degrees. It is possible that the Kauravas are more responsible – but even that is decided long after the event when the perspective of distance becomes possible.

Arjuna's mind has become anxiety-ridden in this dense moment of a war. Nothing is clear. What is going on, and to what extent is it right? And even if it becomes very clear that the other side are the tyrants, the aggressors, then still all his loved ones are standing with them too. Duryodhana may be a tyrant, but what about Drona? Drona is not a tyrant. What about Bheeshma? He is not a tyrant. In fact, both Kauravas and Pandavas were raised and cared for by him when they were children. The enemy is not just one person, it is a host of people. It is difficult to make a concrete decision in the light of this fact, and this is the cause of Arjuna's anxiety.

The socio-ethical laws created by Manu are very ordinary – useful in ordinary situations, but in a special situation like this, Manu will not do. He would only have done under one circumstance: if Arjuna had denied the uniqueness of the situation and quoted Manu to rationalize his action, saying, 'Manu has said it is all right to kill the tyrant and so do I.' But that would not have been a very intelligent step. And it would certainly have not been a very intelligent step for one more reason – because then the Gita would not have become available to you. The Gita was born out of Arjuna's deep inquiry, thought and reflection – out of his quest. If he had accepted the situation in a simplistic way, then all that would have happened would have been the war taking place, one party emerging victorious, the other being defeated... the usual scene. When there is a war, somebody wins, somebody loses – and this gives birth to a story, to a plot.

The Mahabharata has not proved to be as significant as the Gita has. The Mahabharata happened and came to an end, but it is very difficult for the Gita to come to an end. The Mahabharata was just an event, and as time passes, it keeps fading from our memories. Actually, the truth is that the Mahabharata has only remained in our memories because the Gita was born through it – otherwise it was not even worth remembering.

There have been thousands of wars around the world. Man has fought fourteen thousand wars in three thousand years, but ordinarily a war becomes just another footnote in history. The Gita, however, became a far greater, a far more significant event than the war itself. Today, the Gita is not remembered because of the Mahabharata; the Mahabharata is remembered because of the Gita.

Hence, I would also like to say to you that in this world, what is of value is not the events that occur, what is of value is the thoughts, the ideas. Events occur and are then relegated to the garbage, but thoughts, ideas, take on an eternal presence. Events ultimately die, but if some alive, some spirited thought emerges in the middle of an event, it attains an eternal life.

The Mahabharata is not important. Even if it had never actually happened, it would make no difference. But it would make a great difference if the Gita had never occurred. The Mahabharata has become an inconsequential event, and with time it will become increasingly inconsequential. It was a family quarrel between brothers, between cousins. It happened and then it was over. It was their matter, and it finally came to an end. But the Gita has gained more and more importance with every passing day. It attained importance precisely because Arjuna did not have the kind of ordinary intelligence that would have believed in what Manu was saying. Arjuna had the kind of genius that inquires, that raises questions during a crisis.

Normally it is very difficult to raise questions during a crisis. To raise questions while sitting in your house reading the Gita is very easy. To raise questions in the circumstances Arjuna finds himself in is a risky affair. This is not the situation for raising questions. This is not the situation to begin an inquiry into the ultimate reality; this is not the moment in which a master and the disciple can sit under a tree and contemplate. War is at the threshold. War cries have been made, conches have been blown – and in such a moment the mind of this man is stirred.

Arjuna is a courageous man. In the middle of the battlefield he expresses what state he is in, that he is deeply stirred, and moves into thinking and reflection. One who thinks and questions in the middle of a crisis of this magnitude is not an ordinary genius. Manu would not suffice here; a man of Krishna's caliber is needed. Had Manu been there he would have said, 'Read my *Manu Smriti*. There it is written: "Kill the tyrant." Your duty is crystal clear.'

Duty has always been clear only to stupid people. To the

intelligent, it has never been clear. Intelligent people have always been uncertain. The reason is that intelligent people think so deeply, and usually about both sides of the matter so much, that they have difficulty deciding which is right and which is wrong. Thoughtful people are not as clear about right and wrong as ignorant people are.

For the ignorant man everything is so clear-cut: this is right, that is wrong; this is Hindu, that is Muslim; this person is one of us, that one is a stranger. But the more contemplation grows, the more doubts arise: 'Who is mine and who is a stranger? What is right and what is wrong?' And in this world, everything that is of value has always been born from those who have gone through the birth pangs of this contemplative process. In that moment Arjuna suffered this pain, and the Gita is a response and an outcome of this pain. No, Manu is not enough in this situation. A gross law of this kind won't do.

There are traffic rules on the roads. 'Keep left!' is perfectly fine – there is no problem with it. Even if you turn it around and ask people to keep right, there will be no difficulty. In America it is just the opposite: there, the law is to keep to the right, and so people keep to the right. Keeping to the right, keeping to the left – whatever has been decided serves the purpose, but these are not some supreme foundations of life. And if someone raises the question, 'What is so special in keeping to the left? Why not to the right?' – nobody in the world will be able to explain why. It is only functional. And if a very thoughtful person asks, 'Anyway, what is actually left and what is actually right?' it will become a problem.

The system created by Manu is merely functional, and Arjuna is questioning this merely functional system. His questions are profound. He is asking: 'So, I attain the kingdom by killing so many people, by killing my nearest and dearest, but so what? What purpose will it serve? Suppose I win the war, what can it really bring? Granted that the Kauravas are tyrants and if we kill them revenge will have been taken, but what then? What is the meaning of this revenge? Who knows how many unarmed people, how many innocent people will be killed who have nothing to do with it all? They have been dragged onto the battlefield just because they are somebody's relatives. What about all these people?

No, Arjuna's questions are very significant. Manu is not enough here.

'Hence, O Krishna, it is not worthy of us
to kill the sons of Dhritarashtra – our own kinsmen.
For how can we gain happiness
by killing our own people?

'Even though these people,
whose sensibilities are already ravaged by greed,
cannot see the wrongness of destroying their own people
and the sin of betraying their friends.

'But Krishna! Why should not we,
who are aware of this sin
and can see the wrongness that comes from doing this,
avoid it?

'As the clan weakens,
its virtuous traditions decline,
and many transgressions arise within it.'

Arjuna is saying, 'They are thoughtless; if we also start behaving in the same way, how is it going to help? Granted they are wrong, but if we also respond to this wrong by doing more wrong, will that make it right? Does responding to one wrong with another wrong make it right?' What he is asking is: 'If we add our mistakes to theirs, are the mistakes doubled or are they rectified? Their minds are deluded, they are being stupid – does that mean we should behave stupidly too? And is what we will get in return *that* worthwhile, is it *that* useful, is it *that* valuable?'

Take note. Two parallel thoughts are moving in Arjuna's mind.

He is asking if it is worthwhile. There are two motives behind this question. Maybe all of this has a significance, and so if Krishna explains it to him, he can then rationalize his act of fighting. Maybe Krishna will be able to explain that it is worthwhile, that it is beneficial. Maybe Krishna will be able to successfully explain that evil will be negated by evil and then what will remain will be good. If this happens, he will be able to prepare himself for the fight. Man wants to find some rational excuse for preparing to fight.

Both of these points of view are running side by side in Arjuna's mind. The way he is presenting his question suggests that he is saying, 'Either give me permission to run away so I can escape, or give me some clear reason why I should go to war.' He wants to get his mind clear, so that if he does go to war it is with an understanding and with a mind that is totally convinced that what is happening is good.

His other alternative is to run away from the war. These are the two alternatives that he can see. He seems to be ready for either – whichever of the two may occur. This is worth understanding.

Man has always considered himself to be intelligent, thinking, rational. Aristotle went so far as to call man a rational animal, a rational being. He said, 'Man is a rational animal.' But as our understanding of man has grown more and more, we have come to realize that his intelligence is nothing more than an effort to prove that his unintelligence is intelligence. Man's reason has always been involved in justifying the irrational and the unreasonable in him.

If he has to fight, first he likes to prove to himself and others that some good, some blessing is going to come out of the war – then he can move into it easily. If he has to behead someone, first he likes to prove to himself that the act is taking place in the interest of the person who is being beheaded – then he can do his job with ease. If he is going to set fire to something, first he likes to convince himself that this act is going to protect religion – then he will be easily ready to light the fire. Man has continuously tried to justify the utterly irrational elements in him with the help of reason.

Arjuna is in exactly the same situation. Inwardly he is ready to fight – otherwise there would have been no need for him to come to the battlefield at all. His mind is inclined to fight; he wants to acquire the kingdom and he wants to take his revenge for all that has been done to him. That is why he has allowed himself to come so far, to the point where the battle is about to begin. But he is not ready in the same way as Duryodhana or Bheema are. He is not total; his mind is divided, split. Somewhere deep inside he knows that it is wrong, futile – and at the same time he also feels that he will have to do it, that it is a question of his prestige, his ego, his family and a thousand and one other things. Both these thoughts are running in his mind. He is in two minds.

And remember, a thoughtful person is always in two minds. A thought-less person is not. In the state of no-thought there is no split mind. But a thoughtful person is always in two minds.

By 'a thoughtful person' I mean one who is constantly having a dialogue and discussion within himself; one who is constantly debating within himself. He splits himself into two fragments and debates which is right and which is wrong. A thoughtful person is discussing by himself, within himself, twenty-four hours a day.

The same kind of debate must be going on in Arjuna's mind. Somehow he may have convinced himself of the rightness of the war and has arrived at the battlefield. But he was not aware of the full implication of the war.

During the Second World War, the man who dropped the atom bomb on Hiroshima had no idea what was going to happen. All he knew was just this much – that he had to press a button and the atom bomb would drop down. He had no idea that this bomb would kill one hundred thousand people. He didn't know anything. He only had this one order that he had to carry out, and the order was that he should fly to Hiroshima and press a button. He went up to Hiroshima, pressed a button and came back.

He only came to know that one hundred thousand people had been killed when the rest of the world did. Then he couldn't sleep. He started having visions of millions of dead bodies the whole time. He was shaken to his very core.

He started having problems with his limbs trembling. Eventually, he started hurting himself. One day he cut his veins and another day he hit his own head with a hammer. He was admitted to a mental asylum. Later he started attacking others too. He had to be tied up. He lost his sleep completely.

He was suffering from guilt. Just this one guilty thing was weighing on his mind: that he had killed one hundred thousand people. But at the time, he had had no knowledge of it.

Our system of war today is completely inhuman. Even the person who is doing the killing doesn't know that he is pressing the button of death for one hundred thousand people.

It was a different situation during the Mahabharata. Everything was in the open. The war was straightforward and human. People were confronting each other. Arjuna could stand up in his chariot and foresee what the result going to be. He started noticing: 'Here is a friend who is going to be killed. He has small children at home.'

Remember, modern war has become inhuman; hence there is a greater danger now. Even the fighter doesn't have any clear idea about the consequences. Everything is happening in the dark. Those who are taking decisions are also dealing with figures, not with living human beings. They have only statistics: one hundred thousand people will die. Hearing this, nothing real is conveyed. But make one hundred thousand people stand in a row, look down on them and feel that these one hundred thousand people are going to die; then you will also be able to visualize their one hundred thousand wives, their hundreds of thousands of children, their old fathers, their old mothers.... Who knows what innumerable responsibilities these people have behind them.

If the man who dropped the bomb on Hiroshima had been face-to-face with the responsibility of killing one hundred thousand people, I think he would have preferred to die rather than carrying out the order. He would have refused to obey the order. He would have been plagued with the question, 'Should I kill them just for the sake of my job?'

The question arose in Arjuna's mind because the whole scene

was before him, right in front of his eyes. He began to see it all: the crying and weeping widows… and God knows how many of those closest to him would be among the dead; their widows would be there, their pining and suffering children would be there, the ground would become littered with corpses. He foresaw all this with such clarity that any rationalization about the rightness of the war that he might have consoled himself with before simply toppled over.

The other part of his mind started saying, 'What are you about to do? It is a sin! What can be a greater sin than this? Just for the sake of the kingdom or for wealth or pleasure, you are ready to kill all of these people?'

He must certainly have been a thoughtful person. His mind started refusing. But another mind is lurking inside that refusal. That second mind is also speaking: 'If only I could find some rationalization, if only someone could convince me that this is all right, that there is no harm in fighting; that in some ways it is right, then I can pull myself together, become single-pointed and jump into the war.'

While Arjuna is asking Krishna questions, he has no idea what Krishna's response will be, he has no guarantee how the situation will unfold. Men like Krishna are not predictable. Answers from men like Krishna are not fixed, or ready-made. You cannot predict what men like Krishna will say.

With Arjuna, however, it is clear that he wants one of two things. Either it should become established that this war is right, moral, religious, beneficial, and benevolent; that it will bring him happiness in this world and the world beyond – and if this is the case, he will plunge into the war. Or, if it is proved that the war is pointless and that all this is not possible, then he will run away from the war.

These two alternatives are clearly before him. And between these two his mind is wavering; between these two lies the split of his mind. He does have the desire to fight. If he had had no desire to fight whatsoever, then there would have been no need to ask Krishna any questions at all.

Recently I was in a village. A young man came to me and asked, 'I want to take *sannyas*. What is your advice?'

I said, 'As long as my advice is needed, please don't take sannyas. Sannyas is not something that can be taken because of my advice. The day you feel that even if the whole world suggests that you don't take sannyas you still will, is the day that you are ready for it. Only then will the flower of sannyas bring a fragrance to itself – otherwise not.'

Had Arjuna's mind been clear about this single point – that the war is wrong – he would not have asked for Krishna's advice, he would have simply left. He would have said to Krishna, 'Take care of this chariot, lead these horses wherever you want to lead them, and do whatsoever you want! I am off!' And if Krishna had insisted on giving him advice, he would have said, 'Unasked for advice has never been accepted in this world – and it never will be. Keep your advice to yourself!'

But no, Arjuna is asking for advice. In the very act of seeking advice he is revealing his divided mind. He still believes that if he can get the right kind of advice, he will fight. He has this belief and that is why he is putting questions to Krishna. If he had been clear that to go to war was right, then Krishna's advice would not have been needed – because all preparations for the war were already made.

Arjuna is shaky, he is divided. That is why he is raising all sorts of questions. His questions are significant. Such questions invariably raise their heads in the life of anyone who thinks even a little bit – when the mind gets divided and two different answers start coming simultaneously and all decisiveness is lost. Arjuna is in this state of doubt. His decisiveness is lost.

Whenever someone asks for advice, it always indicates only one thing: that the person has lost his self-confidence. Now he has no trust in himself to find the answer. Two different answers are arising from within him with equal force and emphasis: it has become difficult to choose between the two. Sometimes one seems to be right, and sometimes the other.

Man only seeks advice when he is in this situation. Whenever someone is looking for advice, it should be understood that this person has become so split within that he cannot connect with any answer from within himself. This is Arjuna's state. He is talking about his state.

OSHO,
Both Arjuna and Krishna are standing on a battlefield. How can Arjuna get involved with listening to the eighteen cantos of the Gita just before the start of the battle? And how can Krishna find the time to speak the Gita? Both of the armies were present there as well. Does it mean that all the soldiers got involved with listening to this dialogue between Krishna and Arjuna?
Did all this take place in psychological time or something of that nature?

This long discussion with Krishna is certainly questionable. Undoubtedly this question arises. On the battlefield, with the soldiers ready to jump into a fierce fight.... If Krishna had spoken the eighteen cantos in the way that his devotees recite it, such a lengthy book would have taken a considerable time! Even if he had gone on speaking it non-stop, without so much as looking at Arjuna, it would still have taken a long time. So how was it possible?

There are two things to be said in this context. This question has always been in the air, so a few people simply said that the Gita is interpolated into the epic Mahabharata, that it must have been added at a later date – because otherwise it is just not possible. And some people say that the dialogue must have taken place in a much more concise form, and that the poet elaborated on it later on.

According to me, both views are incorrect. To me, the Gita *did* happen and it happened exactly as it is available to us now. But here it is necessary to understand the process of its happening. Had it happened like a normal face-to-face dialogue, in the same way as we are discussing here, then Krishna and Arjuna would not have remained the only protagonists. There were many people there, there was a big crowd all around them, and others would have also joined in with the discussion, others would have also raised questions.

But in the dialogue of the Gita, all these people don't come into the picture at all. So many warriors on this side, so many warriors on the other side, the dialogue between Krishna and Arjuna going on for hours... and no one else is speaking in the middle of it! No one even says as much as: 'This is not the time for discussion! It is time we started the war. The conches have been blown. Enough of this discussion now!' But no, nobody intervened.

As I see it, this discussion is telepathic. This dialogue has not taken place verbally, face-to-face. You need to understand a little of exactly what telepathy is, and then you will be able to comprehend this – otherwise not. I will try to explain with the help of a few examples.

There was a mystic called George Gurdjieff. He went with a Russian mathematician, Ouspensky, and thirty more of his disciples, and stayed in a small village in Tiflis.

He kept these thirty people captive in a huge bungalow – captive, I say, because they had no permission to go out. And they had been asked to maintain a complete silence for three months. Not only were they not supposed to speak through words, but also through signs, eyes or hand gestures. Each one had been told to live in the house for three months as if he or she were utterly alone there, and as if no one else existed. The other was not to be recognized – either by sight or by gestures. If someone passed by, the person was not to be taken note of.

And Gurdjieff had warned, 'If I catch anyone making even the slightest sign or gesture, or recognizing the presence of another – for example, another person is passing by too closely and you try to avoid bumping into him – I will expel that person. You have acknowledged the presence of the other, you have acknowledged that the other person is there; a communication has already taken place. In avoiding that person, the gesture has already been made.'

In the following fifteen days twenty-seven people were turned out. At the end of this experiment only three people remained. It was a very difficult situation. Where there are thirty people present, ten to twelve people sitting in one room, it is arduous to forget the others and to start living as if one is alone there, as if the others simply do not exist... but not as arduous as we might think because actually three people did survive until the very end. Even three is not a small number. And it is not so difficult, because if someone sitting in a forest with closed eyes can be in the crowd, why can't someone be in the crowd and still remain alone? All the functions of the mind are reversible, can be turned back. If someone can be talking to his faraway wife while sitting in the forest, why can't someone be alone while sitting with his wife? There should be no difficulty in it.

Ouspensky, himself a scientist and philosopher, was one of these people. He has written perhaps the most profound book in the past one hundred years on mathematics: *Tertium Organum*. It is said that in Europe three great books have been written so far. One is *Organon* by Aristotle, the second *Novum Organum* by Bacon, and then *Tertium Organum* by Ouspensky. Ouspensky was a great scientific thinker, and he was one of the three who survived the scrutiny.

Three months passed. In those three months he lived as if he were utterly alone there. Not only did he forget all about the other people who were in the room, even the outside world did not exist for him. And remember, he who forgets the other forgets himself as well. In order to keep being reminded of oneself it is necessary to keep remembering others, because 'I' and 'thou' are two ends of the same pole. The moment one of the two disappears, the other drops by itself. Either both remain or both go. If somebody says, 'I will save the "I" and forget the "thou"', it is impossible – because 'I' is the echo and resonance of 'thou'. If the 'you' is forgotten, the 'I' disintegrates on its own accord. If the 'I' is dropped, the 'you' evaporates. They both survive together or else they don't survive at all. They are two sides of the same coin.

It is understandable that Ouspensky forgot the others, but he also forgot himself. Only pure 'is-ness' remained.

After three months, Ouspensky and Gurdjieff were sitting in front of each other, when suddenly Ouspensky heard somebody calling him, 'Ouspensky, listen!' He was startled and looked around to see who was calling but nobody was speaking. Gurdjieff was sitting in front of him. He looked at Gurdjieff minutely for the first time in three months. Gurdjieff started laughing. Again he heard inside, 'Don't you recognize my voice? It is Gurdjieff speaking.' Gurdjieff was sitting silently in front of him; not even his lips had moved.

Ouspensky was perplexed. He exclaimed, 'What am I experiencing?' This was his first utterance in three months.

Gurdjieff said, 'Now your silence has reached to a point where dialogue is possible without words. Now I can speak to you directly. Words are not needed.'

Russian scientists have successfully transmitted messages up to a distance of a thousand miles without using any medium. You can do it too. It is not that difficult.

Try a small experiment in your own house. Find a small child. Put the lights off in the room while the child sits at one end of the room, and you sit at the other. Tell the child to close his eyes and keep his attention on you and on trying to hear whether you are saying something.

Then start repeating just one word inside you, 'Rose, rose, rose…' Don't speak the word; just repeat it silently inside. In half an hour or so the child will tell you that you are saying the word *rose*.

You can also try it the other way around, but it will take more time. If a child starts repeating a word and you want to catch it, you may have to practice for two or more days. Children get it much more quickly!

In what we call life, man does nothing except get spoilt. Old people end up being nothing more than spoiled children. But a child will start catching the word within an hour or half an hour.

Just repeat one word and once that one word can be received then a whole sentence can be picked up after some practice.

In the context of Krishna and Arjuna it is necessary to remember that this dialogue did not take place on the outside. This dialogue is a profoundly inner one. That is why even the people standing near them on the battlefield were not witnesses to it. And that is why it is also possible that those who initially wrote the Mahabharata did not include the Gita in it. This is possible. It is possible that the historian, the person, who wrote the story of the Mahabharata did not include the Gita in it.

But Sanjay hears it. Sanjay, who is able to see from that afar, can also hear from afar. In fact, the world first heard the Gita from Sanjay and not from Krishna. Arjuna is the first person to hear it, but that hearing is very inner. There is no outer evidence that he heard it.

Secondly, I would like to tell you that the Gita is a telepathic communication. It is an inner dialogue in which outer words were not used.

It is said that Mahavira never spoke, that he did not utter all the words that are attributed to him. There were people standing next to Mahavira, and he would speak to them, but not verbally because the thousands of other people who had come to listen to him would not hear a single word. Then one of the men standing next to Mahavira would say out loud what Mahavira had said.

That is why Mahavira's talks have been called silent talks, wordless talks. He never spoke directly. He spoke inwardly to someone and that person expressed it outwardly. It is almost like when I am speaking through this microphone and you are listening. A man can also be used like a microphone.

If Sanjay had not heard the dialogue between Krishna and Arjuna, it would have been lost forever. Many other such things have happened many other times and been lost. Many sayings of Mahavira are not available.

One day Buddha called together all his disciples and came to them with a lotus flower in his hand. Sitting down, he started looking at the flower. He went on looking at it. People were at a loss, and soon they became restless. Some must have started coughing, some must have started fidgeting – because this went on for quite some time. 'Why is Buddha silent? He should be speaking. Why doesn't he speak?'

After half an hour had passed like this, their restlessness reached its peak. Someone stood up and said, 'What are you doing? We have come to listen to you. Why don't you speak?'

Buddha said, 'I am speaking. Listen! Listen!'

The people said, 'You are not saying anything, what is there to listen to?'

At that very moment a monk called Mahakashyapa started laughing. Buddha called him and gave him the flower. Then he said to the others, 'Listen! That which can be said through words I have said to you all. And that which cannot be said through words, which can only be said in silence, I have said that to Mahakashyapa. Now if you want to ask anything about this, you can ask Mahakashyapa.'

Ever since then the monks of Buddha have been asking each other, 'What did Buddha say to Mahakashyapa?' – because whenever someone asked Mahakashyapa about it, he would start laughing and say, 'If Buddha could not say it, why should I get into trouble? Buddha would have said it if he had wanted to. If he did not make that mistake, I am not going to.'

Later, Mahakashyapa silently passed it on to someone else, and in turn, that person transmitted it using no words. In this manner the tradition was passed down through six people. Bodhidharma was the sixth, and for the first time he expressed it verbally.

In the meantime, some nine hundred years had passed. For the first time Bodhidharma put into words what Buddha had been saying to Mahakashyapa in silence. Why did he do this? In China, when Bodhidharma said that now for the first time he was going to put into words what Buddha had said to Mahakashyapa in silence, people asked him, 'Why are you going to speak about this when nobody has said anything up till now?'

Bodhidharma replied, 'Silent listeners can no longer be found.' So I am helpless, and I am about to die. What Buddha said to Mahakashyapa will be lost. Now I want to reveal it at whatever point of purity or impurity I can manage.'

This is another incident.

So the first thing I would like to tell you is that the Gita is a silent dialogue that took place between Krishna and Arjuna.

Secondly, the passage of time during a silent dialogue is totally different. This also has to be understood – otherwise you will think that even a silent dialogue needs an hour, an hour and a half or two hours. 'What difference does it make whether something is communicated outwardly or inwardly? It will still take some time.' If this is your understanding, you still need to understand the concept of the passage of time.

Sometimes sitting in your chair you doze off and start dreaming. In the dream you get married, raise a family, get a job, buy a house, have children, your son gets married and wedding music starts playing all over again.... At that moment somebody wakes you up from your sleep. You look at your watch and find that hardly a minute has passed since you dozed off. So it is very difficult to work out how such a long story was enacted in such a short time. It takes half a lifetime to get through all that hassle! How did all these events, that normally take almost thirty to forty years, take place in one minute?

But it happened. The fact is that dreamtime is different; its timescale is different. The perception of time in a dream is totally different. That's why the story of a whole lifetime can be seen in just one minute.

It is said that when someone is drowning, when he finally goes under, he goes through the complete movie of his life. It is possible; it is not at all difficult.

Time in the waking state is different from the time of your dreaming. And even while you are awake the timescale is not always identical. It is continuously changing, flickering. For example, when you are in misery time seems to be too long; when you are happy time seems to be very short. When your beloved is sitting with you, after an hour you feel as if she has just arrived – just a moment ago! If your enemy happens to visit you, he may have just arrived and you want him to leave, so it feels like a lifetime has passed. According to a watch, the time that has passed is the same, but the mental perception of time keeps lengthening or shortening it.

Someone in your house is dying and you are sitting by his deathbed through the night. The night will seem like an eternity – as if it is never going to end. But when you are dancing all night with your friends, it feels as if time is running away too fast. Night appears to be the enemy; it seems to be in a hurry. It flies quickly away and the dawn breaks – as if there had hardly been a gap between the evening and the dawn. The evening had only just begun and already the morning is coming. The time gap between the two seems to have fallen away.

In moments of happiness, time appears to be shorter. In reality, it not only appears to be so, it *does* become shorter – just as it becomes longer in misery. Even during the day, while you are awake, the timescale is changing.If you ever have experienced bliss, in this state there is no time.

Someone asked Jesus, 'What will be the most special thing in the kingdom of your God?'

Jesus said, 'There will be time no longer there.'

They replied, 'We fail to understand that. How can things happen without time.'

There is no time in the moment of bliss. If a moment of meditation has ever descended within you, if a moment of bliss has ever made you dance, then in that moment there is no time, in that state time evaporates. All the mystics of the world agree on this point. Whether they are Mahavira, Buddha, Lao Tzu, Jesus, Mohammed or anybody else, they all say that the moment of bliss, of self-realization, of the experience of the ultimate reality is a timeless moment, is beyond time.

So the scale of telepathic time is different. Something that may take an hour and a half to write down can be communicated in a moment through telepathy. If you start to write down the details of one moment of your dream, it may take one and a half hours. You will find this strange: the dream that could be seen in a single moment is taking one and a half hours to write down. Why? What is the reason?

This is the third point that I would like to bring to your attention. The reason is this: when something happens inside you, it happens all at once, simultaneously. For example, when I am looking at you, I am seeing all of you in the same moment. But if I get down to counting you all, I will have to count you one by one, and that act will be linear. I will have to count you in a linear way – which will take hours. When I saw you, I saw you all simultaneously, and that happened in a split second. But if I count you, and if I also have to write down your details in a book, that will take many hours.

So when you dream, you see things in a simultaneous mode; when you write it down on paper it becomes a linear phenomenon – it is no more a simultaneous happening. You have to write down the details of events one by one. That becomes linear and takes more time.

When the Gita was written down, or when Sanjay was narrating it to Dhritarashtra – 'This is the dialogue that is taking place between Krishna and Arjuna' – it must have taken the same amount of time that is required by you to read the Gita now. But it will be difficult for you to grasp how long it may have taken for the dialogue to happen between Krishna and Arjuna unless you have had some experience of telepathy yourself. Our timescale is of no consequence in that space.

So it is possible that none of the other warriors and soldiers even got an inkling of what was transpiring between Krishna and Arjuna. It may have happened in a moment. Maybe the chariot came onto the battlefield, Arjuna saw the scene, felt drained and unable to move a muscle, and this whole narrative happened within a split second.

A small story, and then we will take up the next sutra...

I have heard a beautiful story attributed to Narada's life. Narada was constantly hearing from the great sages and wise men that this world is an illusion. So he went to see God and asked him, 'I fail to understand how that which is can be an illusion? That which is, is! How can it be illusory? What does it mean?'

It was noontime. The sun was beating down mercilessly. God said, 'I am thirsty. Please go and get me some water first, and then I will explain the matter to you.'

Narada went to fetch the water. He entered a village. People were taking a nap in their houses because of the noontime heat. Narada knocked on a door, and a young girl came out. Seeing her, Narada forgot all about God. Anybody would! What is the hurry to remember someone who can be remembered at any time? Narada forgot.

When God himself had been forgotten, there was no question of remembering his thirst! He forgot why he had come there in the first place. He went on looking at the girl, completely infatuated. He declared that he had come with a proposal to marry her. The girl's father was out. She told him to rest until her father came back.

He rested. The father returned and he agreed to the proposal. The marriage took place. The story takes off – several children were born to them. It all took many long years. The girl's father, Narada's father-in-law, died. Narada himself grew old, the wife grew old – and there was a whole battalion of children to raise.

During one rainy season there was a big flood and the village was submerged and swept away. In an effort to save his wife and children, Narada tried to escape from the flood in some way. He was old and powerless; trying to keep the children safe, he lost his grip on his wife who began to be swept away, and so was he. The streams were torrential and finally they were all swept away.

Half-dead and in tatters, Narada landed on some shore. His eyes were closed, his tears were flowing, and someone was saying, 'Get up! You took a long time; the sun has almost gone down and I am still sitting here, thirsty. Didn't you bring the water for me to drink?'

Narada opened his eyes and saw God standing there. He said, 'My God! I forgot all about it. But in the meanwhile a lot has happened – and you are saying that the sun has only just gone down!'

God said, 'Yes. The sun has gone down just now.'

Narada looked all around. There was no sign of a flood anywhere. He asked about his wife and children. God said, 'What children? What wife? Were you dreaming? You were asking me, 'How could that which is be an illusion?' That which is, is not an illusion – but seen through the medium of time it becomes an illusion. Seen from a timeless state, from beyond time, all that which is becomes the truth.'

The world is the truth seen through the medium of time. The truth is the world seen through the medium of timelessness.

The Gita is an inner happening and is beyond the periphery of time.

'As these transgressions increase,
the women of the clan become corrupt.
And once our women are corrupt, O Krishna,
descendant of the Vrishni clan,
spurious births take place.

'These spurious offspring, these destroyers of the clan,
are simply doors to hell.
And their forefathers also fall
because the ritual offerings to them
have been forgotten.

'The good and ancient traditions of the clan and its lineage
disappear because of these defects
caused by such clan-destroying offspring.

'O Krishna, those who have lost their noble clan traditions
dwell forever in hell.
Thus I have heard.'

Looking this way and that, Arjuna is trying to discover all the things that can go wrong if there is a war. His mind sees many evils. He is not only thinking of now, but of the future – what will happen to their offspring, how the purity of their caste will be corrupted, how their ancient religion will perish… he is foreseeing all these things.

It all seems very strange. Why is he suddenly worrying about all of this? But if you take a look at the anti-war literature of Bertrand Russell and others like him in the West, you will be amazed. They are all saying the same things: that children will be handicapped, that systems will collapse, that civilization will be destroyed, that religion and culture will be lost. The thoughts that are bothering Arjuna here bothered the pacifists after the destruction of Hiroshima. I am saying 'pacifists'. A pacifist tries to discover all the evils that will come in the wake of a war, but his entire search comes from a need to justify his attitude of escapism.

We find justifications for doing what we want to do, but on the surface it has to appear that we are doing what is right. We look for arguments to justify what we want to do. And in life, everyone has the opportunity to find their own justifications. So man can find reasons to support anything that he wants to do.

An American writer has written a book in which he contends that the number thirteen is bad, and that the thirteenth is a dangerous date. He has described it in great detail. He had done some great research to show how many people, and who, have fallen down from the thirteenth floor and died.

So now, in many hotels in the United States, no thirteenth floor exists because of the influence of this book. Nobody is ready to stay on the thirteenth floor of any building. After the twelfth floor straightaway comes the fourteenth floor!

The writer has shown how many of the people who are admitted to hospital on the thirteenth die, how many accidents happen on the roads on this date, how many people contract cancer, how many airplanes crash, how many cars collide… basically he has gathered details of all the untoward incidents that occur on the thirteenth. All of this must surely be happening on the eleventh or the twelfth as well, but he has ignored all these other dates and collected all his information only about the thirteenth.

If somebody is against the eleventh, he can collect all this information about the eleventh as well. If somebody is in favor of the thirteenth, he will find that there are many children born on the thirteenth, that there are airplanes that do *not* crash on the thirteenth; that a number of good things happen on the thirteenth: people get married, new friendships are made, great celebrations happen.... Everything good happens on the thirteenth as well.

The human mind discovers what it wants to. Arjuna wants to escape; hence he seeks out all these arguments. Up to the day before, he had never talked about any of this. Until then, he had no concern whatsoever for the coming generations. Up to the very last minute before the war these thoughts had never occurred to him; now he suddenly remembers all of this. The escapist in him is getting the better of him, and so he is trying to find all kinds of arguments.

It is very interesting to note that the crux of the matter is that he is afraid to kill his own people, but the arguments that he is putting forward are about different matters. He is finding all sorts of arguments, but the bottom line is simply this: that he is suffering from attachment, from affinity. He is unable to gather the courage to kill his nearest and dearest. This is the whole matter, but he is spinning such a web, so much philosophy around it!

We all do this. It often happens that we avoid the small matter that may be there and the web that we spin around it is something totally different. If someone wants to hit another person, he will find his reasons for doing so. If someone wants to vent his anger, he will find his justifications. If someone wants to escape from a certain situation, he will find some reason for doing so. The doing comes first, and the justifications will follow later.

Krishna sees this and he is laughing inside. He understands that all these arguments that Arjuna is bringing forth are cunning, that they are neither real nor right. These are not Arjuna's own insights

– because so far he had never thought twice before killing anybody. This is not the first time that he is killing somebody. He is an expert fighter. Killing is his lifelong experience and expertise. Killing is his forte, his power. His sword is his very arm, his bow and arrow his very being. He is not a man who having spent his life with some weighing-scales in his grocery store has suddenly been made to stand on the battlefield.

So Krishna must be laughing at his words. He must be looking at the cunningness of the human mind.

All human beings are cunning. We avoid the real issues and gather arguments to support false ones. It often happens that we convince ourselves with false arguments and the basic issue is overlooked. But Krishna would like Arjuna to see the basic issue, because true understanding is born out of comprehending this. But if we push the basic issue under the carpet and try to play with false reasons...

Now, what has what will happen in the future got to do with Arjuna? Since when has he been worried about the destruction of religion? When did he ever worry about the adulteration of his clan? When did he ever give a thought to all of these matters? No, none of these things ever mattered to him before. And then, suddenly, all of these problems descend upon his mind today.

It is interesting to understand why these problems are overshadowing his mind. It is because he wants to escape. But while escaping, he does not want to show that he is doing so out of cowardice. He will have good reasons for escaping. It will look reasonable. He will say that he has dropped fighting because of all these reasons. If he escapes without any reasons people will laugh at him.

This is where his cunning lies. We all have this kind of cunning in us. Whatever we are going to do, we create a network of reasons before we start it, just as we erect a structure first when we build a house. Our network of reasons will justify our action but the real reason behind this action will be totally different. If Krishna could clearly see that what Arjuna is presenting is the real reason for his escape, then I don't think he would be interested in destroying his religion, I don't think he would want to see his clan being corrupted; I don't think he would want his ancient religion and culture to be destroyed. No, he wouldn't want any such thing!

But these are not the real reasons, they are false substitutes, hence Krishna will try to overturn them. He will try to tear them to pieces, to cut them away. He will bring Arjuna to the point where the real reason is lurking – because real reasons can be fought against, but false ones cannot. And so we all hide the real reasons and live in the false reasons.

It is necessary to understand Arjuna's state of mind thoroughly. This is the cunningness of reason, of intellect. He doesn't say directly that he wants to escape; that he doesn't feel like killing his own people, that it is nothing less than suicide. He doesn't say this straight.

In this world, nobody talks straight. Whoever talks straight finds his life going through a revolution. The life of the person who talks in distortions, this way and that, never goes through any revolution. The way he behaves is called 'beating around the bush'. He will save the bush and beat the periphery. He will save himself and find a thousand and one rationalizations.

The problem is simple and very small: he is losing courage. Because of his attachment, his courage is disappearing. But he won't admit to such a straightforward thing and gathers all sorts of false reasons instead.

His reasons are worth pondering. Our minds function in the same way; hence it is useful to understand them.

OSHO,
One of the reasons that Arjuna is giving is that if the family traditions are weakened, the women will become corrupt and give birth to offspring from mixed castes. And as such children will not perform the ritual offerings to their ancestors, their ancestors will fall into hell.

Do dead ancestors starve if they are not offered this kind of nourishment through these rituals, or is this only a misconception in Arjuna's mind?

No. All the reasons given by Arjuna are utterly superficial and meaningless. No ancestor depends upon your ritual offerings. And if the ongoing journey of your ancestors could be affected by your offerings, then it would be a dangerous rite.

Souls continue on their journey according to their own intrinsic patterns. Their journey does not depend on what you have or have not done after they have departed.

But the world is infested with a network of priests. From the cradle to the grave this network is keeping human beings in its grip – and even after their deaths. Human beings cannot be exploited without fear being created in them first. Fear is the foundation of exploitation. A son can be exploited by creating fear in him – even about his dead father.

Arjuna is talking about all of these things. He must have heard them all being discussed; they must have existed in the very air. It is not at all surprising that they existed in those days; they exist even today. It is not at all surprising that Arjuna heard about them five thousand years ago; they prevail even today.

Arjuna is putting into words what the priests must have been explaining all around him, what he must have imbibed from all around. They are not really his concerns, he is just trying to marshal many arguments in front of Krishna so that it can be proved that if he is running away it is right, it is the religious thing to do. This is precisely why he is putting forward all these reasons.

But there is no truth in them. Nothing gets distorted or destroyed through different races or caste-groups mixing. It was just an idea that was prevalent in those days.

Even today some people hold this same opinion. If you ask saints like Karapatri or the religious leaders like the *shankaracharya*, they will hold the same opinion. Everything in the world may change, but some people never change their opinions.

Some people cling so tightly to an idea that their whole life may pass under its shadow, but they will never loosen their grip on it. Mixing races – what Arjuna refers to as *varnasankara* – is the best kind of breeding. Crossbreeding has the potential of giving birth to a superior generation. You make very good use of it with seeds, and when you are doing that, you don't remember that you are going against Arjuna! You are using it with animals too. So far you are not using it with human beings – so the breeding of the human species is not as far advanced as the breeding of animals.

Today we produce the best kind of dog by crossbreeding, but we don't produce an equally superior quality of man. The system of reproduction in human beings is still very unscientific. It must have been so at the time of Arjuna, but even today it is so. Even today, our attention is not towards producing a better man – a man who is healthy and superior in his body and mind, who can live longer, who is a genius. We pay so much attention to seeds – and the seeds of fruits, flowers, wheat have been getting better and better. We have taken care to produce the best breeds of animals… it is only man who has been paid no attention.

In the past it was thought that if people from two different caste-groups or races reproduced, the new generation would be contaminated. But the reality is that all the intelligent races of the world are born out of crossbreeding and all the pure races have remained backward. African tribes are pure, Indian tribal people are pure. All the developing cultures and civilizations are a result of intermixing.

In fact, just as two rivers become richer when they meet and merge with each other, two different streams of life also become enriched by mixing and merging. If Arjuna were right, a brother should marry his sister – that will produce the purest children! But no pure children are produced as a result of the marriage between a brother and sister, only retarded children.

We don't allow brothers and sisters to marry each other. Those who are intelligent even avoid marriage between cousins. Those who are even more intelligent won't even marry within their caste

– and people wiser than them will avoid marrying even amongst their own countrymen. And if today or tomorrow we discover human beings on some other planet or sub-planet, the most intelligent will consider interplanetary crossbreeding.

Arjuna is simply parading his arguments. He is saying, 'This and this is what I have heard. Such and such a calamity will befall us – so let me run away.' He is neither concerned about crossbreeding nor is he an expert on the subject. His expertise and skill do not lie in these areas. Yes, he had heard about such things; such ideas were around in the society, and they still are. It seems natural that they were prevalent in those days, because genetic science was not so evolved then.

At least today it is very evolved, but even today, even though genetic science has evolved so much, our minds have not evolved sufficiently for us to tolerate it or afford to think about it. Marrying into your own caste-group is nothing but marrying your own very distant sister. There is not much of a gap – maybe a gap of ten generations or so. What does marrying into your own caste group mean? It means that some ten or so generations ago the children were born from the same father. Maybe you will have to go back a hundred generations if you are marrying quite distantly, but within the same caste group everyone is nothing but sisters and brothers. If you trace back even further, then an entire race is also nothing but brothers and sisters.

So the more you move away from this, the more that crossbreeding happens, the more enrichment, the more refinements, the more the entire history experienced by different castes, tribes and races over thousands of years becomes available to the child – all encoded in the genes – the more distant the two streams that come together are, the greater the possibility of an extraordinary human being being born.

So races and castes intermixing was a great and insulting abuse in Arjuna's time – and it still is in orthodox religious places like Kashi in India. But all the intelligent people of the world now agree on one point: the further away from each other that groups involved in reproduction are, the more diverse their intermixing, the greater the possibility of their giving birth to the best human beings.

But Arjuna has nothing to do with all of this; he is not really making any statement concerning all of this. He is just gathering arguments in his favor.

OSHO,
Are there such specific places as heaven and hell? It seems that sin and virtue, hell and heaven are merely imaginary conceptions created to frighten or entice human beings. Do you agree with this?

Heaven and hell are not geographical places, but they are certainly psychological states. Man's thinking always converts things into pictures. Man cannot think without pictures. Pictures are supportive to his thinking.

We are all acquainted with the photograph of Mother India that hangs on the walls in millions of households. I don't understand why some of the wise people in our country don't set out in search of this Mother India! Every household has the photo. But nobody is going to find Mother India, no matter how much they search for her. In one or two thousand years from now, if someone says that Mother India had no physical existence, people will not agree with him. They will say, 'Look! Gandhi is pointing towards her in the photograph. Can Gandhi make a mistake? Mother India must have existed. She must be hiding somewhere in the mountain caves because of our sins.'

Whatever he wants to understand, man tries to convert into a picture. In fact, the more we go back into the past, the more we come across pictorial language. All the ancient languages of the world are pictorial. Chinese is still a pictorial language. Even today it does not have words or letters. It has pictures; everything has to be done through pictures. That's why Chinese is very difficult to learn. Even if someone wants to have a working knowledge of

Chinese, it will take ten to fifteen years. You have to learn at least ten to twenty thousand pictures by heart.

If you want to write the word *fight* in Chinese, you have to draw a roof and two women underneath it, and then this conveys the meaning of fighting. No doubt it is a fight! Two women sitting under one roof... what bigger fight could there be?

The more we go back in time, the more pictorial the thinking of the whole world has been. Even now our dreams are not formed in words, they are formed of pictures – because dreaming is very primitive, it is ancient, it is not new. Even in this century it is difficult to have dreams that belong to this century. Our dreaming is millions of years old; its ways, its patterns are millions of years old.

That is why children's books have more pictures and fewer words, because the child understands through pictures, not words. If we want to teach them 'G' we have to draw a big picture and unnecessarily drag the elephant god Ganesha into it. Ganesha has nothing to do with G, but the child will first grasp the Ganesha and then the G. The child is still primitive.

So the more we go back in time, the more we find that all the psychological elements had to be made geographical. Heaven is a state of mind – when everything is joyous, peaceful; when flowers are blooming, when all is full of music. But how is one to explain this state? It had to be placed above, in the sky. And the state of hell, where everything is suffering, pain, and burning, was placed below, beneath the earth.

And this above and below became values. Whatever is 'up there' is good, and whatever is 'down there' is evil, inferior. So raging fire was shown to represent suffering, jealousy, burning. Heaven was depicted as cool, peaceful – air-conditioned. But these are all pictures, depictions of psychological states. Fanaticism was born later. Fanaticism is the priest's contribution. He tells you that these are not merely pictorial depictions, they are geographical places. But now, in this age, he is going to get into trouble.

When Khrushchev sent his men into space for the first time he declared on the radio, 'Our people have circled the moon and they have not seen any heaven so far.'

Now this is a war with the priests. The priests will have to surrender to Khrushchev, because their claims are fundamentally wrong. There is neither a heaven above nor a hell below. But yes, the state of happiness and joy is a higher state, and the state of suffering, the state of hell, is a lower state.

There is a reason why this above and below has been made so geographical. When you are happy, you feel lifted off the ground and when you are unhappy, you feel as if you are sinking into the earth. It is a very psychological feeling. When you are unhappy, it feels as if you are surrounded by darkness, and in the state of happiness, you feel as if everything around you is lit up, aglow. It is a feeling, an inner experience. When you are in pain, you feel as if you are burning, as if there is a fire burning inside you. In the state of blissfulness flowers will seem to be blossoming within you.

These are all inner feelings. But how is a poet to express them, how is a painter to paint them? How is the priest to present them to people? So they created a picture: heaven was placed above, and hell was placed below. But now that language has become irrelevant; now man has transcended that language. It has to be changed.

So I am saying that heaven and hell are not geographical. They are psychological states – but they do exist. And it is not that you will go to heaven or to hell after you die. You visit hell and heaven many times in twenty-four hours! It is not something that happens once, in one go, wholesale. It is retail – it happens around the clock.

When you are in a rage, you are immediately in hell. When you are in love, you immediately ascend to heaven. Your mind is continuously oscillating. You are descending the stairs of darkness and ascending the stairs of light all the time. It is not something that takes place only once. But for a person who spends most of his life in darkness, in hell, the journey beyond life is bound to be towards further darkness.

Under the pretext of rescuing the whole world, poor Arjuna

depicts a picture of immense concern: souls will go to heaven, sons will be able to perform ritual offerings to their ancestors, women will not be widowed; there will not be a rampant mixing of clans and races… but what this man really wants is to run away, and what this man really wants is for Krishna gives his approval.

But in this too he is seeking Krishna's sanction. In this too he wants Krishna to condone his action and say, 'You are right, Arjuna' so that the responsibility doesn't fall on his shoulders, so that the next day he can say, 'It was you who said I could do it, Krishna. That's why I escaped.'

In fact, he doesn't even have the courage to take the responsibility onto his own shoulders and declare: 'I am going!' because if he were to do that, another part of his mind would say, 'This is cowardice.' and that kind of thing is not in his blood. He cannot deal with running away: he is a *kshatriya*, from the warrior caste. He has no courage to turn his back on a war. It is better to die than to turn back. This feeling is very deep in his heart. That is why he desperately wants Krishna to support him and say, 'Yes, Arjuna, you are right to say this.'

Had any other priest or scholar of ordinary mettle been in Krishna's place, he would have said, 'You are perfectly right, Arjuna. It says this in the scriptures' and Arjuna would have simply escaped. But he doesn't know that the person he is talking to cannot be deceived.

Krishna sees right through Arjuna – sharply and deeply. He knows that Arjuna is a warrior and to be a warrior is his destiny. Arjuna is saying all these things as though he were a brahmin, a guardian of religion and religious conduct, but he is not a brahmin at all. He is only talking like one, he is only arguing like one. He is a kshatriya, a warrior. He doesn't know anything except the sword. That is his only scripture. In fact, it is difficult to find another kshatriya like Arjuna in the world.

One of my friends came back from Japan. Someone there had presented him with a statue. The statue holds a sword in one hand and half of its face reflects the sharpness and shine of the sword.

The statue holds a lamp in the other hand and the other half of its face is aglow with the light of the lamp. The half of the face that is aglow with the light of the lamp looks like Buddha's face. The other half, which has the sharpness of the sword, looks like Arjuna's.

He was asking me the secret. I said, 'If it is difficult to find another brahmin, a real brahmin, who knows *brahman*, the absolute reality, and who can be compared with Buddha, then it is also difficult to find a greater kshatriya than Arjuna. This Japanese statue is of a samurai soldier. A samurai is supposed to have the serenity of Buddha and the fighting spirit of an Arjuna. Only then is he a samurai. The daring courage of Arjuna to fight and the serenity of Buddha while fighting – it is asking for the impossible.'

But Arjuna has nothing of the quality of Buddha in him. His peace is merely a self-justification, his talk of peace is merely escapist. Later on he will repent in spite of all his talk of peace. Tomorrow Arjuna will catch hold of Krishna again to complain: 'Why did you support me with my idea? This has only brought me disgrace. The prestige of my family has been eroded.' He will again bring scores of arguments. Just as he is finding scores of arguments right now in favor of escaping, tomorrow he will bring another score of arguments and say to Krishna, 'You alone are to blame. You confused me and made me run away. Now I am dishonored everywhere – and who is responsible for all this?'

That is why Krishna cannot leave him so easily. And in no way is it a matter to be left so easily. This man, Arjuna, has a divided mind. It is absolutely essential to bring him to a state of integration. Then, whatsoever he does out of that integrated mind will have Krishna's approval.

CHAPTER 5

Beyond the Ego

─────────

'Alas! In our greed for the kingdom and its pleasures
we have engaged ourselves in perpetrating the great sin
of being ready to kill our own kinsmen.

'Better for me 'twould be if, armed with weapons,
the sons of Dhritarashtra were to kill me unarmed and unresisting.

SANJAY:
Having spoken thus, the anguished Arjuna, overwhelmed with sorrow
sat in the back of the chariot and put away his bow and arrows.

Seeing Arjuna thus filled with pity, tears, and grief,
Krishna spoke thus.

KRISHNA:
'O Arjuna, how did such a misconception occur to you
at such a difficult time?
For it neither befits the way the noble ones conduct themselves,
nor does it bring heaven or glory.
'O Arjuna, do not yield to impotence; it does not befit you.
Cast off this mean weakness of your heart and arise!'

ARJUNA:
'Oh Krishna, destroyer of enemies
how can I fight with my arrows,
against Bheeshma and Drona, both of whom I revere?

'It is more honorable to live in this world begging for alms
than to slay one's noble elders and teacher.
If I slay them for wealth and worldly desires,
then my every indulgence in them will be stained with blood.

'I know not which is the noblest course for us to take,
whether we will win or they will win.
As for those elders and Dhritarashtra's sons who stand before me
after slaying them I would not wish to live.

'My customary nature has been marred by cowardice,
my mind confused about the rightness of things.
I beseech you to tell me what is good and decisive,
as your disciple, I take refuge in you. Please, enlighten me.

'Even if I attain
the most prosperous and untroubled empire on this earth
or the whole kingdom of the gods,
I see no way in which this sorrow that is withering my senses
can be removed.'

SANJAY:
Having spoken thus to Krishna, Arjuna said to him:
'I will not fight the war,' and became very quiet.

O Dhritarashtra, descendent of Bharat,
Krishna, as though laughing, said the following words
to the sorrowing Arjuna in the midst of the two armies.

KRISHNA:
'O Arjuna, you grieve over what is not worth grieving over
and yet you speak words of wisdom.
But the wise grieve neither for the living nor for the dead.'

S ANJAY DESCRIBES Arjuna as 'filled with pity, tears and grief'. Let us understand this word *pity*. Sanjay does not say 'full of compassion'. He says 'filled with pity'.

Pity and *compassion* seem to be synonymous in the dictionary, and we are also usually found to be using both words in the same way. This creates a big misunderstanding. Pity is circumstantial, and compassion is the outcome of a psychological state. They are fundamentally different.

Compassion means coming from within the heart of the person, having nothing to do with outer circumstances. Compassion will go on emanating from the heart of a compassionate person even if he is sitting alone. It is like a flower blossoming in solitude; it will go on spreading its fragrance. It has nothing to do with any passerby. The fragrance of a flower is not concerned whether somebody is passing by or not. Even if nobody passes by, the fragrance will still permeate that solitary space. If somebody happens to pass by and is enchanted with the fragrance, that is a different matter, but the flower has not blossomed for that person.

Inner consciousness is the fountainhead of compassion. Compassion arises from it like a fragrance. Hence it is wrong to call Buddha or Mahavira 'full of pity'. They are full of compassion; they are supremely compassionate.

Sanjay calls Arjuna 'full of pity'. Pity is born in those who don't have compassion in their hearts. Pity is born under the pressure of circumstances. Compassion is born out of the evolution of the heart. What arises in you when you see a beggar on the streets is pity; it is not compassion.

It is good to understand one more point here: pity strengthens the ego whereas compassion dissolves it. Compassion arises only in those who have become egoless. Pity is a means of nourishing the ego. It is a good means, used by good people, but all the same it is used to nourish the ego.

If you search deep inside yourself in those moments when you are giving something to somebody – when pity arises in you upon seeing a beggar, when you get pleasure from being a giver, from being in the position of being a giver – you will hear the murmuring voice of your ego.

A compassionate person doesn't want there to be a single beggar on the face of this earth, but a man of pity wants beggars to exist, otherwise he will be in difficulty. Societies based on the concept of pity don't eradicate begging, they nourish it. If a compassionate society can be created, it won't be able to tolerate begging – it shouldn't exist! What is churning around in Arjuna's mind is pity. Had it been compassion, he would have gone through a revolution.

It has to be clearly understood that what Krishna is telling Arjuna is worth pondering over. Krishna's immediate response is in answer to Arjuna's ego. He is saying, 'Your behavior is not fitting for a noble person.' The second sutra in this chapter shows that Krishna has pinned down the problem exactly.

The ego is murmuring inside Arjuna. He is saying, 'I feel pity. How can I commit such an act?' Not that the act in itself is bad but: 'How can I commit such an act? I am not that bad.' He tells Krishna that it would be better for him if all the sons of Dhritarashtra were to kill him rather than he commit an act as ghastly as slaying his own people.

The ego can even sacrifice itself. The ultimate act of the ego is martyrdom. And often the ego becomes a martyr – but in its martyrdom it only strengthens itself.

What Arjuna is saying is that he would prefer death to acting wrongly. 'I, Arjuna, just cannot bring myself to commit this wrong act. I feel pity for them. What have all these people assembled here for? I am amazed!'

From the way he is speaking, it appears that Arjuna has not opted for the development of this war in any way, that he has not supported it in any way. It is as if this war has suddenly surfaced in front of his eyes and he has had no inkling of it whatsoever before; he has not been a participant in the emergence of the situation that is in front of him now. He is talking from such a distant standpoint: 'I feel pity for them!' Tears have come to his eyes: 'No. I cannot do this. I would rather die – that would be far better.'

Krishna has detected this streak in Arjuna. This is why I say that Krishna is the first psychologist on this earth. This second sutra of Krishna's is nourishing Arjuna's ego even more. In it he says, 'Why are you talking like an *anarya*, a low-born person?' *Arya* means a noble, an exalted, a highborn person, and *anarya* means a lowly, lowborn person. Arya means the egoists; anarya means the downtrodden. 'How can it be that you are talking like an ignoble person?'

Now, it is worth thinking over – that to have pity means you are behaving like a lowborn person. To have eyes full of pitying tears means that you are behaving like an ignoble one. And Krishna is telling Arjuna that pity will bring him infamy on this earth and no blessings in the other world. Pity!

You may have not thought about it in this way: that Sanjay saying, *Arjuna thus filled with pity, tears and grief,* and Krishna's statement that follows it are not in accordance with each other. The reason is that we have never understood pity rightly. Pity only enhances the ego; pity is also an act of the ego. Pity is the act of a good man's ego and cruelty is the act of a bad man's ego.

Remember, the ego strengthens itself with bad acts as well as with good acts. And it often happens that only when the ego has had no opportunity to strengthen itself with good acts that it tries to nourish itself with bad acts.

Hence, there is no basic difference between those whom we call 'good people' and those whom we call 'bad people'. Both good people and bad people are tethered to the same axis called the ego. The only difference between them is that the bad person will hurt others to fulfill his ego and the good person will hurt himself to fulfill his ego. But as far as hurting is concerned, there is no difference between the two.

Arjuna says, 'I would rather be killed by than kill all these people.' If we use the language of today's psychology, a bad guy is a sadist, and a good guy, while fulfilling his ego, becomes a masochist. Masoch was a man who used to beat and torture himself.

All those people who hurt themselves can become 'good people' very quickly. If I starve you, I will be called a bad guy. The law and the courts can arrest me. But if I go on a fast, no court or law can arrest me. On the contrary, you will turn me into a hero. But if starving the other is a crime, how can it become a good deed if I starve myself – just because the other body belongs to you and this body belongs to me? If I make you stand naked and whip you or make you sleep on a bed of thorns it will be a crime, but if I do all these things to myself, how does it become asceticism? How does just a change of direction, the arrow pointing towards myself instead of towards the other, make something religious?

Arjuna says, 'I would rather die than kill them.' He is saying the same thing. He is still talking in terms of killing and getting killed. There is not much of a difference; just the arrow's point has changed direction.

And remember, one's ego is not fulfilled as much by killing the other as it is by killing oneself – because the other can still show his defiance before dying and spit in the killer's face. But when someone kills himself, he is helpless, unprotected, unable to respond. Killing the other is never complete; that person can survive even in his death. His eyes may proclaim, 'You may kill me but I am not defeated!' But while killing oneself there is no escape. The joy of defeat is utterly complete!

Arjuna is talking of pity and Krishna is saying, 'This talk is not worthy of you; this will give you a bad name.' He is just tickling Arjuna's ego, he is just nudging it.

Krishna's second sutra shows that he is touching Arjuna on the right spot – because it is useless for Krishna to explain to him yet that pity is not right. Even to explain to him that there is a difference between pity and compassion is futile at this point. As yet, Arjuna's ego is his raw nerve. As yet, it is only his ego that is moving from sadism to masochism. At this point he is still only eager to hurt himself rather than hurt the other.

Under these circumstances Krishna says to him in the second sutra: 'What are you saying? How is it that an exalted, highborn, sophisticated man like you is talking like a lowborn, ignoble being? Are you speaking of running away from the war? Is your mind in the grip of cowardice?' Krishna is hitting his ego.

Many a time those who read the Gita miss the basic point at subtle and delicate places like this. Is Krishna calling him an egoist? No, Krishna is only trying to observe that if this pity is arising out of his ego, then it will evaporate if this same ego is pumped up some more. That is why he says, 'You are talking like a cowardly man.' He will use the hardest possible words.

Krishna is speaking like this to Arjuna in order to watch what reaction it brings up in him. It is here that the psychoanalysis begins. It is at this point that Arjuna lies down on Krishna's couch and Krishna takes Arjuna into psychoanalysis. From now on, whatever Krishna is asking, he is trying to assess Arjuna by provoking things in him. He is trying to figure out Arjuna's true depth. From here onwards, Krishna is just a psychoanalyst and Arjuna is a patient. And it is necessary for Krishna to provoke him, to prod him from every direction and watch.

The first hit he makes is on his ego – and naturally, man's deepest and principal disease is his ego. And where there is ego, if there is pity it is false. With ego, any non-violence is false. With ego, any peace is false. And where there is ego, all talk of benevolence, universal good and welfare is false – because where there is ego, all of these things are only there to adorn it.

ARJUNA:
'O Krishna, destroyer of enemies
how can I battle with my arrows,
against Bheeshma and Drona, both of whom I revere?'

But Arjuna fails to grasp this. He repeats the same point, but from another angle. He says, 'How could I battle with Drona and Bheeshma? They are the ones I revere.' He still talks in terms of humility. But the ego often speaks the language of humility, and often the biggest egoists are found amongst the most humble people.

Actually, humility is defensive egotism; it is the ego defending itself. An aggressive ego can get into trouble. The humble ego is already secure, protected; it is insured. So when somebody says, 'I am nothing; I am just the dust beneath your feet,' look closely into his eyes. His eyes will be telling an altogether different story, although his words may be saying something else.

Krishna has put his hand right on Arjuna's pulse, but Arjuna is unable to understand it. He starts the same thing from a different angle. Now he says: 'How can I attack Drona – my teacher – or Bheeshma, both of whom I revere?'

It is important to understand that Bheeshma and Drona are secondary here. What Arjuna is saying is: 'How could I attack them? I am not so bad that I would shoot an arrow at Drona or pierce the heart of Bheeshma. No, I wouldn't be able to do that.' He is saying, 'They are my respected elders. How could I do such a thing to them?' But if we try to probe more deeply and look more closely, what he is really saying is: 'It is impossible for the image that I have created for myself, for the person that I am in my own eyes, to do such an act. It would be better, O Krishna, for me to die. It is better for me to save my image rather than my body; it is better for me to save my ego rather than my self, my being.' This self-image of his…!

Each person carries an image of himself. When you get angry with someone and apologize later, don't be under the illusion that you are really repenting and want to be forgiven. Actually, you are just repairing your self-image again. You have always taken yourself to be a good person and when you get angry with someone you have destroyed that self-created image of yours with your own hands.

In the wake of the anger the question arises in you: 'Aren't I the good person I always thought I was?' Your ego rationalizes: 'No, no. I am still a good person; this fit of anger was just a slip. It happened in spite of me. I have not done it, it just happened – it was forced upon me by circumstances.' So you repent and you apologize.

If you had really repented of your anger, you would not be able to get angry again for the rest of your life. But no, the next day the anger comes again!

No. The problem you felt was not because of your anger, the problem was felt due to something else. You had never thought that a person like you could become angry. So when you repent, your good image, your ego, is once again crowned on the throne.

The ego says, 'Look! I have apologized. I have asked for forgiveness. I am a humble person. What happened was because of the situation, the occasion – it was caused at that particular time. I returned from the office feeling unhappy, I was hungry and tired; it had not been a successful day. I was not in a good mood, something had gone wrong in the business – so the anger was caused by outward situations; it did not come from within me. See! I have apologized; the moment I came to my senses, the moment I realized, I asked for forgiveness.'

In this way, having washed and redecorated your ego, you have reinstalled it on the throne. Before the anger, your image was also sitting on the throne -- it just slipped down during the anger. Now you have put it back in place. Now, in your own eyes, you are back in your same honorable position as you were before – and you are free to become angry again tomorrow. You have regained your former position. Before the anger you were there, after the anger you have returned to that same place; the repentance part in between was just a rehabilitation process for your self-image.

But it seems that someone who apologizes is very humble. I am sorry to say this to you, but the appearance is not always the reality. Realities are often hidden very deep down, and mostly they are just the reverse. That angry man is not apologizing to you. He has fallen in his own eyes and now he is dusting, cleaning and rectifying that fall. After all this washing and cleansing he will be able to stand tall again.

When Arjuna says that because the ones he reveres are among the opponents so how can he kill them, the emphasis is not on their worthiness. The emphasis is on the 'I' of Arjuna: 'How can *I* kill them?' 'No, no. Instead of blackening my image and letting people say in every nook and corner of the world that I killed my own teacher and the ones I revered, it is better, O Krishna, that I myself die.'

People should say that rather than attacking the ones he revered, Arjuna chose to die. He died, he sacrificed himself, but he did not attack his teachers.

What is needed is for him to spot his 'I'. Right now it is not in his sight – it never is in anybody's. The person who can spot his own ego immediately falls out of its grip.

We live very protective of our egos. Arjuna will go on beating around the bush; he will go on looking for substitutes – this way and that – avoiding the only issue that is really there. Krishna has tried to touch on this issue, but Arjuna has totally passed it by. He doesn't talk about noble and ignoble; he doesn't bring the point about cowardice in, he doesn't touch on the issue of having fame and prestige in this world or going astray in the other. No, he doesn't touch on any of this. He picks up something else, as if he hasn't heard Krishna. Arjuna's statements show that he hasn't heard what Krishna was saying in the meantime.

We do not hear everything that is said. We only hear as much as we want to hear. We do not see all that is visible. We see only as much as we want to see. All that we read is not actually read – we read in it what we wanted to read. Our seeing, hearing and reading are all selective; we choose. All the time we are sifting out what we do not want to see.

There is a new psychology called Gestalt. The answer that Arjuna gave to Krishna is an amazing example of Gestalt psychology. Gestalt psychologists say that if the sky is full of clouds, each person will see different things in them. A frightened person will see ghosts, a religious person will behold images of God, and a movie buff will see the faces of his favorite actors and actresses. The cloud is the same, but each one sees their own thing.

Each person lives in a world of his own creation. So don't be under the illusion of there being just one world on this earth. In this world there are at least as many worlds as there are people. If there are six billion people on the earth today, then there will be six billion worlds. And don't think that one person lives in only one world for his whole life. His world also goes on changing every day.

Pearl Buck has written a book: it is her autobiography. She has called it *My Several Worlds*. Now how can one person have several worlds? But in reality they are changing every day, and every person builds walls, fences and doors and keeps guards around his world. And he tells them to allow such-and-such people in and to tell the others that he is not at home. And we don't only do this with people, we also do this with information.

Now Arjuna hasn't heard what Krishna has been saying. His answer shows this; his answer is not at all relevant.

We too don't listen. When two people are talking, try listening quietly as a mere witness and you will be amazed! But it is very difficult to remain simply a witness. Before you know it, you will have jumped into the conversation as a third person. But if you listen to their talk in an uninvolved way, you will be surprised: are they talking to each other or to themselves? What one person is saying and what the other is saying in reply has no connection whatsoever.

Jung has written in his memoirs that two insane professors were admitted to his asylum for treatment. As it is, professors tend to become more insane, or maybe those who are insane are the ones that become interested in becoming professors. So both of them had gone mad. But they were not like ordinary madmen. A common madman is frightened, timid and scared. They were mad professors! In their madness they had become even greater intellectuals. As long as they were awake, they would be engaged in deep discussion. Jung used to hide behind the window to listen to what was going on in their discussions.

They would talk about amazing matters, profound things. Both were well-informed, well-educated, well-read. Their information was not small – perhaps that was the reason for their madness in the first place. If there is too much information in comparison with what one actually knows, that alone can drive a person mad. And often real knowing is nil – it is only information that accumulates, and then it becomes a tremendous burden.

Jung was amazed to witness how much information they had. The subjects that they were discussing were profound and subtle. But what surprised him even more was that what one professor was talking about had nothing whatsoever to do with what the other one had said. But even that is natural for the madmen. What actually amazed him more was the fact that when one of them was talking, the other one was listening intently – at least, it seemed that he was listening. But as soon as one stopped speaking and the other one began, what he said had nothing whatsoever to do with what the first one had said. It seemed that he had not been listening at all, because if one had been talking about the sky the other began talking about the earth. There was no correlation between the two.

So Jung entered the room and asked them, 'I can understand that you are talking about profound matters, all that is clear to me, but what I don't understand is why one of you keeps quiet while the other one is speaking?'

They started laughing and said, 'Do you think we are mad and that we don't even know the rules of conversation? We know that when one speaks, the other one in the conversation should keep quiet.'

In this world only madmen think that they are not mad. If someone starts suspecting his own sanity, that means he has already begun to get out of his madness.

So, they said, 'Do you think we are mad or something?'

Jung replied, 'No, no, how could I make such a mistake? I don't think you are mad. But when you know this much about the rules – that one keeps quiet while the other speaks – what I want to ask is, how come there is no correlation between what you two are speaking about?'

The two started laughing again and they said, 'Don't be concerned about us, because anyway we are considered to be mad. But is there a correlation anywhere in any conversation that maybe taking place on this earth?'

Jung felt nervous and turned away. And he has written in his memoirs that since that day whenever he was talking to somebody he tried to notice if there was a correlation in the dialogue.

We try to establish some semblance of a correlation. When someone is having a conversation with another person and is not insane – which is very unlikely – he starts talking inside himself while the other person is speaking. And the moment the other person stops, he begins to speak. And what he then says is related to his inner dialogue, not to the other person's. The relationship between the two of them is at the most that of a coat and a coathanger. One may catch hold of one word or one point from the other's utterances and hang what was going on all that time inside him onto it. That is all.

Such moments will come up again and again in the dialogue between Krishna and Arjuna. That's why I thought I would tell you about it in detail.

Arjuna has not heard what Krishna has been saying at all. It is as if he had not said anything. Arjuna just goes on listening to his inner conversation. He says, 'The revered Drona and Bheeshma...' This is what he must have been thinking inwardly, and what Krishna was saying must have all been on the periphery. This is what was going on inside him. He says, 'Oh Krishna, how can I kill these dear and venerable people – me, Arjuna?'

Please keep this in mind. He has not heard Krishna.

OSHO,

You just said that professors are mad. You yourself were a professor of philosophy, now you have become an *acharya*, an enlightened teacher.

Just now you were talking about the ego. The question is that there is no projection without the ego and the psychoanalysts say – well, you yourself are a psychosynthesizer – that the personality cannot develop totally without the fulfillment of the ego.

And yet you talk of egolessness. So are you suggesting the annihilation of the ego?

Firstly, I said that a professor is more likely to go mad: I did not say that he invariably goes mad. Secondly, I also did not say that all madmen are professors. It is just that there is a greater possibility.

In fact, wherever there is too great a burden of so-called knowledge, the mind can go mad. Knowledge frees the mind; the burden of knowledge drives it mad. And the knowledge that liberates comes from within oneself. The knowledge that drives one insane doesn't come from within; it always comes from the other, from the outside.

The second thing that you have asked is that psychoanalysts talk of developing the ego and I talk of dispersing the ego. Certainly the psychoanalysts talk about developing the ego – but not all of them. Buddha or Mahavira or Krishna will not do that. Freud or Ericsson will do that – for the simple reason that for them there is no higher truth than the ego. So the highest truth has to be developed. For Mahavira or Buddha or Krishna the ego is not the highest truth. It is only a ladder in between – a bridge. The highest truth is egolessness. Existence is the ultimate truth, not the ego. The ego is only a ladder.

So Buddha, Mahavira or Krishna will tell you to develop the ego and then dissolve it, climb the ladder and then let go of it, ascend it and go beyond it, go higher on it and then transcend it. Since 'is-ness' is also beyond the mind, the last truth of the mind, the ego, will be the first thing to be dropped for the realization of the 'is-ness' that is beyond it. If I want to come to your house from my house, then leaving the last wall of my house behind will be my first step towards entering your house.

The ego is the boundary of the mind. The mind cannot penetrate beyond the ego.

Because western psychology understands the mind to be the highest truth, to talk of developing the ego is justified. I am saying 'justified', not 'true'. Within the boundary walls of the mind, it is absolutely all right. Western psychology realizes – *has* begun to realize – with Jung that the boundary walls have begun to crumble and the realization has begun to dawn that there is something beyond the ego as well.

But as yet, all that is being experienced by western psychology as beyond the ego is still *below* the ego, it is not beyond the ego. There is also something on the other side of the ego, the unconscious, which is below the conscious – but it is not the superconscious, which is ahead of the conscious. Yet this is a very auspicious hour. At least there is something in addition to the ego – even if it is below it. And if there is something beyond the ego in a lower direction, then the obstacles in the way of having something beyond it in a higher direction become fewer. If we accept something beyond the ego, even if it is in the direction of below, then the way for sooner or later accepting something beyond the ego and above it is cleared.

Psychology is bound to want to make the ego more integrated, more crystallized and pure: it should become more clear and synthesized – and that is individuation, that is one's personality. But Krishna would not agree with this. Krishna would say that there is one more step ahead: the integrated, concentrated ego should surrender some day. This is the final step from the ego's end, but the first step from the eternal's.

If the dewdrop can dissolve itself in the ocean, it can certainly become the ocean. And if the ego can dissolve itself in the cosmic ocean it can certainly become the eternal. But before dissolving, it has to be there, the dewdrop has to be there. If there is no dewdrop, if there is only vapor, then it is difficult for it to dissolve in the ocean. If a drop of vapor is soaring in the sky, we will first have to ask it to become a drop of water, and only after it has become a drop of water, can it be asked to jump into the ocean. Vapor cannot jump into the ocean directly; it can try, but it is bound to fly towards the sky. It cannot jump into the ocean, but a dewdrop can.

So western psychology goes as far as creating the drop, and Krishna's psychology goes to the point of turning it into the ocean.

But one has to pass through the stage of western psychology. Those who are in the vaporous state have to pass through Freud and Jung, only then can they reach Krishna. But many drops of vapor try to reach Krishna directly and then they get into trouble. Freud is in the middle and he cannot be bypassed. He is not the end but he is certainly the beginning.

The psychology of Krishna is the ultimate psychology, the supreme psychology. It begins at the point where mind comes to an end. It is at the last frontier. And Freud and Adler are talking about the first frontier of the mind. If you can understand this, there will be no difficulty.

I will say the same thing in another way: integrate the ego, crystallize the ego, so that you can surrender it one day. Only the one who is crystallized can surrender. How can someone whose ego is split into dozens of parts, who is a schizophrenic, in whom even his 'I' is not one but rather many surrender? You may surrender one part, and the other will say, 'Leave it; come back.'

This is how we are right now. According to all the psychological researches, we are poly-psychic. We don't even have just one 'I' within us, we have several, many 'I's.

You go to sleep in the night and one 'I' promises to wake up at five o'clock in the morning – it swears. In the morning, the other 'I' says, 'It's too cold! Just forget it! What were you thinking of? Leave it until tomorrow!' You turn around and you go back to sleep. And later, when you get up at seven o'clock, the third 'I' says, 'You made a big mistake! You had already decided in the evening, so why did you change your mind at five o'clock in the morning?' It repents deeply.

Now, if you were just one person and you had decided to wake up at five o'clock in the morning, then who is this other one who is now asking you to go back to sleep? It is someone inside you who is speaking; it isn't someone outside you. And again, if you went back to sleep at five o'clock, why are you repenting now at seven? You yourself went back to sleep; nobody asked you to. So who is repenting now?

Usually we have the idea that we are one. This creates a lot of confusion. There are many 'I's inside you. One 'I' decides to wake up early and a second 'I' refuses to oblige. The third one repents, and the fourth one forgets the whole thing. No one remembers such things… and life goes on!

Psychology says: integrate the ego first. If there is one ego, surrender is possible. But if there are a number of voices, how can there be any surrender?

The same thing happens in the temple. One 'I' surrenders itself and bows down in front of a statue, and another one stands erect – in the same place. One 'I' prostrates itself at the feet of a statue and another one is looking around to see if anyone is looking. There is only one person but there are two 'I's. One is bowing down and the other is watching people.

If you are surrendering, why do you want others to know about it? One 'I' is bowing down and the other 'I' is saying, 'There is no God. What games you are getting involved in? It's all meaningless!' Or here one 'I' is bowing down to the statue, while another – in that very same moment – is sitting in the shop running the business.

The ego should be integrated. Only then is surrender possible. So I don't see any contradiction between the two, I see an evolution. Freud is not the end but he is important and he is helpful in integrating the ego. Krishna is the end. There, after a certain point, the 'I' has to be surrendered.

'It is more honorable to live in this world begging for alms
than to slay one's noble elders and teacher.
If I slay them for wealth and worldly desires,
then my every indulgence in them will be stained with blood.

'I know not which is the noblest course for us to take,
whether we will win or they will win.
As for those elders and Dhritarashtra's sons who stand before me
after slaying them I would not wish to live.

'My customary nature has been marred by cowardice,
my mind confused about the rightness of things.
I beseech you to tell me what is good and decisive,
as your disciple, I take refuge in you. Please, enlighten me.'

Arjuna keeps repeating his own things over and over again. He appears to be asking Krishna what is religious, but in reality he keeps telling him. He is imploring, 'I am fed up with the darkness of ignorance. I cannot figure out what is appropriate and what is inappropriate,' and at the same time he keeps saying, 'The food that I will eat after killing my own people will be stained with blood. It is better to be a beggar on the street than to become a king by killing one's own people.'

He keeps passing judgment after judgment but saying at the same time that he is fed up with false knowledge. There is no correlation between the two. If he is really fed up with false knowledge, then he should have nothing to say. It should be enough to say, 'I am fed up with false knowledge. Please guide me. I have no idea what is right and what is not.' But no, at the same time he goes on telling Krishna that this is right and that is wrong.

The mind may say that it is fed up with false knowledge, but the ego is never ready to accept this. The ego says, 'Me? Fed up with false knowledge? I know what religion is and I know what irreligion is.'

The other thing worth noting is that the ego always goes for extremes, chooses extremes. It jumps from one extreme to the other. The ego never stays in the middle. It cannot afford to – because to remain in the middle will be its death. So Arjuna says that it is better to be a beggar than to be a king: he chooses between two polar opposites. Arjuna can either be a king or a beggar; he cannot be anywhere in the middle. He will either be number one at this pole or at that pole, but he has to be number one. This is worth keeping in mind.

Bernard Shaw once said: 'Even if I am sent to the heaven but have to take second place, I will refuse it. I would prefer to live in hell and be number one. Number one I must be. What kind of fun will heaven be if I have to be number two? Even hell can be enjoyable if I am number one.'

So it will not be very surprising if all the people who want to be number one gather in hell. The quickest way to the hell is from the political capitals! Go to Delhi and you have already gone to hell. There is no gap between them.

So if the person obsessed with becoming number one misses the chance to become king, immediately his next alternative is to become a beggar.

It is worth understanding this alternative as well, because it is the ego that chooses this alternative. The alternative of extremes is always chosen by the ego. The ego doesn't care whether it becomes a king or a beggar, what is important is becoming number one.

Arjuna says, 'I would rather be a beggar on the street...'. It appears to be a statement of utter humility. He is talking of renouncing the kingdom and becoming a beggar. But inwardly there is not much of a difference: the inner story is the same. The desire of the ego is always to be at the extreme. The desire to be at the polar extreme is the desire of the ego – either at this pole or the other. The middle is not for the ego.

Buddha's psychology is called 'the middle way'. When somebody asked Buddha, 'Why do you call your way the middle way?' he said, 'Only the person who stands in the middle of two extremes can be free of the ego; otherwise it is impossible.'

A small anecdote is associated with Buddha's life...

Buddha arrived at a village. The emperor came to him and made a request to be initiated. Buddha's disciples whispered in his ear, 'Beware of this man! We have heard all kinds of stories about him. This man has never come down from his chariot, he has never walked on foot. He is mostly drowning himself in all sorts of enjoyments and luxuries in his palace. When he climbs the staircases in his palace, they are lined with naked women whom he uses as hand-rests instead of a banister. He has known nothing but wine and women in his life. And today he suddenly wants to become a monk; he wants to renounce everything and be involved in ascetic disciplines. He is likely to drop you on the path.'

Buddha replied, 'As far as I understand human beings, this man will not drop. He is fed up with one extreme, and he is moving to another.'

The disciples were still doubtful because they were looking at his past, but Buddha said, 'I have no doubt about this. These sort of people always move to extremes. Don't worry.'

The disciples said, 'We don't think that he will be able to walk barefoot on the streets or beg for his food, or will be able to bear the heat and the rain.'

Buddha said, 'He will be able to put up with it more than you can.'

They all laughed. They felt that in this case at least Buddha was sure to be proved wrong.

But Buddha proved to be right. From the very next day it was seen that while all the other monks were walking on a path, the king would get off the pathway and walk through the thorns. And if the monks were sitting under the shadow of a tree, he would stand in the sun. And while all the monks were eating once a day, he would only eat once in two days. Within six months he was reduced to a skeleton. He had a beautiful body but now it became dark and his bones started showing. His feet had wounds on them.

Buddha said to his disciples, 'See, you were saying that this man is not to be trusted. He will surpass you in his ascetic disciplines.'

The monks were amazed at Buddha's insight. How could he see this? Buddha said, 'The ego always chooses one extreme or the other; it cannot stop in the middle. He was a king among kings and now he is a monk among monks. He had gathered all the beautiful women of the kingdom; he had all the pathways of his palace studded with gems; now among the monks he is not an ordinary monk, he is an extraordinary monk. You walk on the regular path, he walks on the irregular path. You all avoid walking on the thorns and he looks for them to walk on. You sit in the shade and he stands in the sun. He will be number one no matter where he is. He cannot let go of being number one. He is going to defeat you. He has defeated kings, how can he spare you simple monks? The ego chooses extremes.'

Arjuna is saying, 'I want to drop the whole idea of the empire; it is meaningless. I would rather live by begging.' He can; he is absolutely capable of doing so. The ego can remain nourished by doing that as well – but it cannot remain in the middle. It can easily move from one extreme to the other, but there is no transformation in moving from one extreme to the other.

One evening Buddha went to see the king. Sick and ailing, he was lying by the wayside. Buddha said to him, 'I have come to ask you one thing. I have heard that when you were king you were an expert musician, an accomplished veena player. What I want to ask you is, if the strings of a veena are too tight, will they create music?'

The king said, 'How can that be possible? The strings will break.'

'And what will happen if the strings are too loose? Will they create music?' asked Buddha.

The king replied, 'No. If the strings are too loose, they won't create even a twang – what to say of music.'

Buddha said, 'Now I will leave. Before leaving I would like to remind you that the law of the veena is that its strings should be neither too tight nor too loose. They should be somewhere in the middle. When the strings are rightly tuned, when they are exactly at a mid-point where they can be said to be neither tight nor loose, only then can they create music. The same is the law for the veena of life.'

Had Arjuna talked about the middle point, Krishna would have been sure to say, 'Go wherever you want to go. The matter is over; there is no need to discuss anything.' But he is not talking about the middle point. He is talking about moving from one extreme to the other. And, on that other extreme the ego is reinforced.

Why in the courts of law is one first required to take the oath by putting one's hand on the Gita? Why are the Ramayana or the Upanishads not used instead? Is it because there is faith in Gita? Or for that matter, is it just a blind faith?

It has been asked why does one have to place one's hand on the Gita while taking the oath in the courts of law? Why not on the Ramayana or on the Upanishads?

There is a potent reason for this. I don't know whether the court is aware of this or not, but the reason is significant.

No matter how great Rama may be, the Indian mind does not perceive him as a perfect incarnation of the divine. He is a partial incarnation. No matter how great a sage the seers of the Upanishads may be, they are not incarnations. Krishna is the perfect incarnation. If the divine were to manifest itself on this earth in its totality in a physical form, it would be something like Krishna. That's why Krishna could touch the hearts of the maximum number of people in this country – and for many other reasons.

Firstly, the perfect incarnation has to be multidimensional; touching all aspects of the human personality. Rama is one-dimensional.

Herbert Marcuse has written a book: *One Dimensional Man.* Rama is one-dimensional; he has only one note. Naturally a man of one note may appeal to a one-track mind, but he cannot win every heart. Mahavira, Buddha, all of them are one-dimensional; they have only one note. And that is why Mahavira and Buddha cannot appeal to all human beings. Yes, there will be a cross-section of humanity that will fall madly in love with Buddha or with Mahavira, but it will only be a cross-section, it cannot be everyone.

But Krishna is multi-dimensional. It is difficult to find a man on this earth who cannot find an aspect in Krishna that he loves and admires. A thief can love Krishna, a dancer can love Krishna, a saint can love Krishna… and so can a sinner. A warrior fighting on the battlefield can worship Krishna; a dancer dancing with his girlfriends can adore him. Krishna is an orchestra. There are many instruments, all playing. At least one is bound to fall in love with the music of his favorite instrument. And this is also why there cannot be people who love the whole Krishna. Those who have loved him have chosen some part in him.

If Keshavdas is to love Krishna, he will not bother about Krishna as a child. He will choose Krishna as a youth who is dancing in the moonlight, who has no moral code of conduct, who does not follow any limitations of discipline, who is beyond disciplines, who cannot be caught in any bondage, who is a total chaos. Keshavdas will choose this youthful Krishna and forget all about Krishna as a child.

Surdas loves the child Krishna. He is very afraid of the *gopis* – the girlfriends of his youth. He adores the childhood image of Krishna, it appeals to him. He faces no problems with the phase of Krishna's childhood. Surdas is afraid of the grown-up Krishna, because essentially, he is afraid of the grown-up Surdas. So he has to make his own choice, and he chooses this one aspect.

Until now there has been no one who loves Krishna in his entirety. Only a multi-dimensional person can love Krishna as a whole. Usually we are one-dimensional; usually we have a one-track personality and we go on moving on that one track as though we were on railway lines. But in Krishna everyone can find something fitting with his own track. That is why Krishna is lovable to every kind of person in this country. He can be lovable even to a really bad person.

Remember, good people have to go to a court of law very rarely – in other words, when they have to go, it is because bad people take them there. Generally, a court of law is a place for bad people. If a bad person loves Rama, he won't be before the court of law in the first place – it is meaningless to ask him to take an oath in Rama's name. But he can be asked to do so in Krishna's name. A man who comes before a court of law can love Krishna – because

Krishna is open and available even to the bad guys. His house has an open door even for bad people.

Good people like Rama have only one entrance to their temple. Krishna's temple has many doors. Even an alcoholic will find a door that is open for him. In fact, it is very difficult to find a more large-hearted man than Krishna.

So I don't say that the judiciary might be aware of all this, I don't know about that, but consciously or unconsciously they must have felt that Krishna's range of touching people's hearts is the widest of all, that the maximum number of people can be touched by him. There is not a single person whom Krishna will refuse to embrace. He won't reject anybody. He is there for everyone. This fact is the possible reason.

Furthermore it has been asked: 'Is this merely a superstition?'

No, it is not merely a superstition. In this world, love is a greater truth than truth itself. And it is difficult to be untruthful to someone you love. Actually, we are able to be truthful only towards the person we love. In life, we are only able to be truthful where there is love. And if you are unable to be true even with your lover or beloved, you can be sure that your love is only a deception.

If a husband hides something from his wife and cannot be truthful or if a wife hides something from her husband and cannot be truthful…and it is not necessarily about some big matter, even if small things, inconsequential things, are being hidden, for example one may be feeling anger but trying to hide it – then there is lack of love, there is no love between them. Love uncovers itself until it is completely naked, in every way, on all levels.

So it is not because of superstition. The chord of love has to be touched, only then can the truth be made to speak. I don't know whether the judiciary is aware of all this or not – because it is a little doubtful whether the court is aware of love. But this much even psychology knows: that if you touch the chord of love, there is the greatest possibility of a person speaking the truth. Whether he *will* speak it or not is a different matter. But the greatest possibility is only there when the chord of love has been struck. And where there is no love is the greatest chance of a lie being told – because then there remains no reason for truth.

> 'Even if I attain
> the most prosperous and untroubled empire on this earth
> or the whole kingdom of the gods,
> I see no way in which the sorrow that is withering my senses
> can be removed.

> SANJAY:
> Having spoken thus to Krishna, Arjuna said to him:
> 'I will not fight the war,' and became very quiet.

> O Dhritarashtra, descendent of Bharat,
> Krishna, as though laughing, said the following words
> to the sorrowing Arjuna in the midst of the two armies.

Arjuna is in a state of tremendous indecisiveness.

Sanjay says, 'Arjuna said, "I will not fight the war," and became very quiet.' Such a decisive attitude as 'I will not fight the war' in the midst of such a state of tremendous indecisiveness is worth looking at! Such a decisive statement as 'I will not fight the war' in the middle of such indecisiveness as '*I beseech you to tell me what is good and decisive, as your disciple, I take refuge in you. Please, enlighten me.*' Even while saying, 'Please enlighten me,' he has already taken a decision of his own. He has said, 'I will not fight the war.'

We must go more deeply into this. If you often make very decisive statements, you can be sure that the indecisiveness within you is tremendous – otherwise a steadfast decision wouldn't be needed. If someone says that he firmly trusts in existence, it means that there is no trust inside him. Otherwise what is the need to label it firm trust? If someone says again and again that he only speaks the truth, he is only covering the falsehood that is within him. Otherwise why should he say so?

We try to cover and deny our indecisiveness, the wavering that lurks within, by imposing decisive statements on top. We want to see all that is indecisive inside projected as certainty on our faces.

Now Arjuna is saying something very amusing. He is saying, 'I am not fighting the war.' He has taken the ultimate decision; he has arrived at his conclusion, made the concluding statement. So what has he left for Krishna now? If he has decided not to fight, what remains for him to ask Krishna about? What guidance is he seeking?

Hence the second thing that Sanjay says is very interesting. He says, '*Krishna, as though laughing, said the following words…*'

What is he laughing at? What is the reason for his laughter? Does Arjuna deserve to be laughed at – an Arjuna wallowing in pain and sorrow, an Arjuna facing such a crisis? And here is Krishna laughing at him! But Krishna had not laughed at him so far; he laughs for the first time on hearing his statement.

There is a reason for this laughter. He sees that a person who is in such an indecisive state is making such a decisive statement: that he will not fight. Whom is he deceiving? Krishna laughs at Arjuna's self-deception. Any person who knows would feel like laughing. Krishna sees that deep down Arjuna's mind is torn to pieces. It has disintegrated, it is divided: nothing has been decided in him and outwardly he is saying that he will not fight. In this way he is deceiving himself.

We all do this. Whenever we are talking too emphatically on the outside, we are hiding uncertainty inside. Whenever we are talking too vehemently of love, we are hiding hatred. And when we are speaking the language of the religious person, it is only to hide the irreligious side of us. People always talk about what they are not. What we see on the surface is exactly opposite of what they are inside.

So, Krishna's laughter is appropriate and timely. It is not untimely. It may appear to be untimely. It doesn't feel good. It appears to be very hard that Krishna is laughing at Arjuna – who is grieving deeply and in such a crisis. But there is a reason why he is laughing. He is looking at Arjuna's split mind. Arjuna is saying one thing and deciding to do something completely the opposite.

The statement of a split-minded person is always self-contradictory. And the contradiction here is quite clear. Arjuna is putting down a building block with one hand and taking it away with another! He is constructing the wall with one hand and demolishing it with the other. He is making the house in the day and destroying it by night.

Krishna is laughing at the split in Arjuna's personality. What else can be done with this schizophrenia within him, with this disintegrated personality of his?

There is enough of a hint in Krishna's laughter. But I don't think that Arjuna may have noticed this laughter, that Arjuna may have heard this laughter.

Read one more last sutra.

KRISHNA:
'O Arjuna, you grieve over what is not worthy of grieving
and yet you speak words of wisdom.
But the wise grieve neither for the living nor for the dead.'

What Krishna has said laughingly is even harder. He says to Arjuna, 'You are talking the language of the scriptures but you are not a sage. You are an idiot, a fool, because even while talking the language of the scriptures, the conclusions that you are reaching are your own.'

Arjuna *is* talking the language of the scriptures: 'What irreligious things will come to pass; what will go wrong and what evil will befall us...' He is absolutely talking the language of the scriptures. But he is imposing himself upon that language. He has already reached the conclusions that he wants to reach; now he is only gathering the support and sanction of the scriptures.

There is only one difference between a sage and an idiot. The idiot can also speak the language of the scriptures – he often does – and he speaks it expertly, because there is no contradiction between being an idiot and speaking the language of the scriptures. But an idiot derives the meanings that he wants to from the scriptures. His concern is not about the scriptures, his concern is for himself. He uses the scriptures as evidence for what he is saying.

Simone Weil has written that there are some people who want the truth to support them and there are some who want to support the truth. These are the only two types of people there are. There are some people who want religion and the scriptures to support them from behind their backs and there are some people who have the courage to stand abreast with religion. But it is an extremely revolutionary step to stand abreast with religion because religion will efface you; it won't let *you* survive. But making religion stand in support of you is very conformist, very simple and conventional – because in that way you will find convenience and security to protect yourself.

Arjuna is speaking the language of a sage but his statements have nothing to do with knowledge or wisdom. He wants all the scriptures to stand and support him.

And someone who tries to get the scriptures to stand and support him naturally places himself above them. And there cannot be anything more dangerous than placing oneself above the scriptures, because in this way the person has already assumed that he is right. Now there are no chances of his being wrong. He has already concluded that he is right. Now he is just seeking all the support for himself in the scriptures.

Christian mystics used to say that even the devil quotes the scriptures. He often does! There is no difficulty in quoting from the scriptures; it is very easy to do so. And Arjuna is quoting them in the same way.

And the interesting thing is in whose presence is he quoting the scriptures? When a living scripture is standing before you, only a fool can quote the scriptures. Before whom is he making these wise statements? When wisdom incarnate is standing before you only a fool can talk with borrowed knowledge. Krishna was right to laugh. And he rightly said to Arjuna that he was talking like a wise man but acting like a fool – and in whose presence?

I have heard that somebody went to Bodhidharma with a book of Buddha's. He asked Bodhidharma to explain the book to him.

Bodhidharma said, 'If you think that I will be able to explain this book of Buddha's, then throw away the book and understand me directly. And if you think that I will not be able to explain this book of Buddha's, then throw me away and understand the book directly.'

Krishna's laughter is appropriate. To whom is Arjuna quoting? And the interesting point is that at the same time he keeps addressing Krishna as 'O blessed one!' and then continues quoting the scriptures.

There are some fools who even arrive in front of enlightened people carrying their scriptures. Their stupidity is endless. If by chance they happen to meet an enlightened person, a blessed one, they will still start quoting the Gita. So the enlightened person will have to laugh: 'At least now you can forget your Gita!' But they will not drop it.

Arjuna is repeating the foolishness of the common scholar and Krishna is talking straightforwardly and clearly. It is very, very rare that anything has been said so straightforwardly and clearly, but Krishna can say it and not without reason. However, it is difficult to say whether Arjuna will listen or not. Throughout almost the whole Gita – for a long time – Arjuna behaves like a man who is both blind and deaf. Otherwise perhaps there would have been no need for the Gita. Had he opened his eyes even once and taken a closer look at Krishna, that would have been enough. But he goes on calling him 'the blessed one' while not paying any attention to him.

If an enlightened person is his charioteer, if he really knows that Krishna is awakened and that the reins of the chariot are in his hands, then why is Arjuna unnecessarily taking the burden of sorting things out upon himself? If he knows that Krishna is awakened, then what is there to ask? The reins are in his hands and now Arjuna should let go. But he only calls him 'the blessed one' in words. He does not know it.

We also go on saying 'O blessed one,' but we don't actually know that it is so. Someone is standing in the temple and praying with folded hands: 'I am unemployed. Please Lord, find me a nice job.' If this man knows that he is praying to the omnipotent and the omniscient, then he should also know that the omnipotent and omniscient one must already be aware of his unemployment! There is no need to pass on this information. And if this blessed one does not have the power to know this information on his own, then he cannot have the power to get a job for you either! All this folding of your hands in supplication is futile.

So this is just what any common believer is doing in front of his god: calling him 'the blessed one' and at the same time still worrying about his own son's employment!

In the last moment, as Jesus was nailed to the cross, a sound escaped from his mouth, 'O God! What are you doing to me? What am I having to go through?'

What does this mean? He is complaining! What does it mean? It means that Jesus wanted to see something else happening, but what was actually happening was totally different. It means that he has not surrendered. It means that his reins are not yet in the hands of existence. It means that in this moment Jesus considers himself to be wiser than the whole.

But Jesus immediately collected himself. Arjuna does not become aware so quickly. Jesus became immediately aware. As Jesus uttered these words, 'Why am I having to go through this?' the very next sentence that follows is, 'Forgive me. Thy will be done.' He must have become aware: 'How did I come to say this? A doubt had arisen in me.'

According to me, while uttering the first sentence, Jesus was Mary's son, Jesus, and while saying the second sentence, he became the Christ. In one moment the revolution happened. Up until a moment before he was only Mary's son, Jesus, who was saying, 'What is this I am having to go through?' It was a complaint. There can be no complaint in a religious man's heart. So the next moment he says, 'Forgive me. Thy will be done': whatever you are doing is right. There is no question of anything else being right. And immediately he became the Christ. The very next moment he was no longer the ordinary son of Mary; he became the son of the whole of existence.

Arjuna goes on calling Krishna 'the blessed one,' but it is just a way of addressing him – in the same way that all forms of address are false, formal. As of yet, he does not see existence moving in Krishna. What he sees is that this is his close friend Krishna. 'He *has* come with me, he is functioning as my charioteer, and since he is here I may as well ask his opinion. But if Arjuna really experiences the blessed one in Krishna, there will remain nothing left to ask. He will say, 'You are holding the reins. Thy will be done.'

So Arjuna addressing him as 'the blessed one' has no meaning as yet. In spite of addressing him like this, Arjuna is still making his own decisions. He is saying, 'I will not fight the war.' He is saying, 'the blessed one' and then he is making his own decision: 'I will not fight the war.' If Krishna is laughing at all this and telling him how contradictory the things he is saying are, it is only right.

CHAPTER 6

The Thought-less Mind

'It is not that there was once a time when I was not,
or you were not, or all these kings were not;
nor will there ever be a time when all of us will not exist.
This is absolute, ultimate.

'Just as this being
passes through childhood, youth and old age in this body,
so too it passes through the changing of bodies.
And the serene and tranquil ones do not grieve over this.

'As the senses come in contact with objects, O Arjuna, son of Kunti,
heat and cold, happiness and unhappiness result;
these come and go, are impermanent;
hence, O Arjuna, descendant of Bharat, endure them well.

'O Arjuna, best of men,
the serene and tranquil one whom these do not afflict
who remains unmoved by pain and pleasure both
is worthy to experience deathlessness.'

OSHO,
Actions are triggered by the idea of a goal and when we want
certain results. So if the mind is egoless or thought-less all the

time, how can actions take place? How can the thought-less mind manifest anything? If everybody becomes inactive by remaining continuously thought-less, how can the society carry on? Won't it perish?

ONE DOESN'T BECOME inactive when one becomes egoless. Neither does one become inactive when one is without thought. By becoming egoless only the idea of 'the doer' drops. Action is surrendered to the whole and flows with full momentum. A river is flowing and there is no ego. The wind is blowing and there is no ego. The flowers are blossoming and there is no ego. And in exactly the same way, everything takes place from a spontaneous, egoless life-center – except that no sense of the doer gathers inside.

So when I say that Arjuna's ego has become his constant suffering and torture, it doesn't mean that when he drops his ego his actions will cease. And when I say that thinking creates worry for man and if his mind becomes thought-less – if it goes beyond worrying – it doesn't mean that a thought-less mind will no longer speak or act, or that it will cease to express itself.

No, it isn't like that. The thought-less mind becomes hollow like a bamboo flute. Songs will flow through it but not its own songs, rather those of the divine. Thoughts will emerge out of it but not its own, rather those of the whole.

Such a mind will be surrendered to the whole. It will only speak what the whole makes it speak. It will only do what the whole makes it do. The inner core of the 'I' will disintegrate – and with its disintegration, there will be no anxiety, no anguish.

'It is not that there was once a time when I was not,
or you were not, or all these kings were not;
nor will there ever be a time when all of us will not exist.
This is absolute, ultimate.'

Arjuna appears to be worrying that all these people standing before him will be killed in the war, will be no more. Krishna tells him that that which is has always been, and that which is not is always not.

It will be good to understand this a little.

Religion has always said this but science has also started talking in the same terms. And it is better to start with science, because religion talks about the peaks that most people have not yet reached; science talks about the base, about the ground, where we all are standing.

One of the deepest findings of science is that existence cannot be taken into non-existence. That which is cannot be annihilated. And that which is not cannot be created either. All our scientific information and know-how, all the scientific labs of the world and all the scientists of the world together cannot annihilate even a single grain of sand. All that they can do is transform it, give it new forms.

What we call the creation of the universe, the big bang, is also nothing but the manifestation of a new form – not the creation of a new existence, only of a new form. And what we call the big crunch is not an annihilation of existence, only of the form, of the shape. The forms keep on changing, but what is hidden inside the form is unchangeable.

It is like the wheel of a cart that moves and rotates but the point at its center remains static. The wheel revolves around it. Those who only know the wheel will say that everything is a change, a flux. Those who also know the central point will say that at the center of all movement there is something unmoving, static.

And the most interesting thing is that if we separate the wheel from the axle, the wheel will not be able to move at all! The movement of the wheel depends on that which does not move. The forms change, but the change is dependent on that which is formless, which is unchanging.

When Arjuna says that all these people will die, he is talking about the form. He is saying that all these people will be annihilated: he knows about nothing beyond form. And Krishna is saying that it is not that the people you are seeing today were not there before – they were there before too: I was here before and you were here before. And it is also not that those who are here today will not be here tomorrow. No, we will be here in the future too – always, forever. Existence is from no-beginning to no-end.

So it is necessary to understand that Krishna and Arjuna are talking about two different things.

Arjuna is talking about form and Krishna is talking about the formless. Arjuna is talking about the visible and Krishna is talking about the invisible. Arjuna is talking about that which comes within the range of the eyes the ears and the hands; Krishna is talking about that which is beyond the range of the eyes, the ears and the hands. Arjuna is thinking the way we all think; Krishna is talking about something that will be a blessing to us if we ever come to realize it.

The visible was not always there. *Always* is a big word. The visible was not even there a moment ago. You are looking at my face: it is not the same face that was there a moment ago; and it will not be the same face after another moment. Within one moment so much in my body has died and so many new things have emerged.

Buddha used to say to the people who would come to see him, 'When you leave here, you won't be the same person as the one who came. In an hour many things will have changed.'

In seventy years a man has completely changed at least ten times. Every seven years all the atoms and the molecules of the body are changed. Each moment something in the body is dying and being expelled; each moment something new is being born, something new is emerging.

You are putting the new in through your food. The whole body changes completely in seven years. But we go on saying: 'I am the same person.' To us, similarity of form becomes oneness of form.

You must watch the movies sometimes. If the movie is run very slowly, you will be amazed. For a hand to rise and reach the head, for that much movement, thousands of pictures have to be taken.

Then the sequence of all those pictures is run very fast. Because of this, you see the hand being raised as one normal act. If you watch it in a slow motion, you will notice how many positions the hand has to be filmed in.

In the same way, when we are looking at a person, we are not seeing the same person the whole time. During the time that we are looking at him, our eyes see thousands of his faces. By the time the image is processed and a figure has formed in our minds, things in the face have changed.

And in the same way, there are innumerable stars in the vast sky. The stars that we see are not actually there where we see them. Once they were there. It takes four years for the light from the closest star to reach our planet. And light doesn't travel slowly. The velocity of light is one hundred and eighty-six thousand miles per second. It takes four years for our nearest star to reach us with the light traveling at this tremendous speed. When the rays of light reach us, we see the star where it was four years ago. It is possible that during this time it may have become non-existent, it may have disintegrated. And it is certainly not where it was four years ago. It must have traveled millions and billions of miles in the meantime.

So the stars that we see at night are not where we see them. The night is very misleading, the stars are very misleading – none of the stars are really there where you see them. And these stars are very far away. In the case of some stars it takes a hundred years, for others it takes a thousand years, before their light reaches us – and some of them take millions and billions of years. There are stars whose light started traveling towards the earth before the earth even came into existence some four billion years ago and their light has not reached here yet. Who knows what might have happened out there in those four billion years?

What we are looking at is not exactly that which is. And even during that short fraction of time it is changing. When I look at your face, the rays of light start from your face and reach my eyes, but this too has a time gap. By that time you are not the same.

Everything has changed inside. What to say about forever – the form does not remain the same even for one moment.

Heraclitus has said, 'You cannot step in the same river twice.' Even this is not totally right. It is difficult to step in the same river even once, stepping twice is impossible – because as your foot touches the surface of the river it is flowing away. As your foot goes a little deeper, the water on the surface is flowing away. When your foot has reached a depth of one foot, all around it the water in the river is flowing rapidly on. When your foot is on the surface, the water beneath you is flowing away and when your foot is at the bottom, the water on the surface is flowing away.

Form runs away like a river, but to us it appears to be static. It looks identical because it looks similar. It appears to be the same as what we saw yesterday, it appears to be the same as what we saw in the morning, and so we take it to be identical. But form is changing every moment.

Arjuna has become very worried about the world of forms and shapes; we are worried, too! He says of those who are already dying each moment, 'What will happen if these people die?' He is worrying about those who are already dying, who cannot be saved; he is worrying about impossible things. And the person who worries about impossible things can never become free from worrying.

Worrying about the impossible turns into insanity. It is difficult to save the form even for a moment; the question of saving it forever does not even arise. There is a world of forms – of appearances, of sound, of rays and waves – it is in a constant flux. Everything is continuously changing. Right now, we are all sitting here – all of us are changing, pulsating, wavering. Everything is changing. Anyone who wants to save the changing world from change wants the impossible. Man becomes insane through bumping against the banks of impossible desires.

I am reminded of an incident in Socrates' life. When Socrates was dying, Creto, one of his friends asked, 'You are about to die but you don't look worried or concerned.'

Socrates replied, 'I am not worried or concerned, because if I will be finished after my death, there is no reason to worry – and if I don't survive, then who will be there to worry? Who will be there to know that I have died and to suffer over it? If I am finished, there will be no one to know that I have died. There will be no one to become aware that I ever existed, that there was ever someone called Socrates. So there is no reason to worry. And if I don't die, if I don't die even after death, then what is there to worry about?

'There are only two possibilities: either I will be finished or I will not. There is no other possibility. Hence I am unconcerned.'

Krishna is telling Arjuna that that which is going to die anyway is not going to survive just because of his efforts, and that which is not going to die is not going to be killed even if he tries to kill it – so he should stop worrying unnecessarily.

There is this expansion of the world from the form to the formless. If we look at it from the viewpoint of the form, then too it is pointless to worry, because that which is already dying… dying… dying each moment is eventually going to perish. It is like drawing a line on water – it starts disappearing before it is completed. Before we finish drawing it, the line has gone. And if we look at it from the viewpoint of the formless, then that which is not going to die is never going to die, and it has never died before.

But we are not acquainted with the formless, and nor is Arjuna.

It is also important to understand that Arjuna's worrying shows one more thing. Arjuna is saying that they will all die. This means that Arjuna also considers *himself* to be only a form – otherwise he wouldn't be saying this. What we say about others is actually being said about ourselves. When I see somebody dying and I think – 'My God! That person is dead! That person has vanished forever!' – I should know that I myself don't know anything about my own inner reality, which does not die, which does not perish, which does not disappear.

When Arjuna is expressing concern over their death, he is expressing concern about his own death. He doesn't know the reality within him that is deathless. Similarly when Krishna is saying that they will not die, he is saying something about himself. He has known that which is deathless.

Our outer knowledge is nothing but an extension of our inner knowledge. Our knowledge about the world is nothing but the extension of our knowledge about our own selves. What we know of our own self is what we then extend over the whole as our knowledge of it. And whatever we don't know about our own self can never be known in the context of the other. Self-knowledge is the only knowledge. All other knowledge is based on deep ignorance, and knowledge based on ignorance is completely undependable.

Now, Arjuna appears to be talking about great knowledge, about great religiousness – but he doesn't even know that there is something formless and beyond any shape, that there is something intrinsic to existence that is deathless. He has no idea of this. And the person who hasn't experienced the deathless doesn't know anything. The person who knows only death is engulfed in dense darkness and ignorance.

So this is the criterion: if you know only death, you are rooted in ignorance; if you have known that which is undying, that which is deathless, you are rooted in knowledge. If you are afraid of death – it makes no difference whether it is of your own death or the death of other people – that just proves one thing: that you have not known the deathless. And nothing exists but the deathless.

Death is just a name for the waves on the surface. They *only* exist if the ocean exists, but it is invisible. What is visible is the waves. Have you ever seen the ocean? If you have been to the beach you will say categorically that you have seen it. But what you have seen are mere waves. You have not seen the ocean. The waves are not the ocean. The waves are *in* the ocean but they are not the ocean – because the ocean can exist without the waves but the waves cannot exist without the ocean. The waves are what is seen, they are spread all over the surface of the ocean. Our eyes see only them; our ears hear only their sound.

But the interesting fact is that you can't actually see a wave – because a wave is that which is wavering, changing. Before you even see it, it has changed. The wave is continuously becoming and vanishing. Its becoming and not becoming are simultaneous. It is rising and falling, it is and it is not. It is swaying between the two simultaneously – it is this wave that we see.

One who takes the waves to be the ocean will be anxious: What will happen? The waves are disappearing, what will happen then? But one who has known the ocean will say, 'It doesn't matter if the waves disappear. The water, the ocean that is surging in the waves was there before them and will remain after they have gone.'

Someone asked Jesus 'What do you know about Abraham?' Abraham was an ancient prophet long before Jesus' time.

Jesus replied, 'Before Abraham, I was.'

The man can't have believed Jesus. Jesus was hardly thirty years old, and Abraham had died thousands of years before. How could Jesus say that he was before Abraham?

What Jesus is actually talking about is the ocean, not about the wave that was born out of Mary. He is not talking about the wave called Jesus. He is talking about the ocean which was before the wave and which will be after the wave.

Similarly when Krishna says, 'We existed before. You, I and all these people standing on the battlefield have been before and we will exist afterwards too,' he is talking about the ocean. And Arjuna is talking about the wave. Usually a communication between a person talking about the ocean and a person talking about the wave becomes very difficult – because one is talking about the east and the other is talking about the west.

And this is the reason why the dialogue of the Gita will go on for so long. Arjuna will raise issues about the waves again and again, while Krishna will talk about the ocean again and again. And they do not cross each other's paths anywhere. If they could, the problem would be resolved immediately.

So they will continue for a long time. Arjuna will repeat himself and will come back to the waves. He sees only waves. And what can one who can see only waves do about it? After all, it is the waves that are on the surface.

Actually, someone who just depends on looking can only see waves. If someone wants to see the ocean, it is a little difficult to see it with open eyes. It has to be seen with closed eyes. The truth is that if you want to see the ocean, you don't have to look with your eyes at all, you have to take a dip in the ocean. And when you are diving, your eyes naturally have to be closed. You have to penetrate below the waves, into the ocean. But someone who hasn't penetrated beneath the waves of his own mind cannot penetrate beneath the waves that are arising in others' minds. Arjuna's whole misery amounts to just one thing – self-ignorance.

OSHO,

When Krishna is telling Arjuna: 'You, I and all these people were here before and will be here after,' this only elicits the conclusion, just as you are saying, that the formless content, the being, is more important than the form of the body.

But isn't the other possibility also there – that the formless content cannot have its right manifestation without the form? What is the purpose of clay without its form in pots and pans?

There is difference between existence and manifestation. That which is un-manifest can also exist. The tree is latent in a seed; the tree is not yet manifest but still it *is*. It *is* in the sense that it can become. It *is* in the sense that it is latent, that it is a potential.

A unique experiment is being carried out at Oxford University. It is a scientific experiment and according to me it is one of the most significant scientific experiments that has been going on.

The experiment is being carried out with the help of extremely sensitive cameras that can photograph the tree that is hidden in the seed and will be fully manifest in twenty years' time.

It is amazing! It all happened accidentally while they were taking a photograph of a bud. Many scientific discoveries happen accidentally, because scientists are very conventional – they are

186 · INNER WAR AND PEACE

conformists. Normally a scientist is never a revolutionary. Sometimes revolutionaries become scientists – that is a different matter – but the other way around is not usual. A scientist clings very hard to what is already known by science, and he doesn't allow anything new to enter that world.

The whole history of science shows the amount of opposition each new discovery received from other scientists – but never from anyone else. So new discoveries often happen unintentionally. The scientist is not looking for it and it comes accidentally.

In the laboratory the scientists were investigating flowers with the help of some extremely sensitive cameras. They were trying to photograph a bud but instead of the bud a flower appeared on the film. There was a bud in front of the camera but what the lens captured was a flower! At the time it was thought to have been a fault of the camera: it must have been mistakenly exposed; something must have gone wrong. Nevertheless, they decided to wait until the bud blossomed. And when it actually blossomed, they were surprised. The fault was not with the camera; the fault was with the scientists' understanding. When the flower blossomed, it was identical to the one which had been photographed earlier.

After that they continued further with their research. The scientists came to the conclusion that what is going to happen in the future is actually happening in some subtle world of vibration right now – otherwise it could not have been actualized.

A child is born after living hidden in the mother's womb for nine months. Nobody knows what is happening inside, but when the child appears after nine months, it is not all of a sudden. It has been going through a journey inside the womb for nine months. In the same way, when a bud blossoms into a flower, before that, the electromagnetic waves surrounding it have been evolving into becoming a flower – in the womb. That can be photographed. This means that sooner or later we will be able to photograph the future image of old age in the child. I believe it will be possible.

In this way, astrology can gain a solid scientific basis. Until now, astrology could not become scientific; now it will be able to, from the standpoint that what is going to happen in the future is happening right now at some level. We may or may not see it, but that is a different matter.

The problem is something like this: I am sitting under a tree and you are sitting on the tree. You say you can see a vehicle on the road and I don't see it. I say that there is no vehicle; the road is empty. As far as I can see, the road *is* empty.

For me the vehicle is in the future. You are sitting on the tree, for you it is in the present. You say, 'There is a vehicle,' and I say, 'There isn't one in this moment. There may be in the future.' But for you, it is in the present; you are seeing it.

After a while I also start seeing the vehicle. From the future it has come into the present for me. Then it passes down the road, and once again I can no longer see it. It has gone into the past for me. But from the treetop you say that you can still see it. For you it is still in the present.

For me the vehicle was in the future, and then it came into the present and then it went into the past. For you it has been moving in one continuous present. You are just sitting at a higher level than I am, that's all.

Krishna is seeing from a height, a peak. He is speaking from this peak when he is saying that we all existed before, we all exist now and we will all exist in the future too. In fact, from where Krishna is looking, only the ever-present exists; only an eternal present exists from that height.

From where Arjuna is looking he has to say, 'I don't know if we existed before or not. I have no idea about that.' Arjuna's sight only goes as far back as birth – actually not even that far.

If you look closely, you cannot remember anything before you were four years old. Before that, everything is inferred. People tell you that you were there. Your memory goes back as far as four years of age. If someone is very intelligent, his memory may go back to three years of age. Someone even more intelligent can go back to two years of age. Still, the question remains: Were you there before you were two years old? Nothing can be said. If memory is the only proof, then you were not here before you were two. But then how can you suddenly come into being if you did not exist during those two years?

Even if you can trace your life back to your very birth – and others can help you to do this – you existed in your mother's womb before your birth and you have no memory of that. But in deep hypnosis you can remember even this. If you hypnotize someone deeply, he can recall incidents like when he was three months old in the womb and his mother fell down. The child in the womb is also hurt when his mother meets with an accident. So memories from the womb are also possible. And one can even remember from beyond that, from one's past life. But for us, all of this will be in the past. We have to reawaken the memories of it all.

For Krishna everything is an eternal now; everything is only a now. From this now, from where he can see everything, he can say to Arjuna, 'These people have all existed before and will exist again too. I existed before and so did you.'

There can be a fear that Krishna's statement will be misunderstood, that Arjuna will think that he existed before as a person called Arjuna. Krishna is not saying this. The person called Arjuna never existed as Arjuna before; he couldn't have. The personality called Arjuna is just a garment. The formless consciousness hidden behind that garment *did* exist before. The person called Arjuna will never exist again either: it is just clothing and will disintegrate with death. But what those clothes were hanging on will continue into the future.

No matter how thoroughly Arjuna tries to understand what Krishna is saying, he is bound to misunderstand. The misunderstanding will be that at the most he will be able to think, 'I have existed before as Arjuna and you have existed before as Krishna. All these people standing in front of us have also existed before.' He will repeat the same question: 'So, did these same forms also exist before?'

No, these forms never existed before. But a form is a manifestation. Existence – formless, shapeless existence – is not a manifestation. But existence can also be unmanifest. What is visible is not all there is. The invisible also exists. What is visible to us anyway? A very, very small fraction is visible.

If we ask the scientist today, he has begun to admit that what is manifest is very small. For example, there was no radio a couple of centuries ago. Now there is. Sitting here we can switch on the radio and listen to a voice from London. Does this mean that by turning the knob on the radio you have switched on the voice in London? No, the voice in London was passing by you all the time, but there was no way you could have heard it without a radio set to receive the sound waves. But even when you couldn't hear the voice, it was there in an unmanifest form – it was just that your ears couldn't hear it.

There are thousands of other sounds passing through the atmosphere. According to scientists, we are capable of hearing within a certain range. We can only hear within that range. We can neither hear below it nor above it. There is a limit to our capacity for hearing – and so much is passing by in the ranges above it as well as below it.

What we cannot hear still exists and what we cannot see still exists. But only that much of existence for which we have senses manifests itself to us.

For example, light doesn't exist for a blind man – because the light is unable to manifest itself to him. The blind man doesn't have the medium through which he can see light. Now, if we can imagine a species existing somewhere on some other distant planet which has more than our five senses, we will come to know for the first time that there are other things in the universe about which we have had no idea. Our five senses are not some kind of exhaustive limit.

According to scientists, life exists on at least fifty thousand planets. They are aware of some four billion planets and sub-planets, and almost fifty thousand of them are likely to have life on them. Maybe a very different form of life exists on them. There could be beings there who have seven senses, or fifteen senses, or even twenty senses. They may have knowledge of such things as we can never even dream of – because dreaming too is possible only about things that we know. We cannot dream about anything that we have no idea of. We cannot even imagine it. Our Kalidasa and Bhavabhuti and Rabindranath Tagore, our greatest poets, cannot even imagine in poetry what is beyond the realm of our senses – but still it is. We cannot deny its existence just because we cannot see it or perceive it.

Manifestation is a very superficial phenomenon. Existence is a very inner phenomenon. Actually, one should say that existence is not a phenomenon, it is is-ness, it is be-ing, whereas manifestation is a happening.

For example, I am sitting here, and then I sing a song. As long as I was not singing, whereabouts inside me was this song? It was certainly somewhere, but could a physiologist have dissected my body and captured that song? Would some scientist, some psychologist or neurosurgeon have been able to get hold of my song by operating on my brain? No, nobody could have found the song within me. But if the song had not been inside me, there would have been no way that it could have manifested itself.

The song was unmanifest. It was there as a seed somewhere; it was hidden. Maybe it existed as the subtlest of waves, unmanifest, but it certainly existed somewhere. Then it manifested. It has not come into existence because of its manifestation; it was there before that. And this doesn't mean that it has manifested totally, because in the process my own limitations also created hindrances.

Until the very end of his life, Rabindranath Tagore kept saying that he had not been able to sing the song that he wanted to sing. But how did he know that he wanted to sing something that he couldn't? There was certainly some feeling deep inside, some perception that something needed to be sung. It is something like the feeling you have when you realize that someone's name is on the tip of your tongue but you just can't say it. It sounds crazy when you say that the name is just on the tip of your tongue, but you can't say it. If it is on the tip of the tongue, what more is needed? Just say it! But no, you say it is on the tip of your tongue but you cannot say it.

What does this mean? It means that somewhere deep inside there is a creeping feeling that you do know, but still it doesn't manifest itself, the conscious mind doesn't get hold of it. You are vaguely aware of it. And if you die and you are dissected and we try to look inside you for what was on the tip of your tongue, it will not be found. The tip of the tongue will be there but not the name you were about to utter. We can find the brain and the nerves of the brain and the network of millions of cells, but the unmanifest will not be found. It remains unmanifest, hidden in the recesses of your existence, and disappears.

What Krishna is saying is that you are not only that which has manifested as you, you are also that which has remained unmanifest. And the unmanifest is vast, and that which has manifested is but a fragment. These fragments have manifested many times and they will manifest again and again. But the unmanifest, which is endless, beginning-less and infinite is inexhaustible. In spite of all these manifestations it remains unexhausted.

Certainly, if it is not manifest, we won't be able to recognize it through our senses – because the senses can only perceive the manifest. But we are not only the senses. And if we can learn the art of penetrating the senses, that which is unmanifest will also be perceived, will also be recognized, seen and heard, will also be touched at some deeper core of the heart.

Manifestation is not a compulsion for existence. It is its play. Existence is not compelled to take a form – taking a form is its play. That's why Krishna calls the world, life, nothing but a play.

And a play means that when somebody appears on the stage as Rama, it is just a form; and when somebody appears as a Ravana, that too is just a manifestation in form. They are fighting with each other with bows and arrows in their hands, which again is just a form. A little later, behind the screen, they will be chatting with each other and forgetting all about Sita whom they were fighting over. The fight will be over and they will be having a cup of tea together in the Green Room!

Krishna is talking about the Green Room and Arjuna is talking about the stage. But what has appeared on the stage is just a form, a figure; it is just acting. Existence can be without a form, but form cannot be without existence. As I have said before, there can be no wave without the ocean, but the ocean can exist without the wave.

When Rama and Ravana go backstage and start gossiping and having a cup of tea, where will the forms, the characters that manifested as Rama and Ravana be? They will have disappeared. They were just waves and forms, which vanish if there is no life-force behind them. The form changes, the figure changes, the acting changes but the actor is unchanging. That which is behind all of this is unchanging. This is what Krishna is talking about.

'Just as this being
passes through childhood, youth and old age in this body,
so too it passes through the changing of bodies.
And the serene and tranquil ones do not grieve over this.'

Krishna is saying that just as everything is changing in this body – there is childhood, youth, old age, birth and death – just as nothing is static in this body, everything is in a flux, all is changing. Children are becoming youths, youths are becoming old, and the old are disappearing into death.

This is very interesting. It is not felt in language, because there is no dynamism in words. Words are static things. And because words are static, languages do a lot of injustice to life. Nothing is static in life. So when we impose static words on life, which is dynamic, we are committing a big mistake.

We say, 'This is a child.' Now this is a wrong way of putting it. A child is never in the state of 'is'. A child is always in the state of becoming. Actually we should say: 'A becoming child.' We say, 'He is old,' but this is wrong. Nobody is old; everyone is becoming old.

Everything is a becoming. There is nothing that 'is'. Everything is continuously becoming. We say, 'This is a river.' What a wrong way of saying things! A river and 'is'? A river means that which is flowing, which is rivering.

All words are static, whereas nothing is static in life. That is our big injustice towards life. And using these words day and night, we forget the reality. When we say someone is 'a young man', what does it mean in life, not in the dictionary but in life? In life, youth is nothing but a movement towards old age. You will not find this written anywhere in the dictionary. In the dictionary, *old man* means an old man, aged. But in life, *old man* means one who is moving towards death, who is approaching death – that's all! And movement is not something that has taken place somewhere once in the past. It is happening now. It is continuing to happen.

Krishna is saying to Arjuna, 'Things are not static, even in what you call "this life". The forms that you are seeing in this life were children in the past, then they moved towards youth, and now they are becoming old.'

If a photograph is taken of the first cell when conception takes place in the womb, and is later shown to that person with the information, 'This is you fifty years ago,' the person won't be able to believe it. He will say, 'You must be joking! How can I be this?' A tiny cell which cannot be seen by the naked eyes, which has to be seen through a microscope, which has neither eyes nor ears nor bones, whose sex cannot yet be determined by just looking – would you agree that you were that tiny blip, that tiny point? You certainly wouldn't. But that is your very first photograph. You should keep it in your album. And if you are not this, then you cannot be what today's photograph of you shows you to be – because that image is also going to change very soon.

Supposing we put the photograph of someone taken on the day that he died side by side with one taken on the day that he was born – do you think we will be able to see any similarity between the two pictures? We won't be able to find any connection between the two. We won't be able even to imagine that the old man who is dying right now is this same child who was born many years ago. No, they will appear to be totally unrelated. You won't be able to connect the two. But we never pay attention or give even a thought to this much of the apparently unconnected flow in life.

Krishna is trying to trigger this thought in Arjuna. He is saying that the very forms that he fears will be killed, destroyed, are vanishing every moment. They are continuously disappearing over twenty-four hours. They are in the process of continuously disappearing.

Man is continuously dying his whole life. His whole life is one long process of dying. What begins with his birth ends with his death. The process of being born is the first step and the process of dying is the second. And it is not that death suddenly appears one day. From the very first day of someone's birth, death is coming closer towards that person every day – and that is why it is able to reach him. It takes seventy years for death to reach you, or you can say that you take seventy years to reach death. But the journey starts from the very first day.

Everything is changing, yet we still don't see the point: 'How is it that in the midst of all these changes, I am still carrying a persistent feeling of being the same person who was a child, and then a young man and now an old man?' In spite of all the changes, where and how does this identity, this continuity, this remembrance remains – to whom and why?

There must be one unchanging reality inside, otherwise who will remember?

I can remember something that happened when I was ten years old. One who was present in me at the age of ten must also be present now on some level, otherwise how am I to remember an event that happened at the age of ten? This 'I', as I am today, was certainly not there then. My form as it is visible today was not there then.

So who is it that remembers? Where does this thread of memory lie? There must be a center, an axle, within me around which all the changes have taken place. The paths have changed, the chariot has moved over many, many paths, but there must be an axle that has seen the wheel in all its states. The wheel itself

THE THOUGHT-LESS MIND · 195

cannot remember – it is changing all the time. There has to be an unchanging element here.

So Krishna is saying that there is childhood, youth and old age, but amidst all these changes there is some stable, unchanging, unmoving reality, and it is the remembrance of this reality that we have to awaken.

Then we will not be able to say, 'I was a child', or 'I was a young man', or 'Now I am old'. No, then our understanding of reality will be very different. We will say, 'I was there in childhood', 'I was there in my youth', and 'I was there in old age'; 'One day I was in birth and one day I was in death.' And the 'I' will be disidentified with all these states in the same way that a traveler passes through many stations. At the railway station of Ahmedabad he does not say, 'I am Ahmedabad.' He says, 'I am at Ahmedabad station.' After reaching Bombay he does not say that he has become Bombay. He says that he is at Bombay station. If he were able to identify with Bombay, then he would never be able to become identified with Ahmedabad, and if he were able to identify with Ahmedabad, he would never be able to identify with Bombay.

If you are a child, how can you become a young man? And if you are a young man, how can you become an old man? Certainly there must be someone inside you who is not a child. That is why childhood can come and go, youth can come and go, old age can come and will pass away. The wheel of birth and death rotates, but there is some reality standing in the midst of all this movement that is seeing the coming and going of everything like different railway stations going past on the way.

If we can see that what we think we are is actually only one of our passing states, that our being passes through it but we are not it... Krishna is proposing that we remember this.

OSHO,
The being, the consciousness, leaves this body and enters a new one. So during the period that passes between death and a new birth does the soul only exist or does it have a manifestation too? What is the nature of the soul in this state?

In the gap between leaving one body and taking another one, is there some manifestation or only existence? There is also some manifestation, but that manifestation is not the kind that we become familiar with while we are in the body. The medium of that manifestation changes completely. It is the manifestation of the subtle body. It can also be seen through a special kind of tuning, just as radio can be heard through a special kind of tuning. It can also be touched through such special arrangements, but the usual body – the body that we know, that we have disposed of – exists no more.

But this is not the only body that we have. There are more bodies inside that body. There is a whole network of bodies within that body. In a usual death, only our first body is dropped; the second body hidden behind it travels on with us. Call it the subtle body or the astral body or whatsoever name you want to give it – it travels on with us. It is in this body that all our memories, all our experiences, the imprints of all our actions, the impressions of all our conditionings, are accumulated – and these travel on with us.

This subtle body can be seen. It is not so difficult to see it, in fact it is quite easy. But as the world has become more civilized, it has become slightly more difficult. It was not so difficult before. Certain things have been lost, have become difficult phenomena for us to see. It is just that we are no longer used to seeing them. Our minds have withdrawn from that direction, we no longer pursue things in that direction. Otherwise the subtle body used to be seen very easily.

It can still be seen easily, and now very successful attempts have been made to see it scientifically as well. The subtle body has been photographed in thousands of ways, and has been investigated with scientific equipment.

We are all sitting here, but we are not the only ones sitting here. If some day we can develop the right kind of camera that catches the image of the subtle body too – which is bound to happen because subtle bodies have already been photographed – and a picture of this place is taken by that camera, we will find that not only the people who are visibly sitting here are here, but there are many more who are not visible.

It is said that a great crowd used to gather in Mahavira's meetings. But that crowd consisted of many kinds of beings. There were those who came from the nearby villages to listen to him and there were those who came from the sky.

Such beings are present everywhere, all the time. Sometimes from their side they try to get you to see them. Sometimes they can be seen when you try from your side. But to be seen through these efforts requires special talents. Such sightings are not common.

This subtle body exists during the journey from one body to the next, because without it, rebirth will not be possible. To put it in scientific language, the subtle body is a built-in program, a blueprint, a plan, for the birth of the new body. Without it, it will be difficult to take a new body. All that you have accumulated in this lifetime – all the conditionings, experiences, knowledge, and imprints of actions – all that you have accumulated, all that you are, is in the subtle body.

Have you ever observed that the last thought you have before you fall asleep is your first thought in the morning when you wake up? If you have never noticed this, have a look now. In the night, when sleep is just descending on you, the last thought in that moment will be the first thought that emerges in the morning. The last thought of the night will be the first thought in the morning. Where was it during the whole night? You fell asleep, so it should have been lost by now. But no, it was waiting in your subtle body and no sooner did you wake up than it caught hold of you.

The moment this body is dropped, you set out on a new journey with an accumulated blueprint of all your lifelong desires, passions and aspirations in your subtle body. This blueprint will wait until you take on a new body. As soon as you take a new body, the subtle body will start manifesting all these things whenever the possibilities and opportunities for them to do so arise.

But there is also a kind of death in which even the subtle body doesn't remain with you anymore. Such a death is called *mukti*, *moksha* – the ultimate liberation. After such a death only being remains, only existence remains, without any manifested body.

In ordinary death, you have a subtle body with you. This other death is an extraordinary death, is the great death. It happens only to an enlightened one. Attaining to enlightenment means a person has dissolved his subtle body while he is still alive, he has effaced his built-in program. Now he doesn't have any plans for a future journey. Now he doesn't have a 'five-year plan' or a five-lifetime plan. Now he doesn't have any plan, he is free from all of this. Now, whenever this body drops he will only be an existence, not a manifestation.

Manifestation is bondage, because it can never be a manifestation of the whole. A little part becomes manifest and that which remains unmanifest becomes restless. This is why our being is pining for liberation, is hankering after freedom, because only a small part is manifest. It is as if the whole body of a person is tied down with chains and just a finger is left free. He is moving his finger, he is very troubled, he is saying, 'I want freedom because my whole body is enchained.'

Our whole existence is chained in the same way. There is just a small manifestation through a small door and this feels like bondage. That is our pain. We are restless. We can do two things with this restlessness: either we can go on trying to free ourselves through that small door called the body, which means we go on letting it get bigger…

Someone builds a larger house. It only means that he is making his body bigger, that's all! In the big house it feels as if he has become a little freer. The space is bigger, the place is bigger. In his small cell it felt claustrophobic; a bigger house feels a bit more open. But very soon even this house will start feeling small. So then one creates a palace, but after a while even *that* will feel small.

Actually man's being is so vast that even the whole sky will fall short. Hence, no matter how big the palaces one makes, they will always feel small. One needs the same amount of space as is available to the whole of existence. Nothing less than that will do. Within each person the same also exists. It requires the whole space, it requires infinity – where no boundary ever comes.

Wherever there is a boundary, there will be bondage. And the body creates many kinds of boundaries and limitations: the limitation of seeing, the limitation of hearing, the limitation of thinking – everything has a limitation. And existence is infinite; the manifest is finite. Hence to be free of the manifest is to be liberated from the world.

What in traditional terminology we call liberation from *avagamana*, the cycle of birth and death, is nothing but freedom from manifestation. It is the search for pure existence. It is the search for that existence where there will be no manifestation but only being, only is-ness. And there will be no boundary. In being, in is-ness, there is no boundary.

So whenever someone dies after having attained to enlightenment – after having shattered all the built-in programs, after having dropped all the desires and wishes for manifestation – then no kind of body is left with him anymore, then we cannot photograph that person anymore.

So there cannot be photographs of a Mahavira or a Buddha or a Krishna amongst the photographs that have been taken by psychic research societies in the west. Only the bodies of those people who still carry their built-in programs, only those who have a plan, a certain built-in-program for a body, can be photographed by these societies. There is no way that a photograph can be taken of Mahavira. Existence cannot be photographed. A person can be photographed with existence, but not existence itself. How can there be a photograph of existence? It has no limits. Only that which has limits can be photographed.

So in ordinary death, a body will remain but it will be the subtle body. In extraordinary death – in yogic death, the ultimate death, in nirvana – there remains no body whatsoever, but only existence. There remains no wave but only the ocean.

OSHO,
Can the son or wife of someone do something to give peace to his departed subtle body that is still full of desires? The Gita talks about *pindadan* – the ritual of giving offerings to dead ancestors.

Desire is absolutely personal. Another person can do nothing about it. The desire is yours, your wife cannot do anything about it. Yes, in the name of doing something for your desire she can do something for hers, but that is an entirely different matter.

The husband is dead. The wife tries to make her husband free from his desires – she prays, she does fire rituals, she performs ritual offerings, she does a thousand and one things – but this can make no difference whatsoever to her husband's desires. Yes, it can make a difference to *her* desires – and that is the secret of the whole business.

This whole business of rituals is not to free her husband from desires – because if someone can liberate her husband from his desires, she can also induce desires in him, and then liberation will be impossible in this world! If a Mahavira died and then his wife pulled him back into desires, what would he be able to do? If you can liberate someone, you can also put that person into bondage. And in this case, even liberation will be a bondage – in fact, liberation will be impossible.

No. The secret is something else and it has not normally been revealed. The secret is this: the husband has died and the wife cannot do anything about him. She could not help him even when he is alive, how can she help him now, when he is dead? The other has his own being where we have no entry. Neither the wife, nor the husband, nor the mother nor the father – nobody can enter there. But whatsoever the wife does for the sake of her husband, that prayer, that longing for his liberation from desires will help her to become free from her own desires. Her desires will evaporate.

It is a very interesting fact that when we are arousing the other's desires we are actually only arousing our own desires, and when we are helping to dissolve the other's desires we are actually dissolving our own desires. In fact, whatever we are doing for the other person we basically are doing for ourselves. The reality is that doing something for the other can only be a façade – ultimately all doing is only for ourselves.

So this ritual is useful, but please don't think that it is useful for the other person who has departed on another journey. It is useful for *you*, it is meaningful for *you*.

But if this is said the way I am saying it, perhaps the wife won't even pray. She may say, 'Okay, okay! We will see...' But such a longing arises in her heart to do as much as she can for her dead husband: maybe it will help him to find an easy way ahead, maybe he will find the path to bliss, the door to paradise.

There is a fundamental reason behind such longings arising. While living, we do nothing but hurt each other and create hell for each other. Naturally after the death of the other we start repenting. The husband appears to love his wife more after she has died. He was never seen to be so loving while she was alive! This is the beginning of repentance: things start moving in exactly the opposite direction.

Howsoever the son may have treated his father during his lifetime, he will start behaving quite differently after his death. He didn't respect his father while he was alive, but as soon as he dies the son will put up his father's photograph and garland it. He never served his father while he was alive and in his body, but after his death he will gather up his ashes and take them to the Ganges. If his father had asked him to take him on a pilgrimage to the Ganges while he was still living, the son would have never agreed to do so, but now he is proudly taking his dead father to the Ganges!

In this world of ours, we ill-treat the living so much that it is only after their death that we can ask for their forgiveness – and this is what it is all about. So the wife can do for the dead husband, the husband can do for the dead wife, the son can do for the dead father or for the dead mother what no one would even do for himself.

Hence, there has been an attempt to hand down a very psychological truth for a very wrong reason. The truth is only this much: that we are able to get rid of our own desires through efforts we make to get rid of the desires of the other. And this is not a small achievement. But from now on it should only be done with an awareness of this fact. And from now on, it will only be possible to do this with such an awareness, because times change and minds mature.

Wowee

If some sweets are stored in the house we scare away the children by saying, 'Don't go into that room. A ghost lives there.' There is no ghost, just a box of sweets, but you want to protect the child from overeating. And in that moment there is no way we can make the child understand that if he eats too many sweets his body will suffer, so we have to create a ghost. The purpose is served. The child doesn't go in for fear of the ghost.

But when the same child grows up, the ghost cannot frighten him anymore. He says, 'It's okay. It doesn't matter.' On the contrary, the gossip about the ghost creates more attraction. He is all the more tempted to go where under normal circumstances he may not have gone at all. Now it is better to tell this man the truth.

All the concepts that humanity developed in its infancy are totally upside-down now. Now it is better to tell the truth directly and plainly. The concepts from the primary stages of human evolution – from five thousand years ago, or maybe even earlier than that, when the Gita must have been told – have now all become ridiculous. Now, if we want to save them, it is necessary to reveal their secrets, it is necessary to tell plainly and straightforwardly what the reality behind them is: that there is no ghost, there are only sweets, but that there will be such-and-such a health hazard from eating too many of them.

Man has matured. And as a result he appears to have become, on the whole, irreligious. But this is his maturity; it is not irreligiousness. Actually for the mature man, for the adult man, for an adult humanity, the very core of all the theories handed down to humanity in its infancy needs to be given a new form.

'As the senses come in contact with objects, O Arjuna, son
of Kunti,
heat and cold, happiness and unhappiness result;
these come and go, are impermanent;
Hence, O Arjuna, descendent of Bharat, endure them well.'

One who is born, dies. Everything that is created, perishes. That
which comes to be, disintegrates, comes to an end.

Krishna says: 'O Arjuna, keep this in remembrance. Remember
that whatsoever is created also perishes. And if one is aware of this
– that whatsoever is created, perishes; whosoever is born is going
to die – then there remains no cause for grief when it disappears.
And that which cannot cause any unhappiness when it disappears
will not cause any happiness while it is there.'

Our pains and pleasures, our happinesses and unhappinesses,
are born out of the illusion that what we have will always remain.
When a loved one appears, it causes happiness. But the one who
has come will also go; where there is a meeting there is also a separation. One who sees the separation as intrinsic to the meeting is
neither driven by happiness when the meeting happens nor driven
by unhappiness when the separation occurs. A person's happiness
over birth and unhappiness over death both disappear if he is able
to see death as intrinsic to a birth. And where happiness and
unhappiness both disappear, what remains is bliss.

Bliss is not happiness. Bliss is not a big heap of happiness. Bliss
is not a name for happiness that has become permanent. Neither
is bliss just the absence of unhappiness or an avoidance of unhappiness. Bliss is the transcendence of both happiness and unhappiness – a freedom from both.

In fact, happiness and unhappiness are two sides of the same
coin. One who only sees the union in a union and doesn't see the
inherent separation in it only experiences a momentary happiness.
And likewise, someone who not only sees the separation in a separation but also sees the inherent union in it, only experiences a
momentary unhappiness; whereas, in fact, union and separation

are two parts of the same process, two poles of the same magnet, two ends of one unity.

Hence, one who is happy right now should be aware that he is moving towards unhappiness, and that one who is unhappy right now is moving towards happiness. Happiness and unhappiness, pleasure and pain, are two ends of the same reality. Everything that is born, that is created, will disintegrate. The disintegration of the thing lies in its very making; its destruction lies in its very creation. One who sees this truth completely, totally... But we see only half-truths and become unhappy.

It is a very interesting fact that it is not untruth that brings unhappiness and pain, it is the half-truths that do. Actually, nothing like untruth exists – because the very meaning of untruth is that which is not. In fact it is the half-truths that are the untruths. The reason why they can exist is that they have at least some part of the truth in them. The whole truth takes you to bliss, half-truths only make you fluctuate between happiness and unhappiness.

One doesn't have to become free from untruth in this world but only from half-truths.

Understand it this way: a half-truth is the untruth, there is no other untruth. Untruth has to take the support of truth even to have a semblance of existence. It cannot exist on its own; it doesn't have any reality of its own.

Krishna is saying to Arjuna: See the whole truth. You are unnecessarily becoming shaken, disturbed and upset by seeing the half-truth.

If anyone is getting shaken, disturbed and upset, it has to be because of some half-truth. Wherever there is unhappiness, wherever there is happiness, there must be some half-truth there. And all half-truths are constantly trying to appear to be the whole truth.

So exactly when you are feeling happy, the sand under your feet has already shifted and unhappiness has begun to set in. Exactly when you are feeling unhappy, look attentively and you will notice that somewhere nearby, just behind the unhappiness, happiness is following like its shadow.

It is daybreak, and already the evening is coming. Day is at one end but the night is not very far away. Night descends and the day is already approaching. Life is a continuous journey from one extreme to the other. The waves are moving from one shore to the other.

Krishna says: 'O Arjuna, descendent of Bharat, See the whole truth. If you are able to see the whole truth, you can be undisturbed.'

'O Arjuna, best of men,
the serene and tranquil one whom these do not afflict
who remains unmoved by pain and pleasure both
is worthy to experience deathlessness.'

An awakened one is one who, on seeing the differences between two forms of the two opposite polarities in which our existence is divided, experiences the oneness of their inner existence. One who sees the journey towards death within a birth, the image of pain hidden in pleasure, the separation that is hidden in union – one who becomes capable of also seeing the opposite in every moment – is awakened. It is important to remember that 'one who becomes capable of seeing' and not 'one who becomes capable of believing' becomes awakened. Your beliefs are of no use.

Truths that are merely beliefs topple down and disintegrate with the slightest push from existence. It is only the experienced truths that do not disintegrate. One who comes to know this comes to see this, comes to experience this.

And the interesting thing is that one does not have to go far to experience. Life is giving you the opportunity every day, every moment. Have you ever known a happiness in life that has not turned into unhappiness? Have you ever known a success that has not turned into a failure? Have you ever known a fame that has not turned into infamy?

Lao Tzu used to say that no one had ever been able to defeat him in life…

He is dying. The last moments of his life are approaching and his disciples are asking, 'Please, reveal the secret to us, because this is what we also want: to win, for nobody to be able to defeat us. Kindly tell us the secret of your victory. Please reveal this secret to us all.'

Lao Tzu started laughing. He said, 'You are the wrong people. It is futile to tell you. You didn't even listen to the whole thing and jumped in to ask me in the middle of it. I could only say that no one has ever been able to defeat me – and you didn't allow me to finish, you jumped in in the middle. I was going to say that no one in life could ever defeat me because I didn't want to be victorious over anyone, because I could see clearly that the moment you win, you have started preparing for defeat.

'This is why no one could ever defeat me. There was no way to defeat me because I was never victorious. There was not a single person on this earth who could defeat me. Nobody could defeat me because I had already accepted the defeat on my own. I never tried to win. But you are saying that you want to win, and you don't want to be defeated by anyone. Then you are bound to be defeated because victory and defeat are two sides of the same coin.'

What Krishna is saying also observes this. And remember one thing about this seeing: it is an existential experience. It is our everyday experience, but it is a wonder how we go on missing it, how we protect ourselves from seeing it. It seems we are playing a big trick on ourselves, otherwise it would be astonishing for such a living truth of life to escape our notice.

We experience it every day. Everything changes into its opposite. If you go more deeply into a friendship, it starts turning into enmity. But what is the trick, that we go on avoiding seeing it? The trick is that when the friendship starts turning into enmity, we don't see it like that. We say that the friend is turning into an enemy. And this is the point where we miss: When a friend starts becoming an enemy, we think that *this* friend is turning into an enemy, that had somebody else been in their place this wouldn't have happened, that this person is a cheat. And the other person for whom *you* are now becoming an enemy thinks along similar lines. They also think that they made the wrong choice; that this wouldn't have happened had they chosen the right person.

When a friend becomes an enemy we miss the truth. The truth is that it is the friendship that turns into enmity. But we project it onto the person and start looking for another friend.

A man in America married eight times. He must have been an intelligent man. His first marriage lasted for one year. He found that she was the wrong wife. There is nothing wrong in that. All husbands feel the same way; all wives feel the same way. He felt that she was the wrong wife, that he had made a wrong choice, so he divorced.

Then he chose another wife. After six months, he discovered that again he had made the wrong choice. In this way he married eight times in his life. But as I said, he must have been an intelligent man because if somebody arrives exactly at the truth, even after eight mistakes, he is worth calling an extraordinary man. We don't arrive at the truth even after committing mistakes eight thousand times – because our logic remains the same every time.

He didn't marry again after the eighth time. When his friends asked him the reason, he said, 'Eight times I had a strange experience. Every time I brought the woman home thinking that she was the right one, and she turned out to be the wrong one. The first time I thought, "This woman is wrong," the second time I also thought, "This woman is wrong," but the third time I started doubting myself. The fourth time I could see it very clearly. Nevertheless, I thought to make the experiment a few more times. After the eighth marriage it was crystal clear to me that it is not a question of the woman being right or wrong. From whomsoever you expect happiness you will receive unhappiness because every happiness turns into unhappiness. If you expect friendship from someone, you are sure to get enmity from them, because all friendships are nothing but the beginning of enmity.'

What is the trick of the mind? Where is the catch?

The catch lies in the fact that we project the truth of the

experience, the reality of the situation, onto people and proceed to search for a new person again. You don't have a bicycle so you buy one. Later on, you find out that you had been hoping to get great happiness from this bicycle, and this turned out not to be the case. But it never occurs to you that the bicycle which you were dreaming and thinking about so much, and that you were so happy to get, is not giving you that happiness at all.

We totally fail to see such truths. We start dreaming about a car, and when the car comes we forget to ask ourselves whether the car is giving us all that happiness that we were expecting that it would – and it never happens.

We find unhappiness although what we sought was happiness. We find hatred although what we sought was love. We find darkness although what we sought was light. But we never connect the two ends, we never complete the calculation. And there is one more reason for this, which is worth taking note of. Because there is a time gap between the two ends, we fail to see the connection.

When Western people arrived in Africa for the first time, they were amazed to see that the Africans did not know that childbirth is connected with lovemaking. They never thought that the birth of the baby is somehow connected with making love – because the time gap between the two events is quite big. Firstly, a child is not conceived in every lovemaking, and secondly, there is a gap of nine months. The African tribes never thought that the child had anything to do with sexual intercourse: the time gap between the cause and its effect is so big that they did not relate them to each other.

We live some happiness and, by the time it has turned into unhappiness, there is a time gap. So we fail to see the connection between the two points. We cannot conceive that it is the same happiness that has become unhappiness. No, we fail to connect them. It will take some time for a friend to become an enemy. After all, everything takes time to become something. So there could be a gap of a few years before the friend turns into an enemy and so we fail to correlate the two. We think that the phenomenon of becoming a friend is one thing and the phenomenon of becoming an enemy is another. And then we cannot work it out; then we project it onto the person and say, 'My choice of person was wrong.'

What Krishna is saying to Arjuna is to look as penetratingly as possible in order to see things in their wholeness. The one who sees things in their wholeness becomes a wise man, a sage. Pleasure and pain, hot and cold, do not disturb a sage. By this, you shouldn't think that a sage doesn't perceive hot and cold. I say this because such a misunderstanding has happened in the past. – but then, such a person is not wise, he is just numb, insensitive. Many life-less, insensitive people fall into the fallacy that they are wise just because they cannot feel hot and cold. But with just a little practice this is possible. It is not difficult at all.

Remember, a wise man is not disturbed or afflicted by hot or cold, happiness or unhappiness. He no longer chooses between happiness and unhappiness. Choosing disappears from him, he attains to choicelessness. But this doesn't mean that he doesn't see or feel things. It doesn't mean that if you prick him with a needle, the wise man won't feel it. It doesn't mean that if you garland a wise man with flowers, he won't experience the fragrance, or if you throw something stinking at him, he won't notice the stench.

No, he will be aware of both the fragrance and the stench, per-haps even more so than any of you. He will be more sensitive than the average person. Because he will be more aware of existence, he will be more awake to the moment, his senses will be sharper than yours. But he knows that the fragrant and the stinking are two poles of the same reality.

If you pass by a factory where perfume is being made, you will come to know this. As a matter of fact, it is the stench that is trans-formed into perfume. We put stinking manure onto a plant and it ends up as a fragrant flower. The fragrant and the stinking are the two sides of the smell. If we like the smell, we call it fragrant; if we don't like it, we call it stinking.

It is not that the wise one, the enlightened one, doesn't feel what is beautiful and what is ugly. He feels it very clearly – but he also feels that beauty and ugliness are two sides of the form, that they are two ends of the same wave. That's why he doesn't suffer, he isn't shaken, he doesn't lose his balance, he doesn't waver.

But this has created a big misunderstanding. The misunderstanding is that one who cannot feel the difference between hot and cold has become enlightened. This is too simple. What I am talking about is arduous. If you want to become immune to heat and to cold, it is just a question of a little practice. The skin will become insensitive, and it will feel neither hot nor cold. If you keep on sitting near a stench, after a while the nerve endings in your nose will get used to it and you will stop smelling anything.

So just by sitting near a terrible stench people become *paramahansas*, great mystics! Idiots touch their feet: 'What a great mystic – he doesn't smell that stink!' But does a scavenger, a sweeper, ever smell the stink? His nerve endings have been blunted, but that doesn't mean that he has become enlightened.

Khalil Gibran has written a small story that I would like to tell you.

A village woman came to the city to sell fish. The fish were all sold. As she was returning home, a friend of hers who was now living in the city asked her to stay for the night at her house.

The friend was the wife of a gardener. She had grown a beautiful garden all around her house that was in full bloom. Now there was nothing else with which she could welcome her friend, so she picked plenty of fragrant flowers and arranged them near her friend's bed.

The fish-seller could not sleep that night. She started to toss and turn.

The gardener's wife asked, 'Can't you sleep? Is there some problem?'

The fish-seller replied, 'Yes, there is a problem. Please remove the flowers from here. And another thing, please put my empty fish basket near me and sprinkle some water on it.'

It becomes difficult to sleep in an unfamiliar house or in an unfamiliar smell. The stink of the fish had become a part of her conditioning, but that doesn't make her enlightened.

Nobody becomes enlightened because he cannot feel hot and cold or happiness and unhappiness. An enlightened person thoroughly experiences happiness and unhappiness but it doesn't disturb his equilibrium. An enlightened person sees the presence of unhappiness in happiness and the presence of happiness in unhappiness – through and through, transparently. Only then is a person enlightened.

CHAPTER 7

Death

'No presence of existence in the unreal
and no absence in the real;
both these have been seen
by the knowers of the real nature of things
in their inner world.

'Hence, that which is the whole
know it as subtle, indestructible;
no one is capable of destroying this –
the inexhaustible, the everlasting.

'These physical bodies have an ending,
but the dweller within is said to be
indestructible, incomprehensible and eternal;
hence, O Arjuna, fight.

'The one who thinks it to be the slayer,
and the one who believes it to be the slain –
both do not know.
It neither slays nor is slain.

'No presence of existence in the unreal
and no absence in the real;

both these have been seen
by the knowers of the real nature of things
in their inner world.'

WHAT IS REAL, WHAT IS UNREAL? To know the difference between the two is true wisdom, enlightenment. The greatest attainment of our lives is to be able to draw the line, to differentiate between what can be called existent and what can be called non-existent.

What is dream and what is reality? To be able to see and understand the difference between the two is the way to ultimate liberation.

In this sutra Krishna is saying: That which exists will always exist and has no possibility of becoming non-existent, is real. And that which is now, but did not exist before and has the possibility of again becoming non-existent, is unreal.

There is one point worth understanding here. Generally, we call something that does not exist unreal. But what is the point in calling a thing unreal if it doesn't even exist? It is pointless to call a non-existent thing anything. Even to say that something that doesn't exist 'is not' will be wrong because of the use of the word *is*. In saying 'It is not' we are using the word *is*, which is wrong in the context of something that does not exist. That which is not simply is not. To say anything about it is meaningless.

So *unreal, asat*, does not mean non-existent. *Unreal* means something which is not and yet in some way is, which is not and yet gives the impression that it is, which is not and yet creates the illusion that it is.

For example, you have a dream during the night. You cannot say that it doesn't exist. If it didn't exist, then how could you have had the dream? It isn't possible for the non-existent even to become a dream. You had the dream, you passed through the dream, you lived the dream; but when you get up in the morning you say it was a dream.

What you define in the morning as having been a dream cannot be called completely non-existent. It was definitely there: you saw it, you passed through it. And also it is not that it didn't have any effect on you. For example, if it was a frightening dream, you were shaken with fear. Your whole body trembled with fear, you were scared to the very core, your hair stood on end. Although you woke up out of the dream, your heart kept pounding. When you woke up you realized that it was just a dream and yet still your heart kept beating fast and your limbs were shaking.

If the dream had been a completely non-existent phenomenon, it wouldn't have had any effect on you at all. So it had an existence, but not in the same way and in the same sense as all that is seen when you are awake. In what category, therefore, will you place this dream? Existent? Non-existent? Where will you put it? It was certainly there, and yet it doesn't really exist.

The category of unreal, of *asat*, is not the same as the category of non-existent. The category of unreal is somewhere between existent and non-existent. It is a reality that appears to be real but actually isn't.

But how is one supposed to know this? – because while dreaming, one doesn't realize that what one is seeing has no existence. While you are dreaming, it feels that what you are seeing is definitely real. And another thing: it is not that you only get this feeling when you dream for the first time. You must have been dreaming your whole life, and each time when you wake up in the morning you must realize that the dream has no reality. And yet if you dream again tonight, while you are dreaming you will feel it to be real. It feels absolutely real, it appears to be absolutely real, yet when you wake up you find it is nowhere.

This appearance of being real, this deception about its existence, is what *asat*, the unreal, is.

When it is said that the world is unreal, it doesn't mean that it doesn't exist. It simply means that there is also a state of consciousness when one wakes up from even one's waking state. Normally, when we wake up from a dream and look, we find it has no existence. But when someone awakens even from the waking state, he finds that what he knew as real in the waking state also has no existence.

To wake up from our waking state is *samadhi*, enlightenment. When we wake up from what, as of now, we call our waking state, we realize that what we knew and saw as real during this state is also unreal.

Krishna is saying that whatsoever has no existence before and after, but only in the middle, is unreal. That which was not there some time ago and will not be there again after some time, which only happens to exist between two non-existences, is called unreal.

But that which does not know any non-existence – that which had an existence before, has one now, and will have one in the future; and that which exists at all three levels of sleeping, waking, and waking from waking; sleeping, waking, and samadhi – that which exists in all these states of consciousness is called real. And this reality is forever, this reality is eternal, this reality is beginningless and endless.

Those who come to know this reality become neither happy nor sad upon seeing the waves and whirlpools of the unreal arising between two non-existences, because they know that what didn't exist the moment before will also vanish the next moment. If the valleys of non-existence are on two sides and in the middle is the peak of existence, then this 'existence' is a dream, then it is *asat*, unreal. If on two sides is the infinite expanse of existence, then it is *sat*, real.

Krishna has given a valuable criterion for testing what is real. There is happiness now, it wasn't there a moment ago and it will be gone again in a moment. There is unhappiness now, it wasn't there a moment ago and it will be gone again in a moment. There is life right now, it wasn't there some time ago and it won't be there some time in the future. All that exists in the middle but not at either end only manages to create an *appearance* of its presence, because that which doesn't exist at both ends cannot exist in the middle either. It can only appear to exist.

Everything in life can be tested on this touchstone. And this is what Krishna is telling Arjuna: Test and see. Don't be mesmerized by something that was not there before and will not be there in the future. Even when you see something now, it is not actually there. It only appears to be there. It is a deception. And by the time you have woken up to this deception it will have disappeared.

It is better to pay attention to what was here before, exists now, and will be here in the future. It is possible you may not even see it, but still it exists. Start searching for it, looking for it.

In life, the search for truth begins by recognizing the false. To know the false as false, to know the unreal as unreal is the basis, the foundation, of the quest for truth. Except this, there is no other way of finding the truth.

How do we find out what truth is, what the real is? We can only begin by first knowing what is false.

Sometimes it creates confusion, because you may ask: 'How can we know what is false until we have known what is truth? As long as we have not known the truth, how can we know what is false? We can recognize the false only if we have known the truth, and we do not know the truth.' But the opposite of this can also be said, and the Sophists have been giving this opposing argument. They say: 'Until we know what is false, how will we come to know what truth is?'

It is a vicious circle, like the one about the chicken and the egg. It is like asking which came first, the chicken or the egg? If you say the hen came first, then the trouble is that there cannot be a hen unless first there was an egg. And if you say the egg came first, then the difficulty is that there cannot be an egg unless the hen lays it. But one has to start somewhere, otherwise this vicious circle will have no beginning.

But if you were to look at it carefully, the hen and the egg are not two different things – and actually that's why there *is* a vicious circle. The egg itself is a growing hen, and the hen itself is an egg in formation. They are not two separate things but two parts of the same process, the same phenomenon, the same wave. The vicious circle is born when you ask which came first. Neither of the two came first. They are simultaneous. The egg is the hen, and the hen is the egg.

This question about what is real and what is unreal is of almost the same kind. The basis of what we call 'unreal' is also in the real – because even the unreal has to appear real in order to be perceived.

In the dark, a rope is mistaken for a snake. Now, this appearance is a totally false one. When you get closer, you find it is a rope and not a snake. The rope might have seemed like a snake, but beneath this appearance it remained a rope. The existence of the rope is real. The momentary appearance of the snake – to be followed by its disappearance – was unreal. But deep down, substantially, it was the real that formed the basis for this unreal. The unreal could appear only as a reflection of the real.

Behind the wave is the ocean, behind the mortal is the immortal, behind the body is the being, and behind matter is universal consciousness. So if matter has a form, it is caused by the reflection of the universal consciousness – otherwise it cannot have a form.

You stand on the bank of a river and your reflection forms in the water below. You are certainly not that reflection, but at the same time that reflection is not possible without you either. Certainly, that reflection is not real – it is simply an image appearing in the water – and yet the real is from where the reflection is arising.

The unreal is a glimpse of the real – though only momentary. If we hold tightly onto the form that the real temporarily takes on, we will be holding onto the unreal. But if we recognize the form-less in that momentary form, the attribute-less that has shone through it, we will have caught hold of the real.

But from where we are now, it is a world of forms. From where we are now, only reflections can be seen. Our eyes are looking down in such a way that we can only see the reflection that has formed in the water and not the one who is standing on the bank and whose reflection it is. Hence we will have to start with the reflection, with the unreal. If we are in a dream, we will have to begin from the dream, and if we go on identifying the dream rightly, the dream will start disappearing.

This is very interesting and an experiment well worth trying some time. Every night, go to sleep with one reminder, and stay with this reminder until the very last moment before you fall asleep: 'If I dream during my sleep, I want to remain conscious that it is a dream.'

It will be very difficult, but it is possible. Allow sleep to keep on overtaking you and keep remembering that the moment there is a dream you want to be aware of it. In a few days it becomes possible: this remembrance penetrates your sleep. It descends into the unconscious, and when a dream comes, you are able to know that it is a dream.

But what is most interesting is that the moment you come to know that it is a dream, the dream instantly disappears. Instantly. As soon as you come to know that it is a dream, the dream disappears, ceases. To recognize a dream as a dream is to kill it. It can live only as long as it appears to be real. The basis of its remaining alive is the feeling of its being real.

You must do this experiment sometime. After you have done it, you will be able to understand Krishna's statement very clearly – why he is emphasizing so much to Arjuna that one who comes to recognize the dividing line between the real and unreal attains to true wisdom.

You may start with your dreams in the night, and then later watch your daydreams too – fully awake, remembering that what exists between two non-existent sides is a dream. And then suddenly you will find that something within you is changing. Whereas before the mind wanted to hold on to everything, now it no longer has any grip. While before the mind wanted a situation to remain the same forever, now it wants to move on from it with a smile – because trying to hold on to whatever doesn't exist on either side called 'before' and 'after' is like catching air in your fist.

The more tightly you try to enclose the air in your fist the more it slips away. If you don't try to hold it, it remains. If you try and grab it, you lose it.

The moment you come to see that what exists between two non-existent sides only *appears* to exist and is actually a dream, the hold of the unreal in your life will begin to drop away; the dream will begin to shatter. Then what is left, what remains, is real. Whatsoever you are unable to erase even when you are fully awake, whatsoever you are unable to efface even through your total awareness, whatsoever remains in spite of you, is real. It is eternal, it has no beginning and no end. One should say it is timeless.

This too needs to be understood.

The unreal will always be in the realm of time – because that which was not yesterday, is today, and will not be tomorrow is divided into three chronological parts: past, present and future. But that which was yesterday, is today, and will also be tomorrow cannot be divided into three parts. What past, present or future can be there in this context? It simply *is*. That is why there is no sense of time with the real, no concept of time. The real transcends time, is beyond time. And the unreal is within time.

As I said to you before, you are standing on a riverbank and your reflection appears in the river. You may be standing out of the river but your reflection can only appear in the river. The water is needed as a medium. Any medium that can function as a mirror, any medium that can reflect, is essential. But in order for you to exist, no reflecting medium is needed. And yes, for an image of you to be formed, a reflecting medium will be needed.

Time is this medium of reflection. The real stands on its banks and the unreal is reflected in this stream of time. The reflection that appears on the mirror of time, the stream of time, is the unreal.

And nothing can ever remain steady in time, just as nothing can remain steady in water – because water, by its very nature, is unsteady. Hence no matter how steady the reflection may look, it will always waver. Water, by its very nature, is wavering.

All these wavering reflections formed on the mirror of time were not there yesterday, are here today and will no longer be here tomorrow. Even to say 'yesterday' is too long a time. They were not there a moment ago and will be gone the next moment. So that which is changing moment to moment in this way, which is momentary, is unreal. That which is beyond the moment, that which always is, that alone is real. Krishna is saying that the person who recognizes the line of differentiation between the two attains to true wisdom.

> 'Hence, that which is the whole
> know it as subtle, indestructible;
> no one is capable of destroying this –
> the inexhaustible, the everlasting.'

That which pervades the whole universe is subtle, is indestructible. But that which fills this whole universe is gross, is destructible.

Try to understand it like this. A room is completely empty; there is not a single thing in it. Emptiness is pervading the whole room. Actually, the right thing to say will be that the emptiness existed even when there was no room there. It was only later on that we enclosed that emptiness by raising walls all around. When the room was not there, the emptiness still was. And when the room will not be there anymore, the emptiness will still be. When the room is, then too that emptiness is. The room has been built, it will be destroyed some day. Once it was not, and some day again it will not be. But that emptiness, that space, the void, the sky, was there before, is now, and will be hereafter too.

Using words like *was* or *is* is not appropriate, because to say 'is' to that which has never been non-existent is not right. To say 'is' for things that can also become non-existent is fine. It is all right to say 'the tree is' or 'the man is,' but it is not correct to say 'existence is'. To say 'existence is' in reference to existence is to make a repetition.

Existence actually means 'that which is' so there is no need to repeat it by saying 'existence is', in other words, 'that which is, is'. That's precisely what it means, and nothing else. To say 'is' for something that can never be non-existent is meaningless.

That is why a man of such great religiousness as Buddha never used the words 'the ultimate reality is'. Ignorant people took him to be an irreligious man, but Buddha felt it would be a very wrong thing to say this because *is* should only be used for something that can become non-existent too. To say 'man is' would be fine. We can use *is* for man – 'is' is a phenomenon that has happened to him. In time it will be gone. But to say 'the ultimate reality is' is not right, because *the ultimate reality* means is-ness. Using the word *is* for that which always is, is a very weak expression, is a wrong expression, is tautology.

The emptiness is always there. It was there even when the room was not. Then we placed furniture in the room, we put up wall hangings and pictures, and then we sat there. The room was decorated in all sorts of ways and is full of things. Now there are two things in the room: firstly, the emptiness that has always been there, and secondly, the filling caused by things, which were not always there.

And the most interesting thing is that we never see that emptiness, we only see the filling. In a room we see that which fills it, but not that which is empty. When you enter a room you see only the things that are there. You don't see that which has always been there. You don't see, and also it's invisible. Even if you notice the emptiness, one should say it is in reference to the fillings.

For example, here is this chair. You can see the empty space around it. You can see that there is empty space all around the chair, but you never see that there is a chair in the middle of an empty space. And the reality is that it is the chair that is placed in the middle of emptiness. The chair can be removed, not the emptiness. The emptiness can be filled up but cannot be removed.

You can remove a chair from a room because the chair is not part of the is-ness of the room, but you cannot remove emptiness from the room. At the most you can suppress the emptiness of the room by filling it up with things. If everything was removed from the room, you would say, 'There is nothing here.' You would only see the walls of the room. And if the walls were also removed, you would say, 'There is no room here at all.'

But the walls are not the room. The empty space within the four walls is the room. The English word *room* is good; it means an empty space. The very word *room* means an empty space. But we are not able to see the empty space, even the idea of an empty space doesn't occur to us because we don't have any awareness of it. Actually, the empty space has always been so much around us that we have never felt the need to see it.

It is the same as this vast sky, this space stretching out to infinity, this empty space expanding into endlessness with no boundary or limits, neither beginning nor ending anywhere.

Remember, anything that is emptiness can neither begin nor end anywhere. Only fullness caused by things can have a beginning and an end; emptiness cannot have a beginning or an end. What could the beginning and the end of the emptiness of a room be? Yes, the walls have a beginning and an end, the things in the room have a beginning and an end, but the space doesn't have any boundaries. *Sky* means that which is limitless. This infinite space that you see all around is truth, reality. And within this infinity all that appears, all that is created and withers away is untruth, unreal.

A tree comes into the world, and for some time the empty space is filled with greenery. Flowers blossom, and for a while the empty space is filled with fragrance. Then the flowers wither away, the tree topples down, and the empty space carries on being where it was. But in fact, even when the tree was there and the flowers were blossoming, there was no difference to the emptiness. It remained the same.

Things get created and destroyed. Whatsoever gets created and is destroyed is gross, is visible. Whatsoever is not created and not destroyed is subtle, incomprehensible and invisible. Even calling it 'subtle' is not right, but Krishna is helpless when he uses this word. It isn't right, but it can't be helped – there is no other choice.

Actually, when we say *subtle* we still mean it to be part of something gross. When we say *small* it means part of some larger thing. When we say *very subtle*, we mean a great deal less gross. But in the language used by man, even the subtle is related with the gross, the material. Even if we say *tinier than the tiniest*, it still has a relationship with the gross, with matter. Human language is made of dualities; it consists of pairs.

But when Krishna says *subtle, indestructible*, it is in no way part of something gross. What Krishna is calling *subtle, indestructible* is that which is not gross. It is sheer helplessness; we don't have a word for it. The closest incorrect expression that can be given is *subtle*, the least incorrect word that it can be assigned is *subtle*. There is no word for it, so we have to give it some name.

The words we have created are funny. Even if we find the word that is the most opposite of a particular word, it makes no difference, it will still be related to that particular word. For example, if we say, 'It is limitless,' we are deriving the word *limitless* from the word *limit*.

Now it is very interesting that in the word *limit* there is no sense of 'limitless' but the word *limitless* carries the sense of 'limit' in it. No matter how vast we may imagine 'the limitless' to be, what we actually imagine is, at the most, a vast, vast, faraway limit. Regardless of how much we may think, what we mean is, at the most, to keep on pushing the limit as far as possible. But our thinking cannot comprehend that there will be no limit. That is inconceivable. 'Limitless' is beyond the capacity of our thinking.

When we say, 'This room is empty,' what we mean in our minds is that the room is filled with emptiness. So we also treat emptiness like a thing, an object: 'filled with emptiness' or 'full of emptiness' – as if emptiness were a thing, while what emptiness actually means is 'where there is nothing'. But even if we say 'There is nothing,' we are still using *nothing* as a thing. The English word *nothing* is made out of *no* and *thing*. Even in saying 'nothing' you have to bring *thing* in. The point is that we cannot think without considering the thing, the gross.

So take Krishna's use of the word *subtle* as the helplessness of man. It doesn't mean some part of the gross, of the material; it doesn't mean even the tiniest part of gross. *Subtle* means that which simply isn't gross, that which has nothing to do with gross, with matter.

And what is gross? That which is visible is gross, that which can be touched is gross, that which can be heard is gross – actually whatsoever comes in the grasp of our senses is gross.

But also it is not that if tomorrow you develop a very powerful telescope or microscope and it catches something, then that thing can be called 'subtle'. No. Whatsoever can be grasped is gross. A telescope only increases the capacity of your eyes; it is doing nothing else. It is as if your eyes have become more powerful. But regardless of how profound an instrument we may develop, whatsoever comes within its range will be nothing but gross. All such instruments and mechanisms are nothing but extensions of our senses; they are additions to our senses.

For example, when a man looks through his spectacles, he sees what he couldn't see before without them, but this doesn't mean that he is now seeing something subtle. Scientists are now able to see things that are very far away, *very* far away, but those objects are still gross.

Whatsoever can be seen, whatsoever can be heard, whatsoever can be touched, whatsoever falls within the grasp of our senses is gross. *The subtle* means that which does not, cannot, and will not be made to fall within the capacity of man's senses. In fact, the subtle is that which even thoughts cannot grasp.

Until only yesterday, the atom was the subtlest thing. Now even the atom has been split into electrons, the neutron and the proton. Now the scientists say that these are the minutest, the subtlest, because they are simply beyond the range of any vision. They can only be guessed at or inferred. But even that which can be inferred is not subtle, because even inference is a part of human thought.

Hence, what the scientists are calling 'the electron' is also not what Krishna means by *subtle* by *indestructible*. Even beyond the electron… Actually it would be more correct to say: That which is always beyond, that which remains beyond, wherever and howsoever far or deep you may reach, that which is always transcendental, is the subtle.

Remaining beyond is its very characteristic: That which always remains beyond the reach of your grasp, that which always remains – and will always remain – beyond.

It will be good to understand this thoroughly. We have two words: *unknown* and *unknowable*. Ordinarily, when we try to understand *the subtle* we feel as if it is the unknown. No. Krishna is not calling this 'subtle', because that which is unknown can become known. That is not subtle. That which has the possibility of being known some time, even in infinity, is not subtle. Only the gross, only matter, can be known. It may not be known today, but it will be tomorrow – and if not tomorrow, then maybe some other time. But whatever *can* be known is gross.

Only that which can never be known, that which is always left out of knowing, that which always remains out of the grasp of knowing, is unknowable. *Subtle* is that which just can never be known. So *subtle* doesn't mean that we will be able to know it once we have better instruments.

People come and ask me: 'Will science ever be able to know godliness?'

Whatever science will come to know will not be godliness, because *godliness* means precisely that which doesn't fall within the grasp of knowing. If a scientific laboratory gets hold of godliness one day, it will turn into matter. In fact, up to the point where godliness can be grasped, it is still what is called matter. The beginning of godliness is from that point where it is impossible to grasp.

It is very important to really understand what Krishna means by *subtle*, because only the subtle is reality, truth, *sat*. Whatever can be grasped will be unreal, *asat*. It may be here today; tomorrow it will not be. Only that which cannot be grasped is real, is *sat*.

For example, you enter a room and you see a flower. The flower is fresh in the morning, but by the evening it will have withered away. Beneath the flower is a stone statue. It was there in the morning, it will be there in the evening too; but in one hundred years, two hundred years, three hundred years, or a thousand years from now, it will disintegrate.

The flower withered away in a day and the stone, being a stone, will turn into dust after thousands of years – but that makes no difference. There is only one thing in the room that will never disintegrate or fall apart, and that is the 'roominess' of the room, the emptiness that is there. That alone will never be destroyed. That alone is the subtle; that alone is the real. All the rest that is in the room will be destroyed.

I have read a story about a Taoist painter…

Once, a Taoist master asked his disciples to paint a picture for him.

The disciples asked, 'What should the theme be? What is the subject?'

The master replied, 'Paint a picture of a cow eating grass.'

The disciples showed their paintings to the master. All the paintings were good, except one painting brought by a monk that was rather startling because he had brought a blank sheet of paper.

The master asked, 'Weren't you able to paint anything?'

The disciple said: 'No. I have done a painting. You can see for yourself.'

The master looked at the paper. The other disciples also looked at the paper, and then they all looked at the man and asked, 'Where is the cow?'

He replied: 'The cow has left after eating the grass.'

They asked, 'Okay, so where is the grass?'

He replied, 'The cow ate it all.'

So they asked, 'Then what is left?'

He replied: 'I have painted that which was there before the cow was and the grass was and which remains after the cow has gone and the grass is gone.'

They all cried, 'But this is a blank paper!'

And he said, 'This is all that remains: this emptiness, this blankness!'

It is this emptiness, this blankness, that Krishna is calling 'subtle'. That which remains after the rising and falling of all the waves, that which always remains is the truth, is the real.

Osho,

Which of the two possibilities that you so often mention and explain in your talks, namely that of escaping from or waking up to, should I adopt in the context of nothingness versus every-thing-ness. How do they fit in, in this context? Won't an element of effort enter into all of this?

And what is the place of evil in total acceptability?

Shunya – zero, nothingness – and *purna* – wholeness, everything-ness – are two ways of saying the same thing from two different ends, namely the negative and the positive. When we say 'nothing-ness' we are choosing the negative way. When we say 'everything-ness' we are choosing the positive way. And the interesting thing is that only zero, nothingness, can be whole or complete, and only wholeness, completeness, everything-ness can be nothingness. Only zero can be whole or complete because there is no way a zero can be incomplete. You cannot draw an incomplete zero. You can-not divide a zero into halves and parts. No matter how much you subtract from zero, nothing gets reduced in it. No matter how much you add to zero, nothing increases in it.

Zero means nothing can be added to it or subtracted from it. *The whole* also means the same thing. *The whole* means that there is nothing left to add to it, nothing is left outside the whole that can be added to it. Nothing, no place, is left outside the whole where something that has been subtracted can be placed.

If you take away something from zero, it still remains zero. If you add something to zero, the zero remains as it is. There is no way you can subtract anything from the whole or add anything to it – because, if there is still something left to be added to the whole, it only means it was still incomplete, it was not yet whole, something could still be added to it.

Nothingness and *the whole* are two names of the same truth. We have two ways in which we can name the truth. Either we can use the negative way or the positive way. *Everything* and *nothing* are two ways of saying the same thing. It is our choice how we want to say it. If this is understood, the very foundation of a great debate that has dominated the world falls apart.

There is no dispute between Buddha and Shankara. The difference, the distance, is only about the use of negative and positive words. Buddha uses negative terms. He talks about *nothingness*, *zero*, *nirvana*. Nirvana means blowing out the lamp. Like the extinguishing of a lamp, all becomes nothing.

Shankara says all *is* – the whole, *moksha*, enlightenment *is*. He uses all positive words. And the most interesting point is that they both indicate towards one and the same thing. It is difficult to find any two persons closer to each other than Shankara and Buddha are. And yet, it is around these two persons that the biggest debate in India has arisen.

There appears to be a big difference between *yes* and *no*. You cannot find two words as opposite as these two are; but there is no difference between a total 'yes' and a total 'no'. But we can only come to see this if either of the two becomes our own experience.

I ask you to become aware, not to escape. Yes, to become aware of the whole, of everything, because escaping means we are choosing something from the whole, from the total, to leave, and something else to hold on to. This is the only way to escape. Escaping means, 'We will drop something and hold onto something else.'

If we were to drop everything then where would we escape to? If we were to accept everything then where would we escape? If renunciation is total then escaping is not possible. Where will you escape to? The place you may be escaping to will have already been renounced as part of your total renunciation. Where will you escape to: Mecca? Medina? Kashi? Haridwar? If the renunciation is total then escape is impossible. There remains no need to escape anywhere.

These are all games around something that is incomplete – games around the partial. Those who are living and experiencing half-heartedly have the possibility of holding on, and those who are renouncing half-heartedly have the possibility of giving up. But for those who live wholeheartedly, there is neither anything left to be lived nor anything left to escape from. For them there is only something to be known, to wake up to.

So the question is not of escaping, the question is of waking up. The question is of seeing, just seeing, of looking into the depths. The question is not of running away from the material – because wherever you escape to, the material will be there. The question is of looking deeply into the material so that the divine, the super-conscious can be seen in it – and then there wouldn't be any need to escape.

Where will someone who is running away from forms, from the material, go? He will end up with another set of forms. If he runs away from one place, he will end up in another place. If he runs away from one home, he will end up in another. If he runs away from one crowd of people, he will end up with some others.

Where can you escape to? Wherever you go, the world is there. You cannot run away from the world. Whatever place you reach, you will realize that the world is still there. Then you have to run away from that place, and from the next place... and in this way you will have to keep running.

Even if we were to move at the speed of the light that is coming from the moon and the stars, we would not be able to escape from the universe. No moon or star has ever succeeded in escaping; no ray of light has ever been able to escape from the universe so far. The journeys that light rays make are infinite, but still they are within the bounds of the universe. They cannot escape from it. In fact, the universe will always be there, however far they go – otherwise how can they go? Where will they find the place, the space to go to?

Awakening is possible. A wise person is one who awakens; an ignorant person escapes. Of course, an ignorant person escapes in two ways. Sometimes he runs after women, sometimes he runs away from women. Sometimes he runs towards money, sometimes he runs away from money. Sometimes he faces the world and runs, sometimes he turns his back on the world and runs. But neither can he attain the world by facing it, nor can he drop the world by turning his back on it.

That which can neither be attained nor renounced is called *samsara*, the world. Dreams can be neither attained nor renounced. The unreal can be neither attained nor renounced. One can only wake up to the unreal, to *asat*. One can only wake up to the dream. A person trying to run away from a dream is in an even deeper dream, because one who has chosen to run away from a dream is certain about one thing: that the dream is not a dream. He is finding it worth escaping from. To this extent he is still finding it real.

As you come to understand Krishna, you will see all this clearly. Krishna's whole effort is to prevent Arjuna from escaping. The whole Gita is against escapists. The whole Gita is against this act and emphasizes that the escapists are engaging in exactly the same madness as are the people who keep holding on, but from the opposite end. No madness becomes sanity just by reversing itself, just by standing upside-down on its head. Madness doesn't go away if a madman stands on his head.

Turning in the opposite direction, the indulgers become renouncers, the worldly become monks, but this makes no difference whatsoever. Yes, their direction appears to have reversed, but they remain the same. Just their mode of living has changed, but they themselves remain the same.

Krishna is saying a very unique thing in the Gita, and it is that a sannyasin and a worldly person are not opposites, are not each other's opposites. One doesn't become a sannyasin by running away from the world; one becomes a sannyasin by waking up in the world. And if you wish to wake up, then wake up here! It makes no difference at all where you escape to. There is no special place for waking up. It can be done anywhere. There is no need to see any special kind of dream in order to let go of dreams. One can wake up from any kind of dream.

One man is dreaming that he is a thief; another man is dreaming that he is virtuous. Do you think that it is easier to wake up from the dream about being virtuous than from the dream about being a thief? Both are dreams, and the phenomenon of waking up is also the same. It makes no difference. You will have to do the same thing with the saint's dream as with the thief's dream – you will have to wake up and realize that it is a dream.

Awakening means to know that a dream is a dream. And one who believes that the dream is real has only two options: either he will drown himself in the dream and indulge, or he will run away from the dream and renounce.

The Gita considers both the extremes called indulgence and renunciation to be part of the dream. There is only awakening! It is for the purpose of this awakening that Krishna is asking Arjuna to recognize what is real, *sat*, and what is unreal, *asat*. Recognize this, and this very recognition will become your awakening.

OSHO,
Would you agree to this much, that awakening is escaping from doing a headstand? At least this much effort will have to be made!

No, awakening is not connected with escaping in any way. Becoming awake has nothing whatsoever to do with running away – because in awakening there is no element of escaping at all, not even as an opposing element, not even as a race in the opposite direction. The very meaning of *awakening* is that we are eager to see that which is.

For example, take money. There are two ways of running away with it. One is latching onto the money with all one's might, making sure not a penny gets away. The other is to run away from money in such a way as to never look back at it again.

Someone was telling me that if you put money in front of the Gandhian, Vinoba Bhave, he turns his face away. Such a fear of money! It seems money has a lot of power. If someone were to place money near Ramakrishna, he would jump as if he had seen a snake or a scorpion. Seeing a snake or scorpion in money? Then the dream hasn't broken yet, the dream has only taken another form. Before, money was like heaven, now it seems like hell. But money is something – that thinking continues.

There is nothing in money as such. If there is anything in it at all, it is no more than a wave – neither worth running away from nor worth running after. Awakening is something totally different. An awakened person doesn't need to close his eyes when he sees money, but he doesn't need to hold it tightly to his chest either. The money stays wherever it is, and you remain wherever you are.

Money has never grabbed you, never run away from you. Money has never worried about you as you worry about it. It seems that money is wiser than you are! It doesn't cry when you go away, it doesn't feel happy when you come. It doesn't say: 'Welcome. How nice you came!'

Wherever one is – and everyone is somewhere or other, in one dream or another; someone is in the dream of his *ashrama*, his hermitage, someone is in the dream of his shop – waking up wherever one is, from whatsoever dream one is in, and trying to recognize if the dream is at all a reality is the meaning of awakening. Inquiring, searching: What is this that is visible to me?

No, I am not saying that from now on you should start saying, 'What I am seeing is a dream.' If you have to say, 'This is a dream,' it is not awakening, it is merely an effort. If you have to make an effort and say, 'This is all a dream,' if you have to make an effort to explain to yourself that this is all a dream, then know for certain that you have not yet come to realize that it *is* a dream.

The moment you realize it is a dream, there will be no need for you to say it is a dream. Only the person who has not yet come to recognize this repeats in his mind that it is all a dream.

Once, a Sufi fakir was brought to me.

The friend who had brought him told me, 'This fakir sees God everywhere.'

I asked the fakir, 'Do you see both God and the place?'

He said, 'I see God in each and every particle of the universe.'

I asked, 'You see both? The particle, and God in the particle? Is that how it is?'

He said, 'What kind of questions are you asking me?'

I said, 'If you are just seeing God, then you shouldn't be able to see the particle anymore. And, if you are seeing the particle, then God must be imposed on it. It must just be an outcome of your effort.'

So, a person who claims he sees God in each and every particle is actually seeing two things: he is seeing the dust particle and he is seeing God too. But both cannot be seen simultaneously. Of the two, only one can be seen at a time. If God is seen, then one cannot see the particle – because once God is seen then there is no space left for the particle to be seen. And if one sees the particle then God cannot be seen – because as long as the particle is seen, it is very difficult for God to be seen.

So I said to the fakir, 'You must have made an effort, you must have convinced yourself that it is written in the books that God exists in each and every particle.'

'No,' he said, 'I have been seeing God for years.'

I said, 'And before this you must have been making efforts and rehearsals to see God. Anyway, stay here with me, and for few days don't make any effort to see God.'

Next morning he came to me and said, 'You have ruined everything! Thirty years of spiritual discipline have gone down the drain! Since last night, as soon as I stopped making an effort, I have started seeing trees as trees. Now I don't see God.'

So I said, 'Something that you have been seeing for thirty years disappears as soon as you stop making an effort to see it for a few hours! Then it is certain that you were only projecting a dream of your own onto the trees. It has nothing to do with God; you were only saying that God is in the trees.'

If you go on suggesting things to yourself, you will start seeing them.

But Krishna is not talking about such godliness. You don't have to project it onto the world around you; you simply have to wake up to the world itself. And the moment you become awake, the world disappears, only godliness remains.

You don't have to convince yourself about a dream that it is false. No you just have to see the dream clearly for what it is. And the moment you see what it is, suddenly the dream breaks and vanishes. Then what is left is the truth.

Our efforts are needed for the untruth, but not for the truth, because truth that has to be attained by human efforts cannot be the truth. The truth that is already present without man's effort, that alone is truth. You don't have to create truth; it is not your construction. Truth already *is*. Just kindly don't construct the false, and you will see that which is.

For example, I pull the branch of a tree towards me. Then I ask you: 'I have pulled this branch towards me. Now I want to put this branch back in its original position. What should I do?' Do you think you will tell me to do something? You will simply say, 'Please stop pulling it. Just let it go and the branch will return to its original position all by itself. The branch was already in its original place; it was just displaced because of your kind efforts!'

Man doesn't need to make any effort to attain to godliness. If he can just stop the effort that he has already been making to lose it, then he will immediately reach the original space where he belongs – the space of godliness.

Dreams are our creation. Truth is not our creation.

That is why when Buddha attained to enlightenment and people asked him, 'What have you attained?' he said, 'I have not attained anything. I have only lost something.'

People became very puzzled. They said, 'We thought you have attained something!'

Buddha replied, 'I did not attain anything, I have only remembered that which was already there. Of course, I have lost something. I had to lose all that I had created, constructed. I lost my ignorance, but I didn't attain wisdom, because wisdom was already the case. I was unable to see it because I was holding on tightly to the ignorance. I have certainly lost something, but I have attained nothing. I have attained that which I already had, which I have always had.'

If you understand this rightly, the only thing needed is to look with wakeful eyes. It is simply a matter of looking with open eyes, with your intelligence fully alert, and with full awareness bringing your consciousness to a total awakening to see what is. And the moment we see what is, in this very act, that which is not drops away and that which really is remains.

> 'These physical bodies have an ending,
> but the dweller within is said to be
> indestructible, incomprehensible and eternal;
> hence, O Arjuna, fight.'

To Arjuna, the impending war appears to be very real, the physical body appears to be very real, death appears to be very real – so his difficulty is natural. Arjuna's difficulty is the difficulty of us all: what appears real to us is exactly what appears real to Arjuna.

And Krishna is talking to him about a totally different world. He is saying: 'This body, these people with physical bodies, this whole network that you see all around is all a dream. Don't be bothered about it. Just fight.'

Krishna's exhortation for war has always been a cause of discomfort to the so-called religious people, and beyond their understanding. This is because on the one hand, there are people who preach avoiding stepping on even an ant and only drinking strained water to avoid tiny microbes getting killed as non-violence; and here on the other hand is Krishna saying to Arjuna: 'Fight, because no one really dies or is killed. The physical body is just a dream.'

Generally speaking, it appears that Arjuna is right. Gandhi would have liked Krishna to agree with Arjuna; the pacifists would have liked Krishna not to have had his way, and for Arjuna to have succeeded instead. But Krishna is saying something very unusual. He is saying, 'You are feeling sad about what is only a dream. You are saddened and troubled about something which is unreal, which doesn't exist.' Obviously this is going far beyond the norms of common morality.

That is why, when the translations of the Gita reached the West for the first time, the moralists there were very shaken up. They couldn't believe that Krishna could have said such a thing. Those who had only read the ten commandments of the Bible in the name of religion, those who had only read: 'Do not steal, do not bear false witness, do not cause pain to anybody.' No wonder they were shaken up! It was very shocking to find Krishna saying, 'This is all a dream. Go ahead, Arjuna, and fight!'

So the Western moralists thought that the Gita couldn't be a moral book. 'Either it is immoral or it is amoral. It is not moral, that's for sure. What type of teaching is this?'

And this not only happened in the West. Jaina thinkers also condemned Krishna to hell. They wondered, 'What is this man saying? Total permission to kill? If Arjuna could have had his way perhaps there wouldn't have been any Mahabharata. It was Krishna who caused it.' The current of non-violence that has been prevalent in India also felt the necessity of throwing Krishna into hell. 'This man must be dumped in hell!'

This is a vital issue and needs careful consideration. What must be kept in mind is that morality is not religion. Morality is a very functional arrangement. Morality is purely a social phenomenon. Morality is some systematization in the thick of our dreams. Even in dreams, if you have to walk you will need some rules to go by. Even for living in dreams, you will need to have a system, some discipline, some cultured and ethical behavior.

Morality is not religion; morality is purely a social arrangement. That is why morality can change every day. As society changes so does its morality. What was right yesterday may become wrong today. What is right today may become wrong tomorrow. Morality is also part of the unreal, of *asat*.

But this doesn't mean that religion is immorality. When even morality is part of the unreal, then immorality is bound to be part of the unreal. Religion transcends both morality and immorality. Actually, religion transcends the world. Hence the level that Krishna's assertions are coming from is very rare, and they have hardly ever been understood from the same level as they are being said.

Throwing Krishna into hell was the Jainas way of getting rid of him. Gandhi declared that the Gita was a metaphor. He said this war never actually happened: How could Krishna cause a war? It is not a story about an actual war, it is only a symbolic story, a metaphor about the war that goes on forever between good and evil. This was another trick – more effective, but the intention was the same – to get rid of Krishna. The implication was that the event never took place.

How can Krishna cause a war? How can Krishna say, 'Go and fight'? No, Krishna can never say such a thing! So here is another cunning way of getting rid of Krishna, and that is to say that the war is a metaphor, that it is just symbolic, that it is an allegorical story, that such an event never actually took place; that such a war which may have been incited by someone never actually happened. 'All these characters are symbolic. Arjuna and Duryodhana, all of them, are not real historical figures. The Mahabharata is only a parable, a symbolic tale in which the fight is going on between good and evil, and Krishna is asking Arjuna to fight against evil.'

Now this is distorting Krishna completely. Krishna is not asking Arjuna to fight against evil. If you really understand Krishna, he is saying that good and evil are both part of the same dream; violence and non-violence are both part of the same dream. Krishna is not saying that violence is good. All he is saying is that both violence and non-violence are dreams; one is a bad person's dream and the other is a good person's dream, but dreams they are, and the person who comes to know the entire dream as a dream attains to reality, to *sat*. This statement transcends morality. This statement is not immoral. This statement transcends immorality too.

In this respect it becomes very difficult to understand Krishna's message. Choosing seems to be easy: this is bad, that is good. But good and bad are both dreams so here we lose all ground. Only someone who can keep his feet steady at this point can enter further into the Gita.

So make sure you understand this clearly: Krishna is neither a violent nor a nonviolent person – because the violent person believes he can kill, and the non-violent person believes he is saving someone from being killed. Krishna says since one cannot be killed, the idea of saving is out of the question. You can neither kill anyone nor save anyone from being killed. That which is, is, and that which is not, is not. So both the savior and the killer are simply dreaming opposite dreams.

For example, a man stabs someone and he thinks he has finished that person off for good. And another person who takes the knife out of the victim's chest in time and heals him with medication and bandages thinks he has saved that person from being killed. But both of these men are simply in opposite dreams: one is a bad man's dream and the other is a good man's dream. And if people choose to go on dreaming then we would prefer it that more people have the good man's dream.

Krishna is saying that both are dreams. There is yet another level of seeing from where both the savior and the killer are indulging in the same fallacy. The fallacy is this belief that that which is can be destroyed or can be saved. Krishna is saying: That which is not, is not. That which is, is. Krishna is not urging you to see the bad man's dream. He is saying that both are dreams. And if you have to pass through the dream, then pass through the entire dream so that you can wake up. If you have to go through the dream then don't choose between a bad man's dream and a good man's dream, just pass through the entire dream in its totality and wake up.

It is difficult to say how Arjuna will be able to understand this process of awareness that Krishna is trying to explain to him. Arjuna is talking of highly moralistic things and he is very eager to have a moral dream. He seems to be fed up with immoral dreams. Now he is eager to see a moral dream. And Krishna is telling him that he is still only choosing between two dreams, that he has to wake up from the entire dream.

Let us read one more sutra for now.

'The one who thinks it to be the slayer,
and the one who believes it to be the slain –
both do not know.
It neither slays nor is slain.'

That which *is* neither dies nor can be killed. That which *is* within us is called *atma*, the being, and that which *is* outside us is called *paramatma*, the universal being, the universal consciousness. That which can be killed, can kill or feels that it has been killed, within us is called 'the body' and outside us is called 'the world'. That which is immortal is consciousness, and that which is mortal is matter. The mortal, the unreal, is the wave, and the immortal, the real, is the ocean.

Arjuna's concern, his dilemma, his anguish is: 'How can I get involved in this killing? Better I myself die.' Both these ideas will exist together. One who can think in terms of the other dying can also think of dying himself. One who thinks death is possible will obviously be saddened. But Krishna is saying death is the only impossibility: Death simply cannot happen, death is impossible.

But from where we are living our lives, nothing is more certain than death. Everything else may happen, may not happen, but death alone remains the absolute certainty. Only one thing is certain and that is death. Nothing else is certain, all other changes are possible: someone will be happy, someone will be sad; someone will be healthy, someone will be sick; someone will be successful, someone a failure; someone will be a pauper, someone else an emperor. As far as everything else is concerned all options are open – they may happen, they may not.

Only one option is closed to us: the option of dying or not. It is bound to happen. Everyone will arrive at that place. The emperor will arrive there, the beggar will arrive there, the successful person will arrive there, the unsuccessful person will arrive there, the healthy person will arrive there, the sick person will arrive there. One thing is certain in life as we know it and that is death.

And Krishna is saying just the opposite. He is saying that only one thing is certain, and that is that death is an impossibility. No one has ever died, nor can anyone ever die. Death is the only fiction.

Perhaps all our perspectives on life form around death. Someone who sees death as real proves that in his life there has been no experience deeper than that of the body. Now this is very interesting, because you don't have any experience of death. You have only seen other people dying; you have never seen yourself dying.

Suppose we manage to raise a person who has never seen death, who has never seen anyone dying. Just imagine that a child who has never seen death is brought up. Now will this person ever think that he will die? Will he ever be able even to imagine that he will die one day? It is impossible.

Death is an inference that we draw from seeing other people die. And the interesting thing is that when you see another person die, you aren't actually seeing death, because for you in this situation, the phenomenon of death is simply this much: this person was talking before and now he doesn't, this person was walking before and now he doesn't. You are only seeing a person who used to walk passing into a non-walking state, a person who used to talk passing into a non-talking state, a heart that used to beat passing into a non-beating state. But is all of this sufficient to make you say that what was within the person has died? Is it sufficient? Is this enough? Is this enough to arrive at this conclusion and to call it death? No, it is not enough.

Some years ago there used to be a yogi in South India called Brahmayogi. He demonstrated an experiment in dying at three universities – Oxford, Calcutta and Rangoon. It was a highly valuable experiment. He used to die for ten minutes.

When he demonstrated it at Oxford University, there were doctors present. He said to them, 'Over the next ten minutes, please examine me and then write down on your certificate whether I am alive or dead.' Then he stopped breathing, his pulse stopped, his heart stopped beating, and all symptoms of blood circulation ceased. The ten doctors – all from the medical faculty at Oxford University – wrote him a death certificate saying, 'This man is dead. This man has all the symptoms of a dead person,' and all the ten doctors signed the certificate.

But after ten minutes Brahmayogi came back to life again. His breathing resumed, his heart started beating again, the blood started circulating and the pulse came back. And then he asked the doctors to write another certificate saying what they thought about him now. The doctors said, 'We are in great difficulty. We hope you are not planning to file a lawsuit against us in the court! We have only said what medical science could say... .'

Brahmayogi said, 'Say in writing that any death certificates you may have issued up until now have all become suspect.'

Actually, what we call death is nothing but life slipping out of the body. Just as the rays of a lamp slowly fade away, so the manifestation of life returns to the seed form and takes off on another new journey. But from the outside, this fading away of life is what we believe to be death.

It is as though an electric light was on, you pressed the switch, and the rays disappeared. Now all that surrounds the bulb is darkness. Did the electricity die? No, only its manifestation stopped. We press the switch again and the rays of light once more begin to flow. Did the electricity come back to life? To say something that has not died in the first place has resurrected is meaningless. The electricity was present all along, only its manifestation had ceased.

So what we call 'death' is only the manifest returning again to the un-manifest, and what we call 'birth' is a re-manifestation of the un-manifest.

Krishna is saying that the being neither dies when the body is killed nor is saved when the body is saved. The being neither dies nor is saved. In fact, the being is only that which is beyond dying and beyond being saved.

CHAPTER 8

The Dewdrop and the Ocean

'O Arjuna, he who knows it to be
indestructible, eternal, unborn and everlasting,
how and whom can such a person slay?
And how and by whom can he be slain?

'Just as man discards his old and worn-out garments
and replaces them with new,
so the being discards the old and worn-out body
and moves on to the new.'

OSHO,
'The one who thinks it to be the slayer, and the one who believes it
to be the slain – both do not know. It neither slays nor is slain.'
In the context of the discussion about this verse, if indeed the
being neither slays nor can be slain, then General Dyer's acts in
India and the Nazis' concentration camps can be justified.
Where do these events stand as far as total acceptability is
concerned?

No ONE EVER DIES and no one ever kills. That which is has no possibility of ever being destroyed. Is one therefore to deduce from this that there is nothing wrong in committing violence? Does this mean that the violence committed by General Dyer or the genocide that took place in Auschwitz, Germany, or the total violence that happened in Hiroshima are not condemnable? Are they worthy of acceptance?

No. This is not what Krishna means, and this is worth understanding.

Just because no one is ever really killed doesn't mean that the desire to kill is not bad. Death is not there, but the desire for violence, the motivation for violence, the violent state of mind is there. One who has a desire for violence, one who takes an interest in killing, one who feels happy killing another person, one who takes the credit for killing someone – even though no one ever actually dies, the idea that he killed someone, his taking pleasure in killing, his mental belief that killing is possible – all of this is evil, sinful.

The sin is not in the occurrence of violence. The sin is in the act of committing violence. The occurrence of violence is impossible, but the act of violence is possible.

When a person is committing an act of violence, two things are involved: Krishna says that the occurrence of violence is impossible, but a psychological state of violence is possible.

Let us also consider this from the opposite end. Does this imply that there is no meaning in Mahavira's and Buddha's non-violence? If the violence that took place in Hiroshima and in the Auschwitz concentration camps has no relevance, then does Mahavira's and Buddha's non-violence also lose all meaning? Yes, if you think that the only purpose of non-violence is to save someone from dying and being destroyed, then it has no meaning.

But no, Mahavira's and Buddha's non-violence has a different meaning. This desire, this intent to save and protect, this desire and intent not to kill, this state of having no interest in killing, this mental state of feeling joy in protecting.... For example, when

Mahavira is walking, making sure that not even an ant is killed under his feet, it doesn't mean that the ant was saved because of Mahavira's efforts. That which is going to survive in the ant has already survived forever, and that which is not going to survive cannot be saved by Mahavira either. But this feeling in Mahavira to avoid killing is of great value. This feeling does not cause any particular benefit or loss to the ant, but it certainly does to Mahavira.

Deep down what matters is how one feels, not what happens. Deep down the question is of the feeling, of what the person thinks, because a person lives surrounded in his thoughts. Events take place in reality but the person lives in his thoughts, in his feelings.

Violence or killing is evil. It is evil despite Krishna saying that it doesn't actually take place. And Krishna's statement is not at all wrong. In fact, Krishna is speaking from an existential state; he has discovered this in the layers of existence itself.

When Hitler is killing people, he is not in the same state of mind as Krishna is. Hitler enjoys killing; he delights in destroying, in exterminating. Whether anything actually gets destroyed or not is a different matter, but Hitler has a passion for killing. This passion for killing is violence.

Understood rightly, the passion to destroy, the desire to kill, is violence. Whether death actually occurs or not is altogether a separate issue. And this passion in Hitler to kill is the passion of a sick mind.

It is important to understand that if someone feels an interest in killing and destruction, that person is insane inside. The more silent and blissful a person is inside, the more impossible it will be for him to be interested in destruction. The more blissful a person is inside, the more he will be interested in creativity.

Mahavira's non-violence is a creative feeling, a creative feeling towards the world. Hitler's violence is a destructive feeling, a destructive feeling towards the world. So the feeling is important. But from where we are living, what actually happens existentially is not valuable yet.

Let me try to explain this to you through a small anecdote...

Many of Kabir's devotees used to visit his place. They would sing hymns and songs in praise of the divine, and just as they were getting ready to leave, Kabir would invite them to have a meal. This created a lot of trouble for Kabir's wife and son.

Finally, one day his son said to him, 'This is going too far! How long can we go on borrowing money and supplies? How can we go on feeding people like this? Please stop asking people to stay for a meal.'

Kabir said: 'I completely forget; when guests come to visit, I completely forget that we have nothing in the house to feed them with. But at a time like this, when guests have come, how can one bother about whether there is anything in the house or not? So I go on urging them not to leave without having a meal.'

Angrily and sarcastically the son retorted, 'So should we start stealing now?'

Kabir said, 'That is a great idea! Why didn't you think of it before?'

The son couldn't believe his ears. He never expected Kabir to say such a thing.

But the son was not an ordinary son – after all he was Kabir's son. So he said, 'So shall I go and steal tonight?'

Kabir said, 'Absolutely!'

Testing Kabir even further the son asked, 'Will you join me?' And Kabir said, 'Of course!'

That night, the son said to Kabir, 'Let's go!' He wanted to take the whole matter to its logical conclusion; he wanted to see if Kabir would really be ready to steal.

Kabir ready to steal? It was simply beyond the son's comprehension. And similarly it is beyond Arjuna's comprehension: Krishna ready to kill?

Kamaal, Kabir's son, took Kabir along with him. He started breaking into a house, and as he was doing so he kept looking around.

Kabir asked, 'Why are you so nervous? Why are you so shaky?'

The son finally managed to break through the wall, and he asked Kabir, 'Shall I enter now?' And Kabir said, 'Of course. Go ahead!' The son entered and pulled out a sack full of wheat. He thought Kabir would stop him any minute. It was really too much.

But Kabir helped him to pull the sack all the way out of the house, and then he said to his son, 'Now go inside to where the people are sleeping. Inform them that their house has been broken into, and that we are taking away a whole sack of wheat away with us.'

The son said, 'But what kind of stealing is this? Does one ever disclose the act of stealing?'

Kabir said, 'Stealing that cannot be disclosed is a sin. So go ahead and inform them!'

The son said, 'All this time I was wondering, and it really kept bothering me, how you could allow me to steal.'

Kabir replied, 'I was completely oblivious to it, because since I have come to realize that all is one, I haven't seen anything as mine or as belonging to anyone else. So if this belongs to another, then of course stealing is a sin. But I didn't remember that what we are taking is not ours. I am glad you reminded me. Why didn't you tell me this before?'

Kabir is saying that as long as something belongs to the other, then stealing is a sin. But if nothing belongs to anyone in particular, if everything belongs to the whole, and if the air the other is breathing is as much mine as the air that I am breathing, then in this respect, on this level, it is meaningless to call stealing a sin.

But Kabir is talking about this from an existential level. This is being said by one who has entered the ultimate state of enlightenment.

So Kabir said, 'If you are unable to wake these people up, then return this sack of wheat – because if you are afraid of informing about something to those who are none other than your own self, then the thing in question is certainly not yours. Then it is better to go and put it back. After all, whom are we really trying to hide this stealing from?'

248 · INNER WAR AND PEACE

Now this has become a matter of two totally different levels, two totally different worlds. Make sure you understand this well. One is the existential world, where everything belongs to the whole, to existence, where stealing is impossible. Kabir is living in this world. The second is the world of our minds where the other is 'the other' and I am 'I'; where my thing is 'mine' and what belongs to the other is 'the other's'. At this level, stealing is possible; it is happening, it can happen.

As long as a thing that belongs to the other person is 'the other's', stealing is sin. In reality, stealing never occurs; only objects are moved from one location to another. How can the phenomenon of stealing ever happen on this earth? Neither you nor I will be alive in the future; neither will my possessions remain as mine, nor will your possessions remain as yours. Just the objects will remain here. What difference does it make whether they remain in this house or that one?

Stealing doesn't happen at the existential level. Stealing occurs at the psychological level, at the level of our feelings and emotions.

If Hitler had been capable of saying that there is no violence in killing, that there is no death, then there would have been no need for him to have bodyguards all around him. And if that had been the case, then he could have gone ahead and killed the people in Auschwitz. I would have no objections. But a person like Hitler, who is anxious to save himself and who is eager to kill the other, believes very deeply that one *does* get killed. After all, he is doing everything to save *his* life.

If Krishna were to say to Arjuna: 'These people on the battlefield cannot die, so go ahead and kill them… but please protect yourself, guard yourself lest you die at someone else's hand,' then that would be dishonest. But Krishna is telling him that neither does anyone kill, nor is anyone killed: 'If these people kill you, then nothing will die. If you kill these people, then nothing will die.' We have to remember that what Krishna is saying here is deeply existential.

Violence took place in Hiroshima because those responsible for dropping the bomb did so to kill people. Hitler committed violence because he was driven by the notion of killing people. Whether someone actually dies or not is of course a very different matter – and Hitler has no understanding whatsoever about this.

But as long as someone is keen on saving himself, he cannot be allowed to put forward a doctrine as a rationalization for killing others. As long as a person is saying, 'This belongs to me, let no one steal it,' and at the same time is going and stealing from someone else's house, it will not be the same as Kabir's stealing from a house. Kabir's stealing is not stealing at all; Krishna's violence is not violence at all.

So your question is right. If by listening to Krishna's Gita, to Krishna's message, someone reaches the conclusion that killing someone isn't killing at all – that it is all a fiction – then he can have this understanding, but with this one condition: that as a part of this understanding his *own* death is also not a death at all. Then there will be no problem. But in saving oneself and killing the other... the interesting thing is: we kill others precisely to save ourselves. So if this is the case, it is better one forgets all about Krishna.

Harm has been done. This country uncovered some very deep truths of life, but because of their misuse it has also met with its greatest downfalls. Actually, when very profound truths fall into the hands of cunning people, they prove to be more harmful than lies. This country has uncovered such profound truths that they cannot be used unless they are experienced in their entirety; a partial use of them is not possible.

This country knew very well that all behavior is illusory, is *maya*, is nothing but the stuff of dreams. So it thought if this is the case, then what can be wrong in being dishonest? If, after five thousand years of perpetual search and reflection this country is the most dishonest on this earth, then there is a reason for it. If, after talking about such great things, we show ourselves to be just the opposite in our everyday lives, there is a reason for it. And the reason is that we don't rise to the level of our words. On the contrary, we pull those truths down to our level.

If Arjuna rises up to Krishna's level, then that is fine; but if he pulls Krishna down to his level, then that is going to be harmful. And it often happens that because it feels very difficult to rise to Krishna's level, we pull Krishna down to our own level. Then we are at ease. Then we can conveniently say, 'Everything is just *maya*, illusion,' and are thus able to be dishonest and cunning around it. And the interesting thing is, how can a person who is able to recognize everything as maya, illusion, still have an interest in self-deceptive behavior?

A friend came and said, 'Since I have started meditating, I have become very simple-hearted. A man deceived me and stole my bag. Although I know very well that everything is just *maya*, illusion, this man deceived me; he took away my bag! Should I continue to meditate or not?' And he keeps repeating, 'Although it is all maya…'.

I said, ' "Although it is all maya…" Then why are you so disturbed by losing your bag? "Although it is all maya…" So in what way then did that man deceive you? And "although it is all maya…" So who is stealing whose bag anyway?'

'No!' he said, 'All *is* maya, but what I have come to ask is, if I go on becoming simple-hearted like this, then everyone will start deceiving and cheating me!'

Now these are statements at two different levels. He doesn't see the point that he has heard 'it is all maya' from Krishna, but his reality, where he is standing, is at the point of 'my bag has been stolen'.

Krishna's statement has been made from a certain peak, but from where we are standing things are totally different.

The interpretations that we have made of these high principles and imposed on our lives are the cause of the decline of this country, are the cause of the moral decay of this country and the darkness and ugliness that has filled the life of this country.

So your question is right.

Krishna is not saying, 'Go ahead and start killing people.' What he is saying is: if it becomes your own experience that no one ever dies and no one is ever killed, then, and only then, can you let whatever happens, happen.

But this is a double-pointed arrow. It is not that when it concerns the other's death you go ahead and kill, because 'no one ever dies', but when it concerns your own death you scream and beg not to be killed! But this is what has happened.

We in India are the strongest believers in the immortality of the being, and yet on the whole of this earth, we are the people who are the most afraid of dying. No other people are as afraid of death as we are. Even those whom we call materialists – who do not believe in universal consciousness, who do not believe in the individual being – are not as afraid of death as we are. Even they say, 'It's okay. If the need arises, we will not hesitate to stake our lives.'

But we in this country have remained slaves for a thousand years because we did not have the courage to stake our lives. Of course, sitting in our homes we talk about the immortality of the being. But if the being is really immortal, then this country could not have been enslaved for even a second.

The being is certainly immortal, but we are dishonest. The being is immortal – we are happy to hear this from Krishna – but we know very well that we will die, and we go on protecting ourselves. In fact, every day we chant the words that the being is immortal simply to convince ourselves that we are not going to die. 'I will not die' is the reassurance we are trying to give to ourselves, is the consolation that we are trying to impart to ourselves.

So make sure you understand the disparity, the gap between these two levels well – the level at which Krishna is and the level where you are.

And what Krishna is saying can only be fully meaningful if you rise to Krishna's level. Please don't pull Krishna down to your level – although that is what is easier for you to do – because now he can't do anything to prevent it. You can drag the Gita down to any level you want. Wheresoever you may be living – in your cage, in your basement, in your hell – drag the Gita there and it will oblige.

Kindly don't drag the highest truths of life into the darkest caves of your life. These ultimate truths of life have been realized at the highest peaks. You must also ascend those peaks. Only then will you understand them. These ultimate truths are simply calls and provocations for you to come to those heights where there is nothing but light, where there is nothing but consciousness, where there is nothing but immortality.

But hearing from the dark alleys that you inhabit – where there is nothing but darkness, where not a single ray of light ever seems to reach – that only abundant light exists and that darkness has no existence whatsoever, please don't put out the tiny lamp that you have with you. Don't blow it out, thinking, 'If there is only light all around, what is the need for this lamp?' The alley will get even darker without it.

Where man dwells, there is a distinction between violence and non-violence, and so there is darkness there. Where man dwells, there is a distinction between stealing and non-stealing, so there is darkness there. Hearing Krishna's statements from that place of darkness, do not blow out your tiny lamp of discrimination, otherwise nothing else will happen except the darkness will have deepened.

Yes, listening to Krishna simply understand this much: there is a peak of consciousness where there is no darkness at all and where it would be foolish to light a lamp. But one has to travel to that peak. We will be slowly moving on this journey to the peak, discovering how we can reach there – where life is eternal, where talking of violence and non-violence is childish.

But this is not the case where we are living right now. Here, violence and non-violence are very significant, highly relevant.

'It is never born and never dies,
it has no past, no present, no future;
it is unborn, everlasting, eternal, and ageless –
the indestructible in the destructible body.'

From where we exist, and given how and what we are, there everything is born. Nothing is without birth within the sphere of our knowledge. Whatever we have seen, whatever we have come across, has been born and dies. But there has to be something that is never born that makes this process of birth and death possible. There has to be something, some thread, running through this chain of birth and death – like the thread that runs through the beads of a necklace. You see the beads but you don't see the thread that holds them together. In the same way, in order to hold together the long necklace of births and deaths, there has to be some eternal thread that is never born and never dies.

Without the thread, the individual beads, the individual parts, will fall apart. They cannot stay connected, they cannot stay together, there cannot be any link between them. Although the necklace looks as if it is just one piece, it is not. The parts are just resting together on this thread that is running through them all.

There is birth, there is death. There is coming and there is going. There is continuous change... but behind all of this, the unborn and the undying – a thread that is never born and never dies – is a must. That thread is existence, that thread is being, that thread is universal being. Behind all change, behind all forms, the formless is needed. Without the formless, the forms will not be sustained.

For example, you are watching a movie at the cinema. The pictures on the film are continuously changing, every moment. There is nothing much in the picture – it is just a network of rays, a combination of light and shade – but you need a screen behind it. As long as the film is running you don't notice the screen at all. And it *shouldn't* be noticed, because if the screen becomes noticeable, the film will not be seen. As long as the film is running and the forms appear and disappear, the unmoving screen remains invisible.

But if you remove the screen, these forms cannot manifest, these images will have no place upon which to manifest. In this moving play of changing images, a steady screen is needed to hold them all together. As the first image appears, the screen will remain the same. As the second image appears, the screen will still remain the same. As the third image appears, the screen will remain the same again. The images keep changing but the screen remains the same. Only then will there be a relevance, a continuity, a relationship between the images. That relationship is made possible by the unchanging screen in the background.

The whole of our lives is a vista of images. These images cannot last forever. Birth is an image and so is death. Youth, old age; happiness, unhappiness; beauty, ugliness; success, failure - they are all a flow of images. Something is needed to sustain this flow, something that will not be visible. There is no way it can become visible. As long as you are watching the images, it cannot be seen.

That which remains in the background, like a screen, is existence. Krishna says: It is unborn; it is never born and never dies. But don't ever make the mistake of believing that this is being said about you. You are born and you die – and you have no knowledge of the 'you' that all this is being said about.

The 'you' that you know is born. It has a date of birth, and it will have a date of death too. The dates of your birth and death will be put on your gravestone. When you were born, people celebrated with a band, with music. When you die, they will weep and be sad. Whatsoever you know about yourself is nothing but a collection of images.

It would also be useful to understand whether the person you know as 'yourself' is only a collection of images from a scientific point of view as well. Now people can be brainwashed; now there are scientific ways to erase your memory completely.

For example, take a fifty-year-old man. He knows he has four sons, a wife, a house; that his name is such-and-such, that his ancestors are so-and-so. He has worked in such-and-such a position. This entire story of fifty years can be washed out of his brain. His brain can be cleaned out completely – and yet he will continue to exist. But if this is the case, he won't even be able to tell you his name or how many sons he has.

I have a friend who is a doctor. Once he fell from a train. He was injured and he lost his memory. He had been my childhood friend, we went to school together, so I went to see him in the village where he was living.

I sat in front of him, and he looked at me as if I were not there. I asked him, 'Don't you recognize me?'

He said, 'Who are you?' His father had told me that ever since he had fallen from the train and been injured, he had lost all his memory; he didn't remember a thing.

That man had no past. All images had disappeared. Until the day before, he had been saying, 'I am such-and-such, my name is such-and-such.' All those images were no longer there. That film had been completely erased; everything had been washed away. Now, he was like a blank sheet of paper. Now something new would be written on this blank paper. New memory had started being recorded.

Recently, when I saw him again, he said: 'You may recall that three years ago I fell and was injured.' Now the memory of his last three years has begun building up. But what he was before that has all gone. If someone reminds him that he used to be a doctor before, he says, 'That's what you say, but I know nothing about it. My past came to an end when I was in that accident.'

In times to come, there will be no need to kill any political enemies. What greater murder can there be than to brainwash a person? Just get hold of the opponent and clean his memory; just wash away that person's memory using electric shocks, chemicals and some other psychological processes – and what is left of him? The matter is over. For example, if you were to clean all that is in Karl Marx's brain, the whole of *Das Kapital* would be wiped away and he would have no identity left behind either.

So, that which we call 'I' – the one who was born, who is someone's son, somebody's father, somebody's husband – all of this is nothing but a collection of photographs, an album. Everyone is holding onto his album and going back to it and looking at it again and again... and also showing it to others, to visitors. But the reality is: You are not all of this.

If you think that it is this album that Krishna is calling unborn, eternal, you are mistaken. This is not unborn. This has a birth, and this will die too. That which is born will certainly die. If birth is one end, then death is the other, inevitable end. You are bound to die.

If you can understand this rightly then perhaps you will also succeed in discovering that which never dies. But we keep holding onto this 'I' which was born. This 'I' is not your true self. It is only a collection of images that you have lived through and gathered on your deeper self. Hence, in Japan, when a seeker goes to a Zen master and asks him what kind of spiritual discipline he should follow, the master tells him to go and find his original face that he had before his birth.

How can there be a face before one is born? Imagine someone asking you to find your face that will be there after your death, or to find your face that was there before your birth! But the Zen masters are right. They are saying the same thing that Krishna is saying. They are saying: find out that in you which was never born.

If you can find such a thread, something that was there before your birth, then be assured that it will remain after your death as well. Death will not be able to wipe out that which was there before your birth. That which existed before your birth will continue to exist even after your death. And that which has simply happened after birth will only accompany you until death, and not beyond it.

So when Krishna says there is something unborn which has no birth and no death, which cannot be pierced by any weapon... you and I can be slain, so remember, Krishna is not talking about that which can be slain. He is talking about that which cannot be pierced by a weapon or burned with fire, or drowned in water. We can certainly be pierced, burned or drowned – there is no problem about that.

The discussion here is not about anything that can be drowned in water, burned in fire, or cut with weapons. The discussion here is not about that which a surgeon or a doctor can work upon. A doctor is involved with the mortal. What a surgeon is working on, what is being investigated in a laboratory, is the mortal. Krishna's statement is not in reference to this.

So if a scientist thinks that some day he will be able to catch hold of what Krishna calls the unborn, the immortal, on the table in his laboratory, he is mistaken. He will never be able to catch hold of it. All his superfine instruments can only catch that which can be pierced, cut. But if that which cannot be cut were to become visible, and it certainly does become visible, it can become visible.

When Alexander the Great was leaving India, his friends reminded him that the Greek philosophers had asked him to bring them a sannyasin from here. Now the reality is that the sannyasin is India's contribution to the world – the only contribution, but that is enough. Even if all the rest of the world's contributions were put together and we had given the world just one sannyasin, there would be a balance. And the day that all these contributions from the rest of the world prove to be meaningless, only the sannyasin that we have contributed is going to prove meaningful for the world.

So these friends reminded Alexander about taking a sannyasin with him: 'We have seized much wealth, but there is plenty of wealth at home. We are returning with many precious things, diamonds and jewels, but at home there are plenty of those too. So let us take a sannyasin with us. That is something we don't have.'

Alexander thought that as all these other things were being taken home, what problem could there be in taking along a sannyasin too? So he gave the order for them to catch hold of a sannyasin, wherever one could be found, and bring him to him.

Alexander's men began searching in the nearby villages and inquiring if there was any sannyasin there. The people said, 'There is a sannyasin in this area, but why are you looking? You don't seem to be in the right state to approach a sannyasin. Holding naked swords in your hands… you look crazy. What is the matter?'

They replied: 'We are not crazy, we are Alexander's soldiers. We want to catch hold of a sannyasin and take him back to Greece.'

The people said, 'If you succeed in getting hold of a sannyasin, know well that he is not one. However, go ahead! There is a sannyasin in the village and we will give you his address.

'For the last thirty years a man has been living naked on the riverbank. From what we have heard, from what we have seen, from what we have known of him during these thirty years, we can say he is a sannyasin. But you will not be able to catch hold of him.'

The soldiers said, 'What is so difficult? We have swords, we have chains.' The people said, 'Just go! Go and deal with him yourselves.'

So the soldiers went to the sannyasin and said, 'Alexander the Great has given orders for you to come with us. We will give you great honor, a big welcome, and treat you royally. We have to take you to Greece. And on the journey we will ensure that you have no pain, no problems, no difficulties.'

The sannyasin laughed and said, 'How could I have become a sannyasin if I still cared for honor, for welcome and for worldly joys? So forget all about this! Don't talk about dreams. Come to the point.'

So the soldiers said, 'The point is that if you don't come with us, we will take you by force.'

The sannyasin replied, 'The one whom you can take by force will not be a sannyasin. A sannyasin is totally free. No one can take him by force.'

The soldiers said, 'Then we will kill you.'

The sannyasin said, 'Of course you can do that. But let me tell you, you will be living in an illusion if you think that you have killed me, because the person you will be killing is not who I am. Why don't you bring your Alexander here? Perhaps he will understand something of what I am saying.'

So they went to fetch Alexander and said, 'This man seems to be a very strange fellow. He challenges us to kill him, saying, "The person you will kill will not be me."'

Alexander said, 'Then who is he? I have never heard of a man who doesn't die after he has been killed. How can this be?'

Alexander was obviously speaking from his own experience. He had killed thousands of people. He was saying he had never seen a single person surviving after being killed by him.

With an open sword, he went to the sannyasin and said, 'You

will have to come with me otherwise this sword will chop off your head from your body.'

The sannyasin gave a big belly laugh. He said, 'As far as chopping off my head is concerned, I have already known for a long time that the head is separate from the body. You cannot separate them any more. I have seen that they are so separate that there will be a big space for your sword to pass between the two of them. I have seen that they are quite separate from each other. You can't make them more separate than that.'

Naturally, Alexander couldn't make head or tail of what the sannyasin was saying. Holding out his sword, he said, 'I will cut off your head this very instant! Look, drop all this philosophical talk. I don't have anything to do with philosophy. I am a very practical man. So drop all this great talk, otherwise with one blow your head will be rolling on the ground.'

The sannyasin replied: 'Go ahead! Not only will you see my head rolling on the ground, so will I!'

Now this man is saying the same thing that Krishna is saying: no weapon can pierce or cut it.

As long as you feel that a weapon can penetrate you, that you can be cut, know well that as yet, you haven't come to know anything about your being. Only when something remains untouched within you when your body is pierced, only when something remains uncut within you when your body is cut, only when something remains beyond sickness in you when your body is sick, only when something in you remains outside the suffering and watches it when suffering comes and overwhelms your body will you know that until that moment you had no knowledge of the *you* that Krishna is talking about.

Arjuna is saying the same thing here that Alexander is saying. Of course they are also of the same type, there is not much difference between their types – only in the body. But we are also of the same type.

So be constantly on the lookout. When a thorn pricks your foot, watch: Did something within you remain un-pricked? We are always getting sick. Just look within: Did something in you remain untouched by the sickness? You laugh, cry, feel happy and sad every day – keep looking, keep watching, keep searching to see if something remains unaffected beyond them.

Slowly, slowly, as you continue your search, you will begin to see it. And once it is seen, you will come to realize that what you had been thinking to be *you* was only a shadow; that you were mistaking the shadow to be *you* and were totally ignorant of the one whose reflection the shadow was. You come to realize that you were living by identifying yourself with the shadow. That shadow is nothing but a collection of our memories, an album of our images from birth till death.

'O Arjuna, he who knows it to be
indestructible, eternal, unborn and everlasting,
how and whom can such a person slay?
And how and by whom can he be slain?'

He who knows…! Krishna is saying, 'He who *knows* this.' He is not saying, 'He who believes this.' He could have easily said, 'He who believes that there is no birth and there is no death…'. This would have made everything very simple for us. There is nothing easier than believing, because for believing one doesn't have to do anything. On the other hand, there is nothing more difficult than knowing, because in order to know one has to go through a total self-transformation.

Krishna is saying 'A person who *knows* this.' It is important to understand the word *knowing* clearly, because leaving the word *knowing* aside, all religions revolve around the word *believing*. All the religions on this earth, no matter what name they have, all of them revolve around believing. All these religions exhort you to believe. 'If you believe like this, your life will become like that.' But Krishna is saying 'A person who *knows* like this.'

Now, what does *knowing* mean? There can be two types of

knowing. One is that you can read the scriptures and know. The other is to know through experiencing.

Do these two types of knowing have the same meaning? It is very easy to know from the scriptures – everything is written in them, you read them, and then you know. Just being literate is enough for this. If you know how to read, that is sufficient – it is not necessary to be at all meditative for this knowing. But knowing from reading the scriptures is no knowing at all; it is only a pretence of knowing. It is just information.

This 'just information' can cause self-deception. We read that the consciousness in us is imperishable, immortal, unborn and undying; we just read this and we go on repeating it. By constantly reading and repeating it, we forget that we don't really *know*, that we are merely parroting. By repeating it so many times – day in, day out – we forget that what we are saying is not our knowing.

For example, a man may read all about the art of swimming in a book. He may become an authority on that book, he may like to give talks on swimming, or he may like to write on swimming. He may even earn a Ph.D. in swimming from some university and become a Doctor of Swimming. But don't ever make the mistake of pushing him into a river! His Ph.D. is not going to help him swim. On the contrary, it will drown him all the more quickly, because his Ph.D. is very heavy: it will function like a rock.

To know *about* swimming is not the same thing as to know swimming. Similarly, to know *about* truth is not the same as knowing the truth. To know *about* is equivalent to not knowing at all. To know about truth is equivalent to not knowing truth. But even to say 'equivalent' is not right, it is a little dangerous, because to know that one doesn't know the truth becomes the way towards knowing it. And to know that one knows the truth – without actually knowing it – becomes the obstacle on the way towards truth. So no, it is not even 'equivalent'.

So you really need to understand this word of Krishna's very thoroughly, because it is around this one word, *knowing*, that the birth of an authentic religiousness takes place, and around *believing* that an inauthentic and pseudo-religion is born.

That which is attained through knowing is trust, and that which is attained through believing is belief. Those who are believers are not religious; they believe without knowing.

Knowing is not a small word. It is one of the most significant words, but it has always been misunderstood. For example, the word *veda* means to know, but for most of us *veda* means the compilations, the scriptures known as the Vedas. We have said that veda, knowing, comes from beyond man – that it is not a human endeavor – but the meaning that is commonly taken is that the books called the Vedas were not written by man, that they were written by God.

Knowing is not a book. Knowing is life. But it is very easy to turn knowing into believing, to turn knowing into meaning a book. It is very easy to make knowing dependent on the scriptures, because then nothing much needs to be done. Instead of knowing, all one needs is memory: just memorizing is enough. That's why you will find so many people memorizing the Gita by heart!

Recently I went to a village where people had built a Gita Temple.

I asked them, 'The Gita is so small, so why have you made such a big temple for it?'

They said, 'No, no. The space is already too small.'

I asked them, 'What do you mean?'

They said, 'So far we have already collected one hundred thousand handwritten copies of the Gita and stored them here. And we are running out of space. Thousands of people from all over India are copying the Gita in their own hand and sending it to us.'

I asked them, 'But what is all this? What will it achieve?'

They replied, 'Someone has written the Gita ten times, someone has written it fifty times, someone has written it one hundred times – and through all this writing they will attain knowledge.'

I said, 'In that case all the printing presses must have attained to supreme wisdom! We should all go and touch the feet of the print workers wherever we can find them – because how many Gitas must have been typeset by now! We should be looking for saints and mahatmas in the printing presses and nowhere else.'

Why does all this kind of madness come about? There is a reason for it. People feel they will attain to knowing through the scriptures, but the scriptures can only give you information, the scriptures can only give you pointers. They cannot give you knowing and wisdom. Knowing and wisdom can only come through experiencing life. And don't stop until through living you have experienced for yourself that there is something unborn and eternal within you. Until then, no matter how much Krishna says something, you are not to believe it.

Learn just this much from what Krishna is saying: 'If this man is saying it so emphatically, then I must set out on a search, then I must find out for myself. If this man is filled with such certainty, if he is saying this with such natural assurance, then it shows that he has known something, he has lived something, he has seen something. Let me also see, let me also know, let me also live!'

If only the scriptures could become just an indication and we could set out on our own journeys! But instead, they become holy shrines and we settle down there and idly rest.

So keep this word *knowing* in your heart, because Krishna is going to lay a lot of emphasis on it again and again.

'Just as man discards his old and worn-out garments
and replaces them with new,
so the being discards the old and worn-out body
and moves on to the new.'

The being discards the body like an old and worn-out garment and obtains a new one. But, like garments...! Have you ever experienced your body like a garment – as something which you have wrapped around you, as something that you are wearing, as something which is outside you, as something which you are surrounded in? Have you ever experienced your body as clothing?

No, you have always experienced yourself as nothing but a body. When you feel hungry you don't say, 'I am aware that my body is hungry.' You say, 'I am hungry.' When you have a headache, you don't say, 'I am aware that the head is aching.' You say, 'I have a headache.' Your identification with the body is very deep. One never feels that the body and 'I' are two separate entities; rather one feels that 'I am the body.'

Have you ever closed your eyes and tried to look, and asked yourself for a moment: 'My body is fifty years old, but what is my age?' Have you ever closed your eyes and reflected: 'The face on my body looks like this, but what does *my* face look like?' Have you ever closed your eyes while having a headache and tried to find out: 'Am I having the pain or is the pain happening somewhere away from me?'

During the last world war a very strange thing happened. A soldier who had been very badly wounded was admitted to a hospital in France. One of his feet had been badly injured; his toe was in terrible pain. He kept screaming, shouting and falling unconscious. The moment he regained consciousness he would start screaming again in pain.

Finally, during the night the doctors anaesthetized him and amputated his leg just below the knee because there was a fear that his whole body was getting poisoned.

Twenty-four hours later, when he had regained consciousness, he started screaming again and saying, 'My toe is in terrible pain.'

As a matter of fact, the toe no longer existed. The nurse attending him started laughing. She said, 'Are you sure you have pain in your toe?'

The soldier replied, 'Do you think I am joking? Of course I am in pain. It is unbearable.' His legs were covered with a blanket, so he couldn't see anything.

The nurse said, 'Consider it a little more, look a little more closely inside.'

He said, 'What is there to consider? I am so obviously in pain.'

The nurse lifted the blanket and said: 'Now look! Where is your toe?' There was no toe; in fact, half of his leg was missing.

He said, 'I can see that there is no toe, I can see that my leg has been amputated – but I still have a pain in my toe!'

Then it became very complicated. All the specialists were called in. This was the first case of its kind. How can a toe hurt when it isn't there?

Upon further examination they found out that this is possible. There can be pain even from a missing toe. Now all this sounded very metaphysical, belonging to the spiritual domain. But after a detailed examination, the doctors confirmed that the man was right – he did indeed have pain in his toe.

But upon hearing this, even the soldier said, 'What kind of a joke is this?' Before they had been saying to him, 'What kind of a joke are you making?' and now the man is saying to them, 'What kind of a joke are *you* making? I must have fallen victim to some illusion, but how come even you are saying that there can be pain in a toe that isn't there.'

The doctors replied, 'Yes, you can have pain in your toe that is missing. Although the pain occurs in the toe, it is experienced somewhere else. There is a great distance between the toe and the point where its pain is registered. Consciousness is where the pain is registered, and the toe is where the pain occurs. The nerves that convey the message from the point of pain to the consciousness seem, in this case, to be still mistakenly conveying the message that there is pain.'

When the toe hurts, the tissues in the nerves connected to the toe start vibrating and in this way relay the message – like the tic-tic-tic of the telegraph system. In the same way nerves also start vibrating and relaying the message. This message passes through many 'head offices' before it finally reaches the brain. And then the brain brings the news to consciousness. During all this, many transformations take place, languages and codes change many times – because all these 'head offices' have different languages.

So something of this sort happened so that the message-relaying nerves went on reporting the message even though the toe had been amputated. As they continued to vibrate, the message went on reaching the brain. As the brain kept receiving the message it kept experiencing the pain in the toe.

Is it possible to separate the whole body of a person from the brain and preserve just the latter? Now it is possible. Now the whole body can be separated and the brain can be preserved – just the brain.

Suppose we were to make a man unconscious, remove his brain from the body, keep it in a laboratory and then ask it, 'What do you think of the body now?' The brain would reply, 'Everything is just fine. There is no pain, no disturbance anywhere in the body.' The fact is there is no longer a body there, but the brain will still say: 'Everything is just fine!'

Krishna says being aware of the body is just like being aware of a garment. But it is a garment that we have become so glued to that it is no longer our clothing – it has become more like our skin. For many, many lifetimes we have been identifying ourselves with the body, so much so that 'I am the body' has become our only stance. Until a distance is created between the body and ourselves, we will not be able to understand this sutra of Krishna: the body … *like old and worn-out garments.*

You will start understanding this if you do a few experiments. It won't mean many experiments; just a few will do.

The truth is what is being said here. The untruth is what we have accepted as belief. But those untruths that we accept hide the real truths, they are our beliefs. We are taught them from our very childhood and then they become firmly ingrained in us.

We have believed that 'I am the body.' If the body is beautiful, we believe 'I am beautiful.' If the body is healthy, we believe 'I am healthy.' Whatever happens to the body, we get the 'I' identifying with it and we start believing it. Then this belief, this memory, goes on becoming stronger and stronger, deeper and deeper. Eventually, the body ceases to be a garment; we become one with that garment.

I have a friend. He is quite old; he must be around seventy-five years of age. One day while he was climbing the stairs he fell down and broke his leg.

While I was in his village, people told me this and I went to see him. He was in agony. The doctors had ordered complete bed rest for three months. He was strapped face-up on his bed and he was not allowed to move at all. He is a very active person, and even at the age of seventy-five he is not at ease with sitting quietly, doing nothing and not running around. Three months seemed like an eternity to him.

When I went to see him he had been in bed for only a week. The moment he saw me he started crying. He is quite a courageous person and I could never have imagined that he was capable of crying. He had become like a helpless child, and he said, 'It would have been better if I had died. Death would have been better than being strapped up like this for three months! This will be hell. How am I going to get through these three months? Please pray to God that I will die. I have lived enough. What is the use being bedridden like this for three months? I don't want to live anymore – and I cannot bear all this pain. It is unbearable.'

I asked him to do one small experiment: to close his eyes and try finding out exactly where the pain was, to try pinpointing the pain exactly.

He said, 'The pain is in my whole leg.'

I said, 'Just close your eyes and investigate a little. Are you really having pain in the entire leg?' Because I know man has the habit of exaggerating everything: we neither really suffer that much, nor are we really that happy. We see things in an exaggerated way. Man has a mind that magnifies things. His mind is like a magnifying glass; it magnifies everything it sees. You honor a man by garlanding him, and he starts thinking he is the whole universe. If someone laughs at him a little, he starts feeling everything is lost, that his whole reputation has gone down the drain. His brain is working like a magnifying glass.

So I said, 'Just try to find out. I don't believe that there can be pain in the whole leg because if the whole leg were in pain, as you are saying, it would have affected the rest of your body too. So just search a little.'

He closed his eyes and started searching. After fifteen minutes he opened his eyes and said, 'It is so strange; the pain doesn't seem to have spread in the whole area like it felt it had. It seems the pain is only around the knee.'

I asked him, 'And how big is that area?'

He said, 'The size of a ball.'

I asked him to try again and to pinpoint it even further.

He closed his eyes again. This time he was feeling much more relaxed and assured because the pain had shrunk so much, and he could never have imagined that the mind could magnify it to such an extent. He went on looking. I sat for fifteen minutes while he kept searching.

But he didn't open his eyes. Half an hour passed, then forty-five minutes, and his eyes were still closed. I was watching his face and I could see it was going through a change. After about seventy minutes he opened his eyes and said to me, 'It is amazing. Now the pain feels to be just in an area that can be covered by a pinprick.'

I asked, 'What happened? You were meant to let me know sooner as I am in a hurry. I have already been sitting here for seventy minutes, and you didn't open your eyes.'

He said, 'When I found out that it is not bigger than the area you can press with a pin, I went on looking at it even more closely. I thought to myself, "If it can shrink that much, maybe it can disappear altogether." And then there were moments when it would feel like the pain was not there, and then again it would be there. One moment it felt as if the pain had disappeared, that everything was all right, and in another moment it would seem to be back.'

I said, 'But at least you should have told me so that I could have left.'

He said, 'I would have told you, but then another new thing started happening which I had never thought of. And that is, when

I looked at the pain so intently, it felt as if the pain is in some very far-off place and that I am so far away from it. There was a big distance between the pain and me.'

So I said, 'Now for the next three months, keep using this as a meditation. The moment there is pain, close your eyes and move into this meditation.'

When he met me three months later, he fell at my feet. Again he wept, but this time the tears were of joy, and he said, 'I am so grateful to existence that, before this life comes to an end, it made me bedridden for three months! Otherwise… you know how I am not one of those people to sit with closed eyes. I have found so much bliss that I feel grateful to existence for this very experience.'

I said, 'But tell me exactly what happened.'

He said, 'In the process of eliminating the pain, I came to have the experience of the pain taking place somewhere on the wall of the house while I was the master of the house – very separate from it.'

We need to know the body from the inside. We only know our bodies from the outside – just like a man who only knows his house from the outside. We have never experienced and felt our bodies from the inside; we only know them from the outside. When we see this hand, we only see it from the outside. Just as someone else only sees your hand from the outside, in the same way you too only know your hand from the outside.

You are only acquainted with your body from without. You don't know how your body feels from the inside, and there is a lot of difference between the two. If you look at the house from the outside you see the exterior wall, but if you look at it from the inside, its interiority is seen.

As long as you keep seeing the body only from the outside, it cannot be seen as a garment, a worn-out garment.

Look at it from the inside; close your eyes and try to experience how the body feels from the inside. What is its inner lining like? You know the jacket from the outside, but what type of lining has it inside? How does it feel from the inside? Outside it feels fine, but what about from the inside? What type of stitching does the jacket have? Try to catch its inner contours.

And as you begin to have a greater clarity, you will feel as though a flame, covered all around by glass, is burning. Up to now, you have only been looking through the glass and it has felt as if the glass itself was the light. But now, when you look from the inside, you will come to see that the flame is separate from the glass; that the glass is only an outer covering.

And once you experience, even for one moment, that the flame is separate from the body and that the body is only an outer covering, you will understand that death is nothing more than the discarding of old and worn-out clothes and that birth is nothing more than the putting on of new clothes. You will experience that the body is discarded like old clothes and that it is also taken up as new clothes. And through its endless journey, the being discards old clothes and puts on new ones countless times. Then, birth and death are no longer birth and death to you; they are simply a change of garment. Then, there remains no reason whatsoever to feel either happy or sad.

But what Krishna is saying will not become known to your understanding just by reading the Gita. You will need to know it from within yourself. To experience religiousness one has to turn oneself into a laboratory.

So don't think that you will know it by just reading what Krishna is saying. And don't be under the misconception that you will know this just by understanding what I am explaining to you. At the most all of this can provide you with a challenge.

So begin experimenting with it when you return home. But why even wait that long? While you are walking, try looking within — watch whether inside the walking body there is some nonmoving, an absolutely stationary entity as well. Then, even as you are walking, you will begin to have a glimpse of this stationary entity. Try to find out whether you are this breathing or whether there is someone behind it watching the breathing too. Then you will be able to see breathing as separate and distinct from yourself. And the one who is observing the breath cannot be the breath, because breathing cannot see breathing.

Then try the same thing with your thoughts. find out if the thoughts that are going on in your brain... are you these thoughts? Then you will realize: how can the one who is watching thoughts be the thoughts?

A thought is incapable of watching another thought. No thought has ever seen another thought. The one that is seeing the thoughts, the witness, is separate.

And when you come to see that the body, thoughts, breathing, walking, eating, hunger, thirst, happiness and unhappiness are all separate from you, you will come to experience the meaning of Krishna's statement that this body is discarded like a worn-out garment and a new body is taken on like new clothes. And once you have seen this, then what happiness, what suffering? Then there will be no death in dying and no birth in being born for you. What was, still is. Only the garment is being changed.

OSHO,

If the being, the consciousness, is all-pervading, if it is the whole, then where does the whole go to from the whole? Which body does the being leave in order to go to another body, from which body does it come to enter a new body? How does the fetus live in the womb before the being has entered it?

The being, the consciousness, doesn't come and go; it is the body that does. Broadly speaking, there are two bodies. One is the physical body, which we can see. This is the body we receive from our parents, that is born. And this body has its own limitations, its own capacity to last for so long and then to finish. It is more like a mechanism. It is this mechanism that we receive from our parents. All that our parents do is create the possibility for this mechanism to be in the womb. This body that we see begins with birth and ends with death. It comes and goes.

Then there is another body which you can say is the garment

closest to the being, which you can say is the underclothes. The physical body that you see is the outer covering of the being, and the other one is the inner covering of the being. It comes along with the being from the previous life. This is the subtle body. This body is subtle in the sense that the outer body that we can see is very material, and the inner body is electrical, is made up of only electrical particles. This body that is made up of only electrical particles comes with you from your previous life. It is this body that travels on to take a new body. This body also has its own journey.

This second body – the subtle body – enters the womb, enters the physical body. Its entry is as automatic and natural as water descending from the mountains, flowing into the rivers and entering the ocean. Just as it is a natural phenomenon for water to flow downwards, so it is a completely natural phenomenon for the subtle body to flow into a suitable and fitting physical body.

Hence, when an ordinary person dies, he immediately finds a new incarnation, because throughout the twenty-four hours, millions of wombs are available all over the earth. But when an extraordinary person dies it takes time, because a suitable womb is not so easily available for him. Both an extraordinarily good person and an extraordinarily bad person have a long waiting period. For both, an immediate womb is not available. Only the middle range of people find readymade wombs. For them, wombs are available every day. They die and there is a womb already waiting. One moment they die, the next they are already descending into a womb. It takes no time.

But for an evil man, for a man like Hitler, it becomes difficult. A man like Hitler will have to wait a long time before he finds suitable parents. A person like Gandhi also takes a long time. For such people wombs are not so easily available. According to our timescale it might even take hundreds of years before men like Hitler or Gandhi can be reborn. Not according to the timescale of the departed subtle bodies – their timescale is different – but according to our system it might take hundreds of years. So the moment a suitable womb becomes available, some subtle body enters it.

So the whole journey is of these bodies. Now how does the being figure in all of this?

Actually, man uses metaphors about coming and going, about someone entering and leaving the house. So man uses metaphors, but metaphors are never quite accurate. This idea of coming and going does not fit as far as the being is concerned.

So how to talk of the being in terms of metaphors? And in Krishna's time there were even fewer metaphors available. In fact, metaphors are very crude. But we have to manage with them somehow. Let us take a couple of examples so that you can understand what is being said...

A man lives on a very isolated island in the sea. It is a very rocky island; no flowers grow there. It is full of sand and rocks.

One day, the man sets out on a journey. He lands on a continent where he sees a lot of flowers. After some time he returns to his island. The people of the island ask him, 'What new things did you see?'

He says, 'I saw flowers.'

They ask, 'What are flowers? What you do mean?' Their island does not have flowers.

Now, how should this poor man explain? He looks around, finds a few shiny colored stones, picks them up and says: 'Flowers look something like this.'

Obviously, nobody from that island will question this explanation, because they see no reason to. But the man who has returned after having seen flowers is in difficulty. There is no metaphor available through which he can give an accurate description of the flowers

In the world we live in, *coming* and *going* are metaphors, so we call birth 'coming' and death 'leaving' or 'going'. But the truth is that the being neither comes nor goes. A better metaphor comes to mind which is perhaps the closest and which you might understand.

In the West it is now being realized that we cannot keep driving cars on petrol forever. Petroleum has done so much harm to this earth. It has caused so much pollution in the air that the earth has become unfit for habitation. There is a whole new ecological movement going on in America and Europe. Soon we will have to switch over from petrol to electricity. But the question arises: if we run cars on electricity, how can we provide them with an uninterrupted supply of electricity?

Some scientists have offered a suggestion that appears valuable. They say we could spread electric wires under all the roads, and the moment a car comes along the road it could get a supply of electricity from the wires laid underneath. It is something like how trams run. The only difference is that in the case of trams the electricity is supplied from above, and with this new system it would be supplied from underneath.

It is the tram that moves, not the electricity. The electricity is continuously available from the top and the tram keeps moving. And if the electric current stops, the tram also stops. It runs on electricity, but the electricity does not run; only the tram runs.

In the same way, these scientists say that electricity will be laid under roads and the cars will run on top of it. And that is it: in its very running, the car will go on receiving the electricity. Every car will be fitted with a meter that will add up the figures to show how much electricity it has used. But the electricity won't be moving, only the car will.

In exactly the same way, the being is all-pervasive. It is simply present everywhere, all the time. Only our subtle body keeps changing place, keeps running. And wherever it goes, it keeps receiving life-energy from the all-pervading being.

The day this subtle body disperses, it is like the tram falling apart. The tram is no more, but the electricity remains where it is. And it is not that with the dispersion of the subtle body the being becomes one with the universal being. No, that was always the case; it only appeared separate because of this wall of the subtle body. And now it doesn't.

Actually, as far as transmigration is concerned, the simile of coming and going is a very crude one. It is quite far-fetched, but there is no other way to explain it. What I am saying to you is that the being is present everywhere, both within us as well as without.

For example, there are so many electric bulbs burning here. One is a hundred watts, another is fifty watts, another twenty watts, and one is a mini-bulb – like a firefly – of only five watts. But the same electricity is running through them all. Each bulb is drawing electricity according to its capacity. And then when using a microphone, which is not a light bulb, it is also drawing electricity for its use… and a radio is drawing electricity, and a fan is drawing electricity – each for its own purpose. As far as the electricity is concerned, it is the same in all of them; it is the same everywhere. The difference is in the mechanisms – the light bulbs, the fan and the microphone.

Existence is present everywhere. Existence is all around. We also have a subtle mechanism: the subtle body. We are drawing life and energy from existence according to the capacity of our mechanism. If the capacity of our subtle body is that of five candles, five watts, we will be receiving energy for five candles. And if our subtle body has a capacity of fifty candles, we will receive the energy of fifty candles. Mahavira has a subtle body of a thousand candles; he is receiving the energy of a thousand candles. If one is so poor that he has a subtle body of only one candle, he will receive the energy of one candle.

Existence is not being miserly in this. What we receive depends on how big a vessel we have brought. If we wish, we can have the power of a thousand candles, and then the genius that manifests in a man like Mahavira will also manifest in us.

Then there comes a point when Mahavira says: 'A thousand candles won't do. I want to be an infinite number of candles.' If this is the case, he is told: 'Break the bulb and you will be an infinite number of candles' – because as long as the bulb exists, the limitation of candles, of watts, will persist. It can be of a thousand candles, it can be of two thousand candles, it can be of a hundred thousand candles, or a million candles, but the limitation remains. If one wants infinite light then he must break the bulb. So Mahavira says: 'If this is the case, then I am breaking the bulb; I am liberating myself.'

Attaining liberation simply means, 'I have derived enough from mechanisms. And I have found that each mechanism eventually becomes a limitation, and wherever there is limitation, there is misery. So now I am dispersing my mechanism, now I am becoming one with the whole!'

In fact, it is one of language's linguistic errors to say: 'I am becoming one with the whole.' You were already one with the whole. Because the mechanism was in between, you were receiving less. The moment the mechanism is dispersed, the whole became available.

The being doesn't come or go. It is the subtle body that comes and goes; it is the gross body, the physical body that comes and goes. We receive the physical body from our parents, we receive the subtle body from our past life, and the being is ever-present.

Without the subtle body one cannot receive a physical body. Once the subtle body disperses, it is impossible to attain a physical body. That's why the moment the subtle body disperses, two things happen. On the one hand, as the subtle body disperses, the journey into physical bodies comes to an end. And on the other hand, the boundary that existed between the whole and you disappears.

The dispersion of the subtle body is the whole spiritual discipline. The connecting bridge that joins you with the physical body on one side and the whole on the other falls apart. Breaking down this bridge is what spiritual discipline is all about.

But it is necessary to understand all that constitutes this subtle body. Our desires, our passions, our ambitions, our wishes, our expectations; the actions that we have committed, the actions that we did not commit but only thought about committing, our thoughts, our deeds; whatever we have been – all that we have ever thought, dreamt of, done; all that we have ever experienced, felt –

all of these together with their electrical imprints make up our subtle body.

It is the dispersal of this subtle body that brings about two outcomes. The first is that the journey to the womb comes to an end.

When Buddha attained enlightenment, he said: 'Oh mind, I declare that you, who until now built so many houses called "the body" for me, can now go to rest. Now you don't need to build any more houses for me. I thank you, and I let you go. There is no longer any work left for you to do, because there is no longer any desire left in me. Oh mind, the builder of many, many houses for me, now you need no longer build any.'

Just before Buddha was about to die people asked him, 'Now, as your being will merge with the whole, where will you be?'

Buddha said, 'If I will be somewhere then how can I merge with the whole?' – because one who is somewhere cannot be everywhere. He said, 'Don't even ask this question. Now I will not be anywhere, because I will be everywhere.' But still the devotees kept asking, 'Please tell us where will you be from now on.'

This is like asking a dewdrop where will it be after becoming one with the ocean. The drop will say, 'I will become that very same ocean.'

But the other drops will say, 'That's all right, but still… where exactly will you be? Maybe someday we can come and visit you!'

So the drop that is about to become the ocean says, 'Just merge into the ocean and our meeting will happen.'

But actually the meeting will be with the ocean, not with the drops.

If one wishes to meet Buddha, Krishna, Mahavira, Jesus or Mohammed, he cannot meet them in their drop form. No matter how many statues you may make and keep of them, you will never be able to meet that drop. That drop is now one with the ocean – and actually that is why you have made the statue of it. This is the interesting paradox: the statue has been made because the drop has become one with the ocean. Now it has become worthy of having its statue made.

But making statues is now pointless. Now if you want to meet, the only way is to merge into the ocean itself.

The outer form of the drop comes from our parents. The inner arrangement of the drop comes from its previous lives. And the life-energy, which is the being, is received from the whole. But until we have thoroughly recognized these two layers of the drop, we will not be able to know that which is beyond the two.

Osho Meditation Resort ™

The Osho Meditation Resort is a place where people can have a direct personal experience of a new way of living with more alertness, relaxation, and fun. Located about 100 miles southeast of Mumbai in Pune, India, the resort offers a variety of programs to thousands of people who visit each year from more than 100 countries around the world. Originally developed as a summer retreat for Maharajas and wealthy British colonialists, Pune is now a thriving modern city that is home to a number of universities and high-tech industries. The Meditation Resort spreads over 40 acres in a tree-lined suburb know as Koregaon Park. The resort campus provides accommodation for a limited number of guests, in a new 'Guesthouse' and there is plentiful variety of nearby hotels and private apartments available for stays of a few days up to several months.

Resort programs are all based in the Osho vision of a qualitatively new kind of human being who is able both to participate creatively in everyday life and to relax into silence and meditation. Most programs take place in modern, air-conditioned facilities and include a variety of individual sessions, courses and workshops covering everything from the creative arts to holistic health treatments, personal transformation and therapy, esoteric sciences, the 'Zen' approach to sports and recreation, relationship issues, and significant life transitions for men and women. Individual sessions and group workshops are offered throughout the year, alongside a full daily schedule of mediations. Outdoor workshops are offered throughout the year, alongside a full daily schedule of meditations. Outdoor cafes and restaurants within the resort grounds serve both traditional Indian fare and a choice of international dishes, all made with organically grown vegetables from the resort's own farm. The campus has its own supply of safe, filtered water.

www.osho.com/resort

For more information:

www.osho.com

A comprehensive web site in several languages that includes an on-line tour of the Mediation Resort and a calendar of its course offerings, a catalog of books and tapes, a list of Osho information centers worldwide and selections from Osho's talks.

Osho International
New York
Email: oshointernational@oshointernational.com
www.osho.com/oshointernational